D1309692

Radicalism and Political Reform in the Islamic and Western Worlds

Over the last decade, political Islam has been denounced in the Western media and surrounding literature as a terrorist or fascist movement that is entirely at odds with Western democratic ideology. Kai Hafez's book overturns these arguments, contending that, despite its excesses, as a radical form of political opposition the movement plays a central role in the processes of democratization and modernization and that these processes have direct parallels in the history and politics of the West. By analyzing the evolution of Christian democratization through the upheavals of the Reformation, colonization, fascism and totalitarianism, this book shows how radicalism and violence were constant accompaniments to political change and – despite assertions to the contrary – are still part of Western political culture. In this way, it draws hopeful conclusions about the potential for political, religious and cultural transformation in the Islamic world, which is already exemplified by the cases of Turkey, Indonesia and many parts of South Asia. The book marks an important development in the study of radical movements and their contribution to political change.

Kai Hafez is a professor (chair) and currently also the director of the Department of Media and Communication Studies at the University of Erfurt, Germany. He was a Senior Research Fellow of the German Middle East Institute in Hamburg and a Visiting Fellow at the University of Oxford. Hafez has been a frequent advisor to German governments regarding the Western-Islamic dialogue and is a member of the German Islam Conference. He is the author of *The Myth of Media Globalization* and the editor of numerous books including *Arab Media – Power and Weakness* and *The Islamic World and the West: An Introduction to Political Cultures and International Relations*.

Alex Skinner holds degrees in German and Danish (the University of Edinburgh) and social anthropology (London School of Economics and Political Science). He has translated the work of leading German scholars, including *The Myth of Media Globalization* (2007) by Kai Hafez and *Social Theory* (Cambridge 2009) by Hans Joas and Wolfgang Knöbl.

Radicalism and Political Reform in the Islamic and Western Worlds

KAI HAFEZ
University of Erfurt, Germany

Translated by
ALEX SKINNER

CAMBRIDGE
UNIVERSITY PRESS

CAMBRIDGE UNIVERSITY PRESS
Cambridge, New York, Melbourne, Madrid, Cape Town, Singapore,
São Paulo, Delhi, Dubai, Tokyo

Cambridge University Press
32 Avenue of the Americas, New York, NY 10013-2473, USA

www.cambridge.org
Information on this title: www.cambridge.org/9780521137119

First published in German as *Heiliger Krieg und Demokratie,
Radikalismus und politischer Wandel im islamisch-westlichen
Vergleich* by Transcript 2009
First English edition by Cambridge University Press 2010

Printed in the United States of America

A catalog record for this publication is available from the British Library.

Library of Congress Cataloging in Publication data
  Hafez, Kai, 1964–
  [Heiliger Krieg und Demokratie. English]
  Radicalism and political reform in the Islamic and Western worlds / Kai Hafez ;
  translated by Alex Skinner.
     p.   cm.
  Includes bibliographical references and index.
  ISBN 978-0-521-76320-2 (hardback)
  1. Jihad.   2. Islam and politics.   3. Democracy.   I. Title.
  BP182.H2713 2010
  320.5'57–dc22   2010010412

ISBN 978-0-521-76320-2 Hardback
ISBN 978-0-521-13711-9 Paperback

Contents

Introduction

Going beyond superficial consideration of wars, crises and conflicts, this book investigates whether the contemporary Islamic world is also the scene of appreciable political change. Can we discern a deeper political rationality behind the facade of radicalism, extremism and terrorism that is served up to us daily in the news? Or do we have to face the fact that a core region of the world, stretching from West Africa to Southeast Asia, from Southeastern Europe to the Sahara, will remain in a permanent state of political chaos?

There are grounds for hope, and they rest upon a very simple idea. The West's current state of prosperity, modernity and global power is due, not only to enlightenment, science and democracy, but just as much to wars of religion, revolutions and colonial exploitation. Radicalism and political violence were, strange though it may seem, constant accompaniments to the development of democracy in North America and Europe. In view of this in-built world historical paradox, it seems legitimate to ask whether, despite political radicalism and violence, positive political developments are possible in other parts of the world as well. Has the evolution of the West not shown that crises – even of epoch-making proportions – may usher in positive change?

The Islamic world, and especially North Africa and the Middle East, has for decades been replete with political contradictions. Islamic fundamentalists oppose the secular state, sometimes violently, and at the same time constitute the strongest opposition to authoritarian dictatorships in the region. Their relationship to democracy is anything but clear-cut, and yet they do very well in the rarely held free elections. Even beyond the Islamic fundamentalist parties, which call for the introduction of Islamic states, Muslims are rebelling against the interpretive sovereignty of the modern clergy; at the same time, they often seek refuge in a new, intolerant Puritanism. Societies are being torn apart by the concurrent wish for change and for continuity with the past, for progress and tradition, while the neo-Islamic movements, which now exist in almost all Islamic countries, embody perfectly the kind of internal contradictions also inherent to radical Protestantism in the modern history of Europe and America, with religious revival and challenges to authoritarian power existing alongside religious fanaticism and intolerance.

RADICALISM AND POLITICAL CHANGE IN THE ISLAMIC AND WESTERN WORLDS

If we accept the parallels between the Western historical processes of the Reformation and contemporary conditions, it seems inevitable that the Islamic countries face a period of unbridled religious wars. And there is, in fact, much to suggest this: civil wars between different groups of Muslims such as Sunnites and Shiites in Iraq and between secular nationalists and Islamic fundamentalists in Palestine, which are occurring against the background of a 'holy war' declared on the West by a handful of globally active terrorists. Like the Turks at the gates of Vienna in the Reformation era, the Western military presence in the Middle East seems to fuel internal discord and encourage tendencies towards rebellion.

Yet it is by no means inevitable that the Islamic world will slide into an age of religious wars. Comparing political developments in different regions of the world helps to sensitize us intellectually – rather than foster a fatalistic worldview which assumes that history must endlessly repeat itself. Of course, the contemporary Islamic world and Reformation Europe are not identical, though some of the mechanisms of radical religious opposition are similar. Those who reject violence and dread the unpredictability of political radicalism may draw comfort from the thought that alongside numerous parallels with the era of Christian Reformation, the contemporary Islamic world also features markedly different tendencies. In Turkey, Indonesia and Bangladesh, a considerable swathe of Muslims already line their lives under democratic regimes. Alongside fundamentalism, there exists a reformist Islam that promotes the pluralist modernization of Islam through an Enlightenment-style critique of sources.

Despite its many problems, the Islamic world of today is in some respects more advanced than 'the Occident' was during the era of Reformation, partly because of the West, which has been viewed as a model of modernization for the last two centuries. Yet the appeal of the West has waned in recent times. The political turn to Islam is *in part* the consequence of neo-imperialist Western policies, the self-inflicted injuries to human rights in Guantánamo and a 'war against terror', which is both hopeless and in breach of international law, that has claimed many thousands of victims. Can such policies still be viewed as exemplary? Is the West even aware of how violently its seemingly peaceful democracies have acted, especially against the oil-rich Middle East? Was the problem really just George W. Bush or is the hegemonic foreign policy that is characteristic of the United States and Europe systemic in nature? If we wish to improve our understanding of the Middle East, we must explicitly confront our own history, examining both domestic and foreign policy aspects. Martin Luther was no liberal but a fiery breaker with tradition, and the secular humanism that he despised has for centuries degraded people in the non-European world, making them objects of racist scholarship and colonial subjugation.

Particularly with regard to the use of political violence, the West and the Islamic world tend to stare at one another uncomprehendingly. While the internally pacified West rejects Oriental despotism and religious radicalism, scarcely noticing the authoritarian nature of its own foreign policies, large numbers of people in the Middle East now embrace any political movement that promises to change the political status quo, that implies resistance and new strength, even, we have reason to fear, if this means quasi-fascist Islamic regimes. Yet the notion of an eternal struggle between Orient and Occident is too simple. The Western model has lost some if its appeal but has left a deep impression. And though we must be aware of the risks to human rights arising from religious fundamentalism, we should also recognize its political potential far more clearly than is often the case.

Islamic fundamentalism is that political-religious movement which explicitly rejects all forms of secularization and which aspires to a social order whose 'fundament' is Islamic law. This is why I use the term 'fundamentalists' rather than simply 'Islamists', as they are very often called today – though, as we shall see, there are certain differences between the contemporary forms of Islamic fundamentalism and Christian fundamentalism.[1] Islamic fundamentalism, which has existed in organized form since the establishment of the Egyptian Muslim Brothers in the 1920s, began to develop into a mass movement in almost all Islamic countries

---

[1] For further explanation of the term 'Islamic fundamentalism' see Lawrence 1987, 1989.

in the wake of the Iranian Revolution of 1978–9. We must understand
the political rationality of this movement on the basis of our own historical experiences and in light of its internal dynamics, without denying its
contradictory aspects. The broad centre of this fundamentalism, rather
than its extremist-terrorist edges, features a large number of processes
running parallel to Western history, which are often difficult to decipher
because their temporal development is not synchronous with that of
the West. Who can really explain why a country like Egypt introduced
female suffrage after the First World War, twenty years earlier than Italy
and France and half a century before Switzerland did so? Not even the
mass Islamic organizations contest these political rights. Even within the
Islamic fundamentalist political spectrum as a whole, the Afghan Taliban
were ultra-radical forces and not representative. Their Stone Age Islam
was quite out of keeping with the mix of intolerance and progressivism
that characterizes contemporary Islamic fundamentalism across much of
the Islamic world. This movement blends and has always blended issues
relating to reformation, the critique of authoritarianism and social justice, issues which were largely worked through consecutively in Europe.
Reformist upheavals, the Peace of Westphalia, democratization and the
labour movement – in the Middle East, many of these developments have
already occurred in the last century, though they have often combined in
an unstable way.

De facto secular politics also have a far longer history in the Middle
East than is often assumed. The process of separating religion and politics began with the death of the Prophet Muhammad in 632; it remains
incomplete to this day. Two opposing trends can be discerned in the
political culture of the contemporary Islamic world: a public desire for
secularism, liberalism and pluralism is evident within the hugely popular
new media, where the broadest range of views is frequently expressed.
The countervailing trend, which also enjoys great momentum, is a
process of morally strict, at times rigid, but inconsistent re-Islamization.
The fact that fundamentalists are fighting once again against secularism
has much to do with political tactics and the simple fact that secularism
has been administered in authoritarian fashion in recent decades. For
those opposed to dictatorship, religion becomes the ally of political and
social transformation. What is happening here within the Islamic world
is in principle no different than in Buddhist Tibet or other parts of Asia.
Slogans opposing secularism become elements in political campaigns. But
does this really mean that the political culture of the Islamic world is
fundamentally a revivalist movement which seeks to restore traditional

forms of autocracy? Is it opposed to political change up to and including full-blown democracy of the kind that has taken hold in other parts of the world – not just in the West but in many countries in Latin America, Africa and Asia?

Today, Islamic politics itself consists of numerous currents, and much of it is a bewildering mix of religious intolerance and an incipient process of 'Christian democratization', which took off in the West only centuries after the Reformation. Not just in Turkey but also in many other countries of the Islamic world a debate is currently taking place along the fracture lines of modern politics. But this is an argument which cannot be resolved *before* the development of democracies, but only *within* the process of democratization, and this, too, should sound familiar to Europeans and Americans. Was Western democracy solely the product of 'cultural democrats', citizens engaged in civil society and non-governmental organizations (NGOs) anchored in human rights, currently the most favoured partners of Western aid projects? Not at all. Ireland is only now undergoing a process that has occurred in many places in Europe since the Second World War. Rather than democracy being achieved by movements specifically dedicated to its attainment, it is formerly radical and militant forces that are bringing about a 'democracy without democrats' in which no political force achieves its ultimate aims while each attains its minimal ones. In Germany, 'democracy without democrats' rouses bad memories of the failure of the Weimar Republic, which too few people really wanted and which was destroyed jointly by reactionaries and undemocratic leftists, who helped the fascists gain power. But why are we so quick to forget the successes of democratization in the northern Mediterranean region, in Spain, Portugal, Greece and Turkey, where Falangists and communists, colonels, militarists and Islamic fundamentalists, none of them 'cultural democrats', managed to attain the radicals' democratic peace? For the most part, political radicalism is not democratically inclined. But neither is it inevitably violent. And its total determination to change the political system may help put an end to repressive regimes.

The scant regard for the Islamic world's potential for political development common in the West also has something to do with the evaluation of a political culture shaped by Islam. Fears of 'Islamofascism' are rooted at least in part in the assumption that Muslims are the leading anti-Semites of the present era. This observation is not entirely unfounded. Fundamentalism has often produced an ideology of hostility towards 'the Jews' out of its – at least partly – justified critique of the state of Israel. Yet Jews and Muslims have coexisted for so long, and the recognition of Judaism as a religion is so well-established within Islam, that any comparison with German anti-Semitism is out of the question. Even where we might most expect them, in the revolutionary Iran of Khomeini and Ahmadinejad, there have as yet been no incidents even remotely comparable to the German Night of the Broken Glass, let alone the Holocaust.

Comparisons are useful, but this by no means implies that everything compared is identical. There can be no justification for identifying the Islamic world with the deformities of fascism and religious hatred found within one's own civilization while overlooking the complex realities of the modernization also taking place there. A country such as Iran, whose authoritarian character is easiest to discern, took social revenge on the Western-oriented middle classes, establishing (and this, too, is quite familiar from Western history) a dictatorship made up of the winners of the Revolution, a kind of caste of *nouveau riche* clergy. Resistance to this caste has been building up within Iranian society for years. President Ahmadinejad is a '20-percent president' favoured by electoral law. The rest of society, including Islamic circles, have long questioned the dominance of the clergy.

THE GLOBALIZATION OF THE TWO VELOCITIES

But there seems to be very little awareness of all these complexities in the West. Opinion polls indicate, for example, that 70 to 80 percent of Germans are afraid of Islam. Openly racist tracts such as the books by Italian journalist Oriana Fallaci sell millions of copies. Anti-Islamic populists like the American Daniel Pipes or the Netherlands' Geert Wilders are eagerly embraced by the established media. Islamophobia is socially acceptable. In the shape of the Swiss People's Party founded by Christoph Blocher, Switzerland has gone so far as to put in power a party that supports a general ban on minarets. Alexis de Tocqueville himself warned against the tyranny of the majority. Democracy demands, not only the procedures of an electoral system, but also a consensus on a culture of liberalism. Particularly in view of the Muslim immigration to Western states over the last few decades, this culture must consciously include Muslims. Today, it is no longer enough to foster a Christian-Jewish dialogue; the need is for a trialogue that incorporates Islam (Hafez and Steinbach 1999).

We must not underestimate the role of Western mass media in this regard. Coverage of Islam focuses on terrorist violence against the West and violence against women, but there is no understanding of the – often seemingly paradoxical – trends and developments of neo-Islam (Deltombe 2005; Hafez 2000; Poole 2002). Many young Muslim women with head-scarves are undoubtedly the victims of societal and familial repression, but they are just as often conservative educational and political activists or are simply characterized by the kind of 'healthy' double standards familiar for centuries to Catholic Christians. Just as in the West many people revere the Pope without obeying his strict commandments, in the Islamic world pre-marital sex – what is known as 'Islamic temporary marriage' – and the commercialization of the system of religious adjudication ('online fatwas') are now far from unusual. Individuals both opportunistically circumvent and openly break with tradition, part of a process of re-Islamization blending orthodoxy, community and individuality. Here, political fundamentalism often seems to function as a useful idiot. Protest voters lend it their support for the sake of political protest, but engage in everyday practices that make a mockery of its reactionary precepts.

It is highly doubtful that the Islamic world and the West have much understanding of one another, ensconced as they are within 'information ghettos' still thriving in this media age (Pintak 2006, 72). It seems more appropriate to speak of the 'globalization of the two velocities'. The often Islamophobic popular and media cultures in the West contrast with active informational elites in academia, the media and social organizations, who have kept the dialogue between Islam and the West going for decades. The consequences of this bifurcation of globalization are as yet unclear. The coexistence of a popular culture with no understanding of Islam and an elite culture with enlightened views is an old phenomenon in the West familiar since Goethe's *West-Eastern Divan*, a work far ahead of its time.

That not all knowledge elites are also truly global elites is evident in the relationship between Islam and the West. In a now famous polemic, Edward Said criticized the widespread 'Orientalism' of Western scholarship (Said 1978). Much has happened since, and entire generations of students are aware of Said's critique. But the Western academic system continues to produce culturalist bestsellers such as Samuel Huntington's *The Clash of Civilizations and the Remaking of World Order* (Huntington 1993, 1996) in which the author works on the assumption that Islam and the West are irreconcilable, a perspective which seems diametrically opposed to cross-cultural comparison. Many leading Western scholars regularly pass judgement on an Islamic world whose thinkers they do not know and whose realities they have, at best, observed while passing through. Hence, alongside the gulf between Islamophobic mass cultures and global informational elites, there is a rupture between ethnocentric and inter-culturally oriented scholars in the West. Edward Said has had an impact – but the key targets of his critique endure.

How have these different camps come about? Why was Huntington, a Harvard professor, an academic star for many while others regarded him with nothing short of intellectual loathing? One simple reason is that there are experts on either the Orient or the Occident, but rarely on both. Research on America, Europe and the rest of the world is often carried out in quite separate institutional worlds. The big Western-oriented disciplines contrast with their small 'Orientalist' counterparts. But because the theoretical work is done mainly within the large disciplines, it is unsurprising that we still lack a viable theoretical bridge capable of dealing with the comparative analysis of political developments in both the Islamic and Western worlds (see also Faath 1999, 238 f.). Theoretical vitality depends on empirical comparison, which too few scholars place at the centre of their work.

In response, some of the leading lights of international and intercultural comparison such as Fred Dallmayr, Bikhu Parekh, Hwa Yol Jung and Charles Taylor have called for a change of theoretical direction (Jung 2002; Parekh 2002; Parel and Keith 2003; Taylor 1992). Roxanne Euben observes that Western scholarship features a latent tension between the aspiration to produce a universal theory and a – still widespread – near-exclusive focus on Western texts (Euben 1999, XI). Fred Dallmayr would like to see a comparative political philosophy as a counterweight to the neo-imperialist mindset that has increasingly gained traction in the West since 11 September 2001 (Dallmayr 2004, 249 f.).

The case of Michel Foucault demonstrates the need for a shift towards a post-Orientalist comparative political analysis. In the late 1970s, this guiding intellectual figure of discourse analysis and the critique of power – who had long been part of the French intellectual establishment and was one of the most influential thinkers of the modern era – expressed enthusiasm for the Islamic Revolution in Iran, about which he wrote reports as correspondent for an Italian newspaper. Events there seemed to lend support to certain aspects of his critique of modernity. Foucault was almost unanimously criticized for this by Western intellectuals (Afary and Anderson 2005) – and quite rightly so. It is true that the vehemence of the reaction to Foucault's attempt to understand the revolutionary conditions in Iran rather than condemn them as an irrational religious reflex, reveals the Eurocentric bias of Western scholarship. Yet Foucault was ill-prepared for this intellectual adventure beyond the European world, and his very naive ideas on Shia Islam, which he viewed as the avant-garde of a new liberation movement, were so open to attack that even Edward Said, otherwise a great admirer, distanced himself from Foucault's views. Foucault was punished for daring to consider the strengthening of religious resistance as an exemplary case of the critique of Western-style modernization. But he also came to grief because of his own political romanticism, which was a far cry from any systematic theoretical position.

Foucault's Iranian excursion is representative of the scholarly mistakes that may ensue when one compares cultures. Attempts to establish a dialogue tend to presuppose that the poles on either end of the dialogue are ontological givens. Another example of this is the well-known communitarian Amitai Etzioni. His attempts to achieve the ethical renewal of the 'world community' entail the revival of old cultural stereotypes of the individualist West and community-oriented Islam (Etzioni 2004). While such approaches are geared towards achieving peace, they do as little justice to the diversity of cultural phenomena and the growing trend towards individuation within Islam (Roy 2006) as Huntington's notion of a clash of civilizations. Post-Orientalist comparative scholarship is conceptually open. It closes its mind to neither the specific nor the universal. It seeks to transfer theoretical knowledge of the West to the East while at the same instant distrusting its own simplicity. It remains open to new theoretical approaches (Somjee 2002, 122; see also Benhabib 2002). The developmental elements of the non-European world may appear quite familiar to the West individually, but their temporal sequence, combination and interactions convey the *specificity within the generalizable* of the non-European world.

For the observer, this state of affairs is neither entirely sealed off and comprehensible only in its own terms nor simply a re-run of Western history, which in any case presents no uniform picture. Like the West, the Islamic world features quite different developmental models. The West has seen revolutions, both successful and unsuccessful, and reforms from above and below. In the Muslim world, monarchies, revolutionary regimes and democracies exist side by side. Hence, in contrasting the West and the Islamic world, geopolitical and religious entities respectively, we are not attempting to pin down eternal dissimilarities. Such comparison is a vehicle for intellectual rapprochement and a concession to the – present – major significance of religion to political and social change within the Islamic world, though it carries very different weight in different countries. It is therefore essential that comparisons of world regions be accompanied by comparisons within those regions.

A good example of the relationship between universalism and particularism in Islamic-Western relations is the question of democracy. Is it legitimate to declare democracy the point of departure for any analysis, assuming it to be the common political goal of both hemispheres? We quickly find ourselves in a catch-22 situation here. To answer 'no' means that we consider the Islamic world incapable of producing democratic conditions, recalling Huntington's culturalism. 'Yes', on the other hand, tallies with old-school modernization theory, which represented another kind of Eurocentrism, in line with the motto: 'The barbarian is capable of development if he models himself on us'. But neither of these is relevant to us here. To observe the Islamic world from the vantage point of Western modernization and democracy does not mean tying it once and for all to these developments. But from a logical point of view, democracy would have to be introduced in the Islamic world, at least briefly, in order to furnish proof of its lack of fit with Islamic culture. Only in this way can people express themselves as bearers of culture, either professing their belief in democracy or correcting its mechanisms, or even abolishing it. Observations on the incompatibility of Islam and democracy made *before* any process of democratic opening are irrelevant in that they merely represent individual opinions. By considering the actual state of existing dictatorships in most of the Middle East, alongside already existing democracies in Muslim Asia and shifts towards future democracy in many other countries, this book takes into account the possibility that democracy may not take hold in many Islamic countries for a long time to come. Are these regimes simply authoritarian or are they fascist? This question is more relevant than ever to the present era.

Michel Foucault's oeuvre is crucial to the work of the modern-day cross-cultural political researcher in several respects. While his remarks on China or Iran underline the dangers of thinking without theory, his trademark combination of discourse analysis and (post-)structuralism shows us much of the way forward. The critique of discourse helps us come to grips with what the ideas and ideologies of the Islamic world and the West have in common and where they differ. But discourse alone does not constitute a reliable scientific basis. Foucault, quite rightly, always took account of the unspoken, of that not contained within discourse (Foucault 1981, 41 f.). Without returning to Karl Marx and his ideas of the primacy of the economy over consciousness, we can acknowledge that there is a world beyond discourse, amenable to observation and explanation. The people killed by Western wars in the Middle East and Islamic fundamentalist terrorist attacks are facts we cannot simply ignore as we indulge in post-modern discourse. To liberate ourselves from the 1400 years of misunderstandings and misperceptions that have blighted the relationship between Islam and the West, it is thus not enough to grapple with ideas and political programmes on religion, modernity, democracy and political violence, whose relevance to reality must always remain questionable as long as they are not tested against it. This book therefore proceeds consistently along twin tracks. Alongside the necessary critique of ideology, it includes consideration of political cultures, defined as public attitudes to politics and the political order, as well as analyses of social movements and the sociology of political transformation. It would, after all, have been impossible to foresee the deep-rooted democratic change that was soon to come solely by considering the opinions of Spanish Catholics, Falangists and communists in the early 1970s. Public opinion and social processes are valid indicators for any comprehensive political analysis.

The discipline of international relations also plays a key role. Today more than ever, it is the international environment that may foster as well as hinder political developments in a given country. The fact that the Islamic world features a greater orientation towards religious fundamentalism than other world regions is due *in part* to the fact that it finds itself in a unique situation globally. Nowhere else does the West provide such unconditional support to the worst dictatorships – in Morocco, Algeria, Tunisia, Egypt, Jordan, Saudi Arabia and many other places. Nowhere else is any other than the United States prepared to take military action on such a massive scale in order to secure its oil interests. The turn towards the region's own religion, Islam, and the abandonment of Western political concepts must be understood to a considerable extent as a pointer, as a message to the West to stop interfering and allow the Islamic world to develop. The West now finds itself confronted with the question of whom it ought to cooperate with and support and whether it should exert pressure in order to encourage political change in the Islamic world. A radical reorientation, away from power politics and towards the politics of principles and rights will be required. Martin Luther's Christian Reformation took off in part because of the Turkish threat to Europe and the failures of its rulers. But military pressure, which may sometimes block developmental processes that would otherwise be possible, does not always help. Does the West today have more to offer the Islamic world than war and exploitation?

THE BOOK

This book takes a step-by-step approach to understanding the role of political radicalism in the West and in the Islamic world. Chapter 1 (in Part I on Modernity) examines the most important secular and religious currents of political thought in the Islamic world. As will quickly become apparent, each camp consists of many strands, characterized by varying degrees of moderation and radicalism. These strands are distinguished by specific ideas about modernity and tradition. In particular, I probe the religious-political thought of the Islamic world, bringing out the similarities and differences with respect to European Protestantism, while also making a more rudimentary comparison with Catholicism and humanism.

Chapter 2 then attempts to determine the social location of ideological currents within the Islamic world. To which commonly held attitudes – characteristic of the political cultures of Islamic countries – do they correspond? Which social constellations, classes and social movements form the underpinnings of political thought and which political forces and parties embody this political thought?

Chapter 3 (in Part II on Democracy) provides a more finely-tuned comparison of the various forms of political modernity by examining contemporary secular and Islamic discourses on the question of democracy. Many internal differences can be discerned, and these are analyzed against the background of Western political currents – among them constitutionalism, conservatism, Euro-communism and American Christian neo-fundamentalism. I demonstrate that, notwithstanding numerous points of contact, Islamic fundamentalism has as yet made no clear commitment to democracy, and retains, to some extent at least, an anti-democratic radicalism.

Chapter 4 provides another shift of analytical perspective, from ideological critique to an interpretation rooted in functionalist political science. The key issue here is the consequences or possible consequences for democratization of the Islamic fundamentalists' radical politics. I deploy modern theories of political transformation to demonstrate that political radicalism – not violence – may render an opposition better able to engage in political conflict than precipitate moderation, which all too often enables authoritarian regimes to nip opposition movements in the bud.

Part III continues to flesh out the comparison between the Islamic world and the West by examining forms of political violence as practiced by some Islamic fundamentalists, as well as their antagonists – the regimes of the Islamic world and Western 'imperialists'. Chapter 5 aims to provide a systematic comparison of political systems, contrasting the authoritarianism of many states in the Islamic world with European fascism. This is supplemented by a section on anti-Semitism. One of the key findings here is that the authoritarianism of the Islamic world has little in common with European fascism. The partial modernization and liberalization of the authoritarian systems of some Islamic countries and the problems with democracy in the Western world – as are evident in Guantánamo and the 'modern slavery' of illegal workers – lead to a discussion of the categories deployed by comparative research on political systems.

Chapter 6 investigates the role of violence in international relations. The key question here is whether Western democracies are really more peaceable than autocracies in the Islamic world. As well as providing a phenomenology of the recent history of Western policies on the Islamic world and reflections on Islamic imperialism, I examine modern Western discourses on the 'new imperialism' and discuss theoretical perspectives on the links between democracy, war and peace.

Finally, Chapter 7 considers terrorism and its exponents, the self-proclaimed opponents of both autocrats and imperialists. It compares 'Islamic terrorism' with terrorism in other parts of the world and examines the various schools of thought on the causes of Islamic fundamentalist terrorism. This comparison is complemented by an introduction to the – frequently overlooked – activities of non-violent resistance in the Islamic world. This shows once again that, whatever the differences in the detail and in timing, the relationship between radicalism and political change in the Islamic world and in the West is often very similar.

I

MODERNITY

In the history of the West, the term 'modernity' refers to a profound social and political shift. But this shift did not occur from one moment to the next but through a slow process extending from the Middle Ages through the Renaissance, Reformation and nineteenth-century industrialization. What typifies modernity is its capacity to break loose from tradition. The uprooting of traditional values and their replacement by laws geared towards reason; the dissolution of traditional social structures through processes of urbanization, mobility and individualization; the development of a specific form of political autonomy, taking in the individual, the public sphere and the separation of state and religion: all these things are implied by modernity, which has become the leading concept for describing the development of Western society.

The critique of modernity, which has always existed, is part of modernity itself. In a paradoxical way, critics in fact corroborate modernity, for the critique of existing conditions is itself an achievement of modern rational, scientist and liberal thought. This means that Western modernity cannot be overhauled by the left or right. It is a system of thought in which critical voices, assailing such things as the destructive privileging of economic growth or Western modernity's advancing anonymization and distance from religion, must be regarded as contributions to the ongoing process of change and, thus, as the salvation of the project of modernity itself.

In recent years, the genetic derivation of the concept of modernity in the work of classical figures such as Max Weber has been replaced by questions about changes in modernity itself, the 'modernization of modernity' or 'reflexive modernity' (Beck et al. 1994). But this does not mean that Weberian thought is absent from the contemporary scene. It lives on, for example, in the debate on the relationship between Islam and modernity. In his attempt to tease out the specific contribution of religion to modernization, Weber contrasted Christianity with Islam, drawing on the scholarship of his day. From Weber's point of view, while Islam offered no significant perspective on salvation, its most impressive feature being the formal legalism of Islamic law, he saw Protestantism's achievement as preaching a concurrently worldly and otherworldly religious orientation. In Weber's view, the return to religious freedom and the striving for salvation in the hereafter (which, particularly in Calvin's doctrine of predestination, kindled a zeal for progress in this world) was a case of Protestantism inventing the central dualism of modernity. Weber failed to take heed of the fact that Islam created latitude for modernization through cyclical reforms (Salvatore 1997, 102 f.).

Even today, the view that Islam's supposed developmental deficits explain why the Middle East lags behind in the achievement of modernity is widespread among Western politicians, churches and media. But as Timothy Garton Ash of the University of Oxford has rightly pointed out, while the Islamic world needs to be modernized in a number of respects, it is not so much religion, a system always open to differing interpretations, that is responsible for the current state of politics and society, but rather the crisis-ridden history of the Middle Eastern states and peoples (Ash 2005, 147 f.). The problem with the neo-Weberian equation of Islam with hostility to modernization is that Catholicism – often seemingly archaic – has not ultimately impeded development and, what is more, for many long centuries the Islamic Middle East managed to keep pace with Europe, even functioning as an agent of modernization for the West in the Middle Ages and early modern period. At a time when there was little sign of the European revival of ancient thought, Arab philosophers such as Al-Farabi (ca. 870–950), Ibn Sina (Avicenna, 980–1037), Al-Ghazali (1058–1111) and Ibn Rushd (Averroes, 1126–98) had long since reconciled rationality and faith. It is no exaggeration to state that the European rediscovery of the ancient world began in Muslim Spain in the eleventh century and that, without the stimulus provided by Arab scholarship, which drew on both Greek traditions of thought and a Mediterranean culture that was subject for millennia to a process of unification, European modernity would never have got off the ground. The notion that Islam is hostile to modernity can be maintained only if we assert a direct continuity between Greek civilization and the Western Enlightenment, ignore the influence of Arab thought on the development of the West and look upon Islam as a religion that, unlike Christianity, impedes rather than fosters modernity.

This denial of the link between Western and Arab traditions of thought is the second key element in the Western view of the relationship between the Middle East and modernity. Prior to the Christian Reformation, suppression of the Arab contribution to a Western modernity that was starting to gain traction was already underway in Europe (Lockman 2004, 33). Since then, and up to the present day, the notion of two fundamentally different attitudes towards modernity has taken hold on a virtually mythological scale in the popular image of Islam. Notions of an unbridgeable cultural divide are conveyed through abstruse over-statement, as exemplified by a lead story in the largest German news magazine, *Der Spiegel*, in 2006:

In the Orient [in antiquity], the air was everywhere thick with the sweet aroma of religion – an opium for the people, lived out in ecstatic cults, (which) provided people with internal stability and welded them together into one great community. (...) Things were quite different among the Greeks. It was not faith but knowledge to which they aspired. (...) Nothing changed in the Orient. Buddha, Jesus, Muhammad – all come from the East. (...) The Greeks, meanwhile, blew away the mists of the sacred. (...) More than 2,500 years ago, East and West had already begun to drift apart. Today, the gap has become a chasm. Western thirst for knowledge versus the strength of Eastern faith – this front is still a living reality.[1]

The Islamic Middle East serves as a pre-modern mirror image for Western culture. The idea that the world is divided into a rational and progressive West and a religious and backward East is fuelled not only by Western media but sometimes also by Western scholarship, and has had a marked impact on Western thinking on modernization. Only in recent years, as many Asian economies have caught up with the West, has a more nuanced view of the comparison between Western and Eastern modernity, in the shape of the concept of 'multiple modernities', begun to take hold.

In what follows, I examine whether it is generally legitimate to take an oppositional notion of this kind as our starting point. Are there any areas of overlap between the notion of political modernity in the West and in the Islamic Middle East? It is vital to take into account not only intellectual currents but also their social practice, so I shall also discuss the social

---

[1] 'Die Entdeckung der Vernunft' ['The discovery of reason'], lead story in *Der Spiegel*, 27 November 2006.

and political bases of notions of modernity in the Islamic world. As we shall see, different currents of thought in contemporary Islam, up to and including fundamentalism, embody very different projects of reform or even reformation. Even when rationality is ultimately rejected, this stance is nonetheless often politically and socially logical in that it represents a radical break with the existing political rationality that marks the mainstream politics of Middle Eastern autocracy.

I

Conceptions of Modernity: Reform, Reformation and Radicalism

Western modernization theory has long been concerned with the question of why the West has attained a hegemonic position in politics, economy, and science over the last five hundred years, while other parts of the world have lagged behind. After the Second World War, a number of Western authors took the view that the key reasons for underdevelopment could be found in a tendency to cling to traditions and traditional values, not in specific political constellations or the injustice of the global economic order. For the Middle East, renowned theorists of modernization such as Daniel Lerner (1958) and Leonard Binder (1964) recommended the wholesale adoption of the Western developmental model. Modernization theory was applied in a wide variety of ways to political theories about the Middle East, such as neo-patrimonialism (Pawelka 1985; Springborg 1979) and neo-patriarchy (Sharabi 1988). These approaches shared a common orientation: they emphasized the weaknesses of modern state institutions when compared with the traditional loyalties of the tribe, village, and clientele, which seemingly undermine such institutions, covertly reinforcing stagnation.

Despite the justified criticism it has received, modernization theory was no classical colonialist hypothesis in scholarly garb. This key American notion was a marked improvement on the colonialist-racist doctrines that were widespread in Europe for many decades. Even as modernization theory insisted on the necessity of imitating the Western path, it nonetheless held out the prospect of such a process of learning and development in the non-European world. The difference between the old, racist European Orientalism and its new universalist American counterpart thus found expression in modernization theory.

Tellingly, the high point of modernization theory was in the 1950s and 1960s, before Western modernization manifestly came up against its own limitations over such issues as, for example, as environmental protection and economic growth. Alongside internal contradictions, developments on the periphery in Asia, Africa and Latin America stimulated a revision of modernization theory, the effects of which are still being felt. The first major phase of critique was rung in by the neo-Marxist theory of dependency and imperialism. Instead of the internal barriers of traditional cultures, this school of thought emphasized the effects of the world economic system on the developing countries, above all, the exploitation of their natural resources by the West; as an alternative to this system, these critics proposed protectionism aimed at achieving autonomy (see, for example, Galtung 1972).

Meanwhile, a shift in thinking had begun in the international debate on modernization. No longer anchored solely in neo-Marxist ideas, it often rested on a capitalist developmental logic. What was already known from the case of Japan has become a certainty in light of developments in China, namely that economic and social modernization may go hand in hand with the partial preservation and re-evaluation of traditions and may even culminate in forms of political and social modernization other than those familiar in the West (Roetz 2006; Schwinn 2006). One of the leading exponents of this line of thought is Shmuel N. Eisenstadt with his concept of 'multiple modernities' (Eisenstadt 2002).

But the notion of the diversity of modernity also has its opponents, who point out that China, too, is ultimately following the path of Western modernity, while practising 'vulgar Confucianism' (Berger 2006) to provide ideological comfort. There is no doubt that other countries have other customs – but does this mean that they are also characterized by a different model of political and economic modernity? This insistence on the unity of modernity and the challenges to the Eisenstadtian approach are certainly worth considering. They touch on crucial questions: What is the role of tradition in the Middle East and does an Islamic Middle Eastern modernity have any claim to independence? It is implausible to emphasize the Arab contribution to Western modernity in the Middle Ages and Renaissance while at the same time denying the Western influence on the Middle East from the Age of Enlightenment to the present. Is 'modernity' not ultimately something of a challenge cup, won by whoever represents the hub of progress in a given era and opens up new horizons to humanity as a whole?

On the other hand, why do the advocates of the 'one' (Western) modernity deny that, a mixing of indigenous traditions and borrowings from elsewhere occurs during such processes, in other words, that new variants of modernity may arise? No one would claim that Western modernity can be derived entirely from medieval Arab models. The modernization of the West proceeded so rapidly over the last two hundred years that we often lose sight of the fact that many aspects of what is now the West are not 'modern' at all, but represent local traditions that are by no means universal (we need only think of German federalism and the centralized French state). At no point in time has it been necessary for a territory to conform to the dominant developmental model in any *total* way – socially, politically and culturally – in order to achieve the latest standards of scientific and technological progress.

THE MINIMUM CONSENSUS OF WESTERN MODERNITY

There does, however, appear to be something of a minimum consensus on modernity. Comparative political scientist Fred Dallmayr distinguishes between two currents of thinking about modernity in the West: one is a view of the Enlightenment which places a rationally anchored human autonomy (as found in the work of thinkers such as Habermas) centre stage, which can succeed only if the traditional institutions of society and politics take a back seat and the relationship between citizen and bureaucratic state is founded anew through a democratic alliance (Dallmayr 2002). According to this view, it is the autonomy of the individual that crucially distinguishes the political framework of socioeconomic modernity. For Dallmayr, the other side of the coin is the critics of this model, who counter the radical modernizers by pointing out that it is characterized by the dissolution of traditional social cohesion and loss of values. As the originator of an intermediate position, Dallmayr identifies Charles Taylor, who distances himself from the logo- and anthropocentrism of a philosopher like Habermas and thus facilitates the rediscovery of the community, community responsibility and the religious community (Dallmayr 2002). At the same time, Taylor wishes to salvage the emancipatory achievements of the Weberian and Habermasian legacy by underlining the autonomy of the individual, whose inalienable rights he regards as universal.

As we shall see as we grapple with Islamic fundamentalism, it is above all the idea of the democratic fundamentals – primarily the constitutional state, within the framework of a popular sovereignty that is discursively founded and secured by electoral procedures – that represents a consensus in mainstream Western thought, though certainly not at its radical margins. Decisions about traditions and modernity should be made within a democratic and constitutional framework; decisions which are by no means, as Anthony Giddens thinks (Giddens 1994), restricted to founding a 'post-traditional society', but which may also leave space for traditions as long as these are compatible with the democratic consensus.

If we disregard for the moment the fascist and some other extremist derailments of the twentieth century, there seems at present to be no fundamental questioning of the democratic consensus about Western modernity, at least in the West. Modernity appears in traditionally imbued variants, from French presidential democracy to Swiss grassroots democracy and from the Swedish welfare state to American liberal capitalism, but fundamental counter-models, such as a neo-authoritarian anti-modernity, find practically no resonance in Western thought. Despite marked regional differences in the emphasis placed on 'caring societies', the West supports in principle religious freedom and the equality of the individual and of the genders. These pre-state rights define the autonomy of the individual and stand in stark contrast to fundamentalist counter concepts of the pre-state nature of a divine law from which human rights may, at best, be derived in appellative contexts and on a case-by-case basis (Kühnhardt 1991). It is possible in the West for communities to form within society (mostly in private, but sometimes assisted and subsidized by the state, even though the state is considered secular and neutral). At the same time, the individual must be protected from encroachment by communities. This dynamic is the basis of permanent, reflexive modernity.

Hence, two key questions arise when comparing the political thought of the West with that of the Islamic-Middle Eastern world:

- Which political traditions and structures can the Middle East retain if it wishes to join the Western minimum consensus on modernity?
- When retaining its own traditions, must the Islamic Middle East ultimately limit itself to moving towards a Western model of political modernization? Or is there a sustainable vision of a political modernity which, though not breaking entirely with the Western consensus, challenges, or even extends, it?

This assumption of a minimum consensus in Western political culture leaves out of for the time being problems of practical implementation. Since the attacks of 11 September 2001, these threaten to undermine democracy, the key terms here being 'Guantánamo' and 'Big Brother state'. Yet the main contradictions of the democratic consensus today lie, not in the relationship between theory and practice, which is characteristic of Western democracies' *domestic* policies, but rather in the imbalance between pacified domestic politics and belligerent *foreign* policies (see Chapter 6). Our next step, however, is to compare political ideas within Western society and the Islamic world.

SECULARISM AND POLITICAL ISLAM: IDEOLOGICAL DUALISM

A systematic view of political thought in the Islamic Middle East has become firmly established that distinguishes following currents: secular modernism, liberal reformist Islam, conservative reformist Islam and Islamic fundamentalism. This list, however, leaves out the largest single grouping, orthodox Islamic scholars, merely paying attention to the liberal, neo-conservative or fundamentalist 'offshoots' of this 'Establishment' Islam. This is justifiable in that it is impossible to refer straightforwardly to coherent 'political thought' among Islamic scholars who specialize in the casuistic interpretation of the law.

Francois Burgat is right to say that the historical 'Islamic state' was in fact always virtually secular in character. Contrary to appearances, religion was no more fundamental to the political systems of the 'East' than to those of the West (Burgat 2003, 132 f.). Along with the French Orientalist Jacques Berque, he points out that it was worldly dynasties and other social forces that dominated Islamic polities rather than Islamic legal scholars. The Ottoman sultan ruled by decree, though he allowed an Islamicized penal and marital law and occasionally took legal counsel.

Then and now, the Western view of Islam has clearly reflected an unenlightened mindset. Solitary figures such as the American Islamic studies scholar Bernard Lewis – who, like Samuel Huntington, is largely isolated in expert circles and has fallen out with the influential Middle East Studies Association (MESA) – has managed to get on to the *Time* magazine's list of the one hundred most important contemporary thinkers. In contrast to earlier Western Oriental studies, analyzed so impressively by Edward Said in *Orientalism* (Said 1978), mainstream scholarship no longer passes sweeping judgements, particularly with respect to the old dictum of the Islamic world's 'inseparability of religion and politics' still being expounded by Lewis (see, for example, Lewis 2003).

There are grounds for the assumption that the dualism of secularism and religious fundamentalism has been a core dynamic in the Islamic world that has followed a different path than in the West in terms of historical timing, but which has unfolded in a manner far more similar to Western developments than is often thought. Modern Islamic fundamentalists are *not* traditionalists. They do not wish to re-establish an old, non-secular order but to invent entirely new political systems by drawing on selective elements of Islamic teachings and aspects of the past to produce new political theories, as exemplified by the supremacy of the top Islamic legal scholar in the present-day Iranian constitution.

In Iran, the state and the parliamentary-democratic sphere are subordinated to Islamic law in the name of religion. But this has not been the universal model of government and society in the Islamic world over the last few centuries. The *umma*, as the community of the faithful held together through divine law, is indeed anchored in the Koran as the fundamental source of social order. Historically, however, from the time of the successors to the Prophet Muhammad onwards, Islamic legal interpretation and political rule were separated institutionally. A political order such as the one headed by Ayatollah Khomeini in Iran was entirely new in Iranian history and not based on any historical model. In theory, it was the ruler's obligation to see to it that practice conformed as closely as possible to Islamic law. This nonetheless demonstrates that worldly and spiritual power were not the same thing. The origins of the notion of 'religion and state' (*din wa dawla*) do not lie in any Koranic principle. Since the time of the successors to Muhammad, political organization has de facto been left to worldly forces and dynasties, which could neither be appointed nor toppled by legal scholars, but merely advised by them (Ayubi 1991; Crecelius 1980; Hurd 2008, 128 ff.; see also Karsh 2007, 33, 46).

This de facto secularism differs markedly from the anti-secular politics of Islamic fundamentalists, who demand clerical supremacy in the Iranian Shia case and, at least, the precedence of Islamic law over worldly positive law and discrimination between religions in the Sunnite case. Fundamentalist visions are a clear break with Islamic traditions of clerical coexistence with the rulers. At the same time, this secular history of the Islamic world bolsters the cause of contemporary secular liberals, left-wing or conservative governments and opposition forces, who can hark back to an Islamic tradition of secular political organization when advocating further and more consistent secularization of Muslim states and institutions.

A party such as the National Progressive Unionist Grouping (NPUG) in Egypt, for example, despite its strong neo-Islamic tendencies, nonetheless sees itself as champion of the secular legacy of Arab socialism propagated by former Egyptian president Gamal Abdel Nasser. It supports a laicist social order and rejects an 'Islamic state' (Koszinowski 1999, 101 ff.). The same goes for the economically liberal Wafd party, which has a secular orientation in part because this brings it votes from the Coptic Christian community – who, after all, make up 10 percent of the population. In recent years, however, some of these parties have entered into electoral alliances with the Egyptian Muslim Brothers, the oldest fundamentalist organization, in an attempt to profit from the neo-Islamic upsurge. Many see this as a weakening of the secular parties' ideologies, prompting factional disputes and resignations. But these very conflicts reveal a cultural dualism of secular and Islamic political justifications. While secular ideologies have been on the defensive since Nasser's death, they have not disappeared. The weakness of the secular opposition parties is rooted less in their secular orientation than in the internal encrustation of both personnel and structure, something which is particularly off-putting to the young (Hegasy 2000; Koszinowski 2005, 118; see also Chapter 4 of this book). In short: even though the performance of many secular parties is poor it would be too simplistic to conclude that secularism in general is finished in the Islamic world, now or in the future.

The history of the Islamic world may be told quite differently. Not only was it mostly ruled by worldly dynasties and other forces, but the full-fledged secularization of the legal system began as early as the nineteenth century. The Ottoman empire proclaimed that all subjects (excluding women and slaves) were equal before the law in 1839, marking the beginning of law-making by the state alone (Haarmann 1994, 384 f.). The policy of reform (*tanzimat*), influenced in part by Europe, kicked off a similar separation of religion and state as had taken hold in Europe, stimulated by the Peace of Westphalia of 1648 and the retreat of the Inquisition. The roots of the modern-day politics of states, such as Morocco, Egypt or Kuwait, in which Islam is the state religion but Islamic law has been almost entirely replaced by a secular legal system, lie in these early attempts to secularize the state. Countries such as Bangladesh and Malaysia have followed a similar trajectory. These countries do not see themselves as 'Islamic states' in the style of Iran or Saudi Arabia. It is clearly impossible to speak of a homogenous political culture with respect to the position of religion in an 'Islamic world' that is so often viewed as a single entity; we may at most refer to a long-standing dualism of secular and Islamic views on the status of religion, which coexist and, at times, conflict with each other.

The Bertelsmann Transformation Index (see Chapter 3) shows that a number of countries have made great progress on the path to secularization, especially Syria, Turkey, Tunisia. However, like countries which have anchored themselves in Islam (Saudi Arabia, Iran, Sudan, etc.), secular states, such as Tunisia and Syria, are among the most authoritarian in the Islamic world. In part, and crucially, this has something to do with the fact that their regimes have attempted to end the dualism of political cultures, that is, the competition between Islamic and secular political legitimation, by favouring one or the other aspect in an artificial and repressive way. If we can learn anything at all from recent Islamic history of the Islamic countries, it is that, with the possible exception of Turkey, attempts to impose a radical 'catch-up' secularization by force have been as unsuccessful in creating democratic orders as they have been in attempts to achieve revolutionary Islamization.

Again, this observation implies that secular modernization and democratization, free competition between secular and Islamic parties, rather than revolutionary Islamization or authoritarian secularization, would be the true cultural reflection of any 'just' politics in the Islamic world. Such a compromise would facilitate a constructive approach that mediates between the goal of the Islamization of the state, on the one hand, and the total laicization (on the Turkish or French model), on the other. Hence, it may be that exemplary compromise solutions will arise neither in Islamic fundamentalist states (such as Iran or Sudan) nor in 'secular' states (such as Tunisia or Syria), which differ greatly on the question of secularism but are very similar in their authoritarianism, but in the broad centre ground of the 'soft' authoritarianism seen in states such as Morocco or Egypt or in electoral democracies such as Indonesia, where Islam is the state religion but does not define the legal system.

Finally, critics of Western pressure on the Islamic world to secularize rightly point out that in the West, too, secularism generally exists in a far from pure form. Blasphemy laws in the United Kingdom, which have for centuries primarily protected the Christian religion; the levying of the church tax by the German state; religious education in state schools; creationist influences on the laws of numerous US states: these are just a few of many examples which show that Western states would rarely achieve the highest score on the Bertelsmann secularism index (Webster 1990). Western societies that had long since been described as democratic were basically half-secular entities in which Christian religious groups, because they formed democratic majorities, laid down the rules of the political and social game for smaller religious groups. The political system itself was not fundamentally religious in nature, but traditions of Christian hegemony evolved at the sub-constitutional level. The fact that, in countries such as Germany, Islam is moving ever closer to achieving recognition as a public organization with the same rights as the Christian churches, shows that democratic systems are capable of self-correction. A democratic system can belatedly secularize itself. In a fundamentalist system, on the other hand, the legal gap between Muslims and non-Muslims remains unbridgeable.

Empirical research on political culture has produced some interesting findings on the character of Islamic political culture, located as it is at the tense intersection of secularism and Islamization. Research on political change generally assumes that civic democratic values develop within a society very slowly, indeed, only after the introduction of a democratic system that crucially facilitates corresponding processes of political education (Merkel 1999, 143 ff.). But obviously, this does not apply in the same way to the fundamental question of secularization or the relationship between politics, state and religion. Mark Tessler's thorough empirical surveys in countries such as Morocco, Algeria and Turkey have shown that Islam has an astonishingly small influence on the formation of political opinions. A comparison of political attitudes among those with a strong or less strong religious orientation showed no significant divergence (Tessler 2002, 2003; Tessler and Altinoglu 2004, 34).

Is it not possible, therefore, that the actual political ideas of Islamization and the fundamentalists' hostility to secularization do not arise from the broad political culture but are the concern of a minority of Islamic fundamentalist devotees who wish to achieve a general legal privileging of Muslims and to force Muslims to practice their religion devoutly? Would the religious basis of politics be contested in a free democratic society if it were up to the Islamic public? There is a significant difference between the popular re-Islamization of the last few decades and Islamic fundamentalism. After the Iranian Revolution of 1978–9, Duran Khalid pointed out that, while organized Islamic fundamentalism 'feeds' on the general process of re-Islamization (the neoconservative trend towards public prayer, the building of mosques, the wearing of veils, and the like – developments that have been with us for three decades), it has remained a 'foreign body' within the movement (Khalid 1982, 21 f.). Religious fundamentalist forces use Islamization as a token ideology without representing a thoroughly Islamic political culture.

The fact that religion has played such a major role in the politics of the Islamic world for a number of decades thus has less to do with long-term political attitudes, values and cultures than with the fact that secularism remains a live issue. The Islamic world has seen nothing comparable to the Peace of Westphalia. Further, secularism was often imposed by authoritarian leaders, provoking a quite logical counter-reaction from an opposition which deployed Islam against the existing regime. The inseparability of religion and state is no uniform cultural model in the Islamic world, but an ideological alternative to secularization on the margins of global society, a process which is associated with Western interference and exploitative indigenous elites. Anti-secularism thus defines a new anti-elite ideological battlefield, not least because secularization and early attempts at democratization in the Islamic world were always in part processes of social repression (see Chapter 2).

While history allows many comparisons, it does not unfold in unchanging patterns. Parallels between temporal phenomena by no means imply any metaphorical claim to totality on the part of explanatory models. What matters for the moment is merely that neither the ideological models nor the political cultures of the contemporary Islamic world can be reduced to a state of unity between politics and religion. 'Thirty years' wars' in Sudan occur side-by-side with processes of secularization in Turkey. The Islamic countries do not share the secular consensus of the West, but on the issue of democracy they have already undergone the kinds of developments which occurred in Europe only in the twentieth century: female suffrage, constitutionalism and parliamentarism. Secularism, too, is nothing new; it is but the current pivot for ideologically charged turf wars.

LIBERAL REFORMIST ISLAM: REFORMATION WITHOUT MODERNITY?

In his deprecatory view of Islam, Max Weber took no notice of the cyclical reform movements that have always distinguished it (Salvatore 1997, 102 f.). Interestingly, the current of liberal reformist Islam seems to flow with both the Western consensus on modernity and Middle Eastern secular modernism, though in the Islamic tradition there is a very different ideological point of departure. Despite the separation of natural and human rights in this school of thought, however, the method of religious-text interpretation deployed in liberal discourse seems to display certain fundamental democratic qualities. How else can we explain the fact that no thinker in the liberal reformist camp would reject the political modernity of the West – the legal autonomy of the individual, protection from the arbitrary exercise of state power, etc.? Another phenomenon is taking hold within reformist Islam: rationalism as an epistemic point of departure conceived of, not as a philosophical act of individual self-creation, as for example, in the case of Descartes (*cogito ergo sum*), but as a symbiosis of faith and rationalism.

Muslim liberal reformist thinkers are a heterogeneous group of intellectuals and authors who wish to devise a modern Islamic society. In line with their great popularity and numerous books, speeches, essays and media appearances, the arguments they put forward are far from uniform. Yet, they share a core conviction that identifies a coherent school of thought, namely, the assumption that every interpretation of the key Islamic texts, the Koran, the Hadith (reports of Muhammad's deeds) and Sharia (Islamic law), is influenced by historical conditions. Every understanding is subjective and arises out of current circumstances. Rational interpretation of the sources (Arabic *ijtihad*) facilitates a permanent modernization of the faith that dovetails with the modernization of state and society.

The Egyptian philosopher Nasr Hamid Abu Zayd, for example, stresses the need for a new, contemporary interpretation of the Koran and underlines that processes of interpretation are always subjective, drawing primarily on the work of Hans-Georg Gadamer (Abu Zayd 2006; Abu Zayd and Nelson 2004). From the same starting point, Muhammad Shahrur of Syria is moving towards a critique of Sharia when he asserts that, if all interpretation is subjective and time-bound, then Sharia cannot function as law (Mudhoon 2006, 141). Abdullahi Ahmed an-Na'im comes very close to this position when he calls for a revision of the Sharia and its adaptation to international legal norms and human rights (An-Na'im 1996). An-Na'im argues that the originally humanistic and enlightened idea of the Sharia must once again become recognizable. Medieval Islamic law was, after all, an early attempt to establish a constitutional order, not unlike the contemporaneous endeavours embodied in the Magna Carta, at a time when monarchical and feudal despotism still prevailed across much of Europe. But according to An-Na'im, if Islamic law is not to degenerate into dictatorship, it must be open to reinterpretation. Farid Esack also advocates religious pluralism. He criticizes the scholarly Islamic orthodoxy as quietist for failing to engage with processes of modernization. Esack wants an Islamic theology of liberation which is compatible with democracy (Fix 2006).

But the reformist thinkers' privileging of reinterpretation does not take into account the fact that subjectivism alone is incapable of qualifying the validity of religious laws (which is necessary in order to ensure the acceptance of the individual's autonomy, irrespective of religious affiliation) because the religious sources are retained as the basis of textual interpretation. Compared with the Western consensus, what is still missing is the anchoring of the law in humanitarian human rights. Many reformist thinkers have therefore gone a step further, showing a tendency to decouple Sharia from jurisprudence (*fiqh*), in other words, to move away from the juridical components of the Sharia; this ultimately reconciles reformist Islam with the secular constitutional state (Jacobs 2006) as the Sharia is now no more than one possible *source* of law – we might also say 'inspiration' – but not the law itself.

Soheib Bencheikh takes the argument further by stating that the Sharia, Catholic canonical law, and the Jewish Talmud are not compatible with positive law. Rather, only the Koran is holy, but not the prophetic writings, let alone Islamic law. For Bencheikh, the guidelines they contain, such as the prohibition on changing religion (apostasy), are thus null and void (Jacobs 2006, 15, 19). The Iranian reformist thinkers Abdolkarim Soroush and Mohammad Shabestari both reject the idea of divine sovereignty expressed in Islamic law for human beings can never obtain divine truth (Shabestari 2003; Soroush 2000). It is thus no surprise that Fred Dallmayr regards thinkers like Soroush as the direct counterparts of Western intellectuals like Charles Taylor: they are attempting to find a middle path between rational and religious, individual and group-oriented modernism on the basis of human rights (Dallmayr 2002, 102–4).

Islamic liberal reformists refute the Western modernization theorists who view Islam as an obstacle to development. They represent a virtually paradigmatic attempt to create a kind of 'Islamic Protestant ethic' and thus demonstrate the compatibility of Islam and modernity. Reformist Islam is entirely compatible with the Western political consensus on modernity because it denies the supreme authority of religion and rejects interpretations of Islam that overemphasize its legal aspects. Its intention, however, is to improve on a Western modernity that it regards as being to some extent bereft of meaning, criticism also heard from Western authors. Even Jürgen Habermas, one of the leading interpreters of secularism, has rediscovered the significance of religion as a source of meaning and guidance for the West. A secular society, as he concluded in his acceptance speech on receiving the Peace Prize of the German book trade in 2001, is not completely without religion, but religion loses its coercive character through the process of secularization (Habermas 2001).

Reformist Islam's quite self-conscious aspiration to improve on Western modernity through religion is apparent in the work of Fazlur

Rahman, a contemporary reformist thinker, when he expresses his view of the relationship between human beings, nature and community:

> It is true that earlier societies were much more dogmatic in certain respects and therefore exposed themselves to dangers, while modern sophistication means less dogmatism, overtly at least. But this competence of modern societies to adjust to necessary change is often like a doctor who treats symptoms rather than the disease. (...) It is to be feared that modern civilization, while sophisticating means and methods to almost no end, has developed cardinal deficiencies in basic insights into human nature. (...) There is a considerable body of what might be called social thought in the Quran, which talks incessantly about the rise and fall of societies and civilizations or 'the inheritance of the earth', of the function of leadership, of prosperity and peace and their opposites, and especially of 'those who sow corruption on the earth but think they are reformers' (Rahman 1982, 161).

Again, in this respect reformist Islam continues the Islamic tradition of integrating and developing other religious ideas and world views, as the Koran does when it identifies Christianity and Judaism as predecessors. This attempt to close the gap between faith and rationality is thus the wellspring of a global ecumene and a harbinger of a future cosmopolitan culture of modernity. Is this not what the evidence suggests?

However, an orientation towards indigenous Islamic sources seems ill-suited to spreading reformist Islamic modernity beyond the boundaries of Islam. The universalist appeal of Western political modernity consisted above all in its success in dealing with the question of power and creating stable orders. The retrogressive reform of a religion, geared towards its own particular traditions and texts, such as being attempted by liberal Islamic reformists, can scarcely be considered exemplary, in part because the basic texts do not adhere to any scientific form. Their analysis belongs to the field of theology, and it requires special knowledge of a stock of linguistically complex traditional sources (Koran, Hadith, Sharia) which are distributed unequally across the globe and concentrated primarily in the Arab world. It is hardly possible to approach this project of reform with the tools of the modern humanities and social sciences.

Hence, liberal reformist Islam is concerned with a kind of reformation which represents a significant, even essential, but not a sufficient element of modernist political thought. It is a particular form of the traditional arguments for political modernity – but is it modernity itself? This would be like claiming that the Protestant Reformation itself established the thought that is characteristic of Western modernity, though it was, in fact, just one stage of a chain reaction of modernization. In light of the controversy surrounding Max Weber's emphasis on the role of the Protestant ethic within modernity (Weber 2006), to overemphasize the role of Protestantism in modern academic thinking would in any case be a particularly dubious notion. It is certainly justified, therefore, to recall Johannes Berger's distinction between local inflections and the preservation of a cohesive (Western) modernity (Berger 2006). In this view, liberal reformist Islam is certainly evidence that it is possible to revitalize an Islamic tradition of progress, a tradition that is of the utmost importance to Muslims' identification with modernity. But this would not be a future-oriented, independent modernity beyond the Western constructs of human rights and the democratic constitutional state.

Islamic liberal reformers claim that they contribute to and supplement (Western) modernity arises less from the universality of their message than from the exemplary quality that their particular fusion of rationality and religion, were it ever to take hold in the Islamic world, might have for other regions. While religious and other critics of modernity have always existed in the West, they are few and far between, and they are at present clearly more at home in the Islamic world, at least when it comes to political thought (having had, at any rate, little effect on the expansive dynamics of Western modernity that have led to environmental destruction, catastrophic climate change and global poverty). This may justify Islamic reformers' claim, if not to universal validity, then certainly to the status of the role model for those aspiring to renew other traditional religious and cultural discourses of modernity.

CONSERVATIVE REFORMIST ISLAM: A LUTHERAN LOGIC

More successful and popular in recent years than the liberal reformist school is that of the conservative Islamic reformers, who may be described, with certain qualifications, as treading a middle path between liberal reformist Islam and fundamentalism. This school is referred to as 'centrism' (*Wasatiyya*) by some scholars (Baker 2003). However, like the liberal reformers and in contrast to the fundamentalist organizations, it is characterized by a very limited number of fixed organizational and group structures, although the relevant thinkers frequently refer to one another and see themselves as an intellectual school. This school finds reflection in a number of organizational forms, such as the Egyptian Wasat party (*Hizb al-Wasat*). The conservative reformers are interesting not only because, as in all other schools of thought, they are open to technology and progress, but because they aspire to a more flexible interpretation of traditions of political and social doctrine, one that is not liberal but modern conservative, and often highly contradictory.

One of the best-known conservative reformers is Islamic studies scholar Tariq Ramadan, whom the USA's *Time* magazine has identified as one of the most influential contemporary thinkers. The grandson of Hassan al-Banna, founder of the Egyptian Muslim Brothers, he lived in Switzerland for many years before moving to France and the United Kingdom. In 2004, he was refused entry when he went to the United States to take up a chair in religion and conflict resolution at the University of Notre Dame in Illinois. The American authorities gave no official explanation. Today, Ramadan maintains contact with a number of academic institutions, such as St. Antony's College, Oxford, but he is essentially a freelance author and leading thinker. For Ramadan, next to the Koran, the Hadith and the Sharia are the most important foundations of social order; in principle, he takes the view that everything that is not forbidden is allowed. Unlike the liberal reformers, Ramadan does not want to reduce the Sharia to a non-binding moral code, but argues instead in favour of a new interpretation of the law. For the 'layman' Ramadan, who did not attend a religious school, it is important that this new interpretation be achieved, not only by orthodox Islamic scholars, but also by the entire community of Muslims. And, in the final instance, it should depend on the conscience of individual Muslims (Ammann 2006, 28 f.).

While this may appear to constitute a significant shift away from orthodoxy and the orthodox teachings of the Sharia, Ramadan's system of thought still has an extremely tense relationship with the demands of the constitutional state in which the (religious) conscience of the individual is subordinate to (trans-religious, positive) law. On the one hand, Ramadan encourages the reinterpretation of and debate on Islamic rules, and underlines the human character of Islamic law, as well as the fact that the essence of the Islamic law of the Sharia is the internal process of embracing an Islamic ethics: this idea may promote the integration of Muslims into secular society because in interpreting the law Ramadan distances himself from the fundamentalist loyalty to the text. On the other hand, he does not adopt an unambiguously critical stance towards Islamic law as a legal system that is in competition with secular orders but criticizes the liberal reformers for submitting to the Western dictum of the privatization of religion (Ramadan 2004; see also 2006, 67 ff.). This undecidedness may be quite deliberate, and it has earned Ramadan much criticism when, for example, he merely demands a moratorium on *Hadd* punishments (including the stoning of women for adultery) rather than their abolition.[1] In his attitude towards the legal character of the Sharia, Ramadan is at least close to the positions of the fundamentalist mainstream (though, as we shall see, this mainstream often tacitly ignores Islamic law through a selective and passive approach to the Sharia; see Chapter 3).

The ambiguity of Ramadan's thinking is captured by Ludwig Ammann: 'Within the cultural struggle of the two reformist velocities that is going on in the Islamic world [Tariq Ramadan] sides with the people, overwhelmed by change. This makes him a conservative reformer, but not a reactionary' (Ammann 2006, 31). Ramadan appeals most to middle-class Muslim circles in Europe who are socially established but lack cultural recognition by the West. Ramadan's assertion of the independence of Islamic modernity lends them a new self-confidence. But we should not overlook the lack of consistency that characterizes this kind of thinking. Ramadan calls for the acceptance of Western laws but not for the abolition of the legal character of the Sharia. He provides no way out of this dilemma.

This is also true of other thinkers within the conservative reformist grouping. Yusuf al-Qaradawi is considered the founder of *Wasatiyya*, which propagates neither simple adherence to Islamic norms nor their fundamental interpretive openness, but rather, in the case of Al-Qaradawi, a process of reinterpretation and modernization led mainly by Islamic scholars (Baker 2003). The fact that teachings such as those of Ramadan or Al-Qaradawi are unlikely to endure over the long-term, and that these thinkers represent transitional phenomena, becomes clear the moment we recognize that their ideological production is largely anchored in their personal situations. Ramadan is leading an intellectual revolt against the interpretive monopoly of the traditional learned Islam of Al-Azhar University in Cairo as did his grandfather Hassan al-Banna. Al-Qaradawi, former student at Al-Azhar, the key stronghold of Sunnite teachings, uses the mass media to reform the world of Islamic legal scholarship, placing it at the forefront of a process of intellectual and social modernization. Here, among other things, Al-Qaradawi is certainly considering the possibility that legal scholars might have a monitoring function vis-à-vis state power. This may be interpreted positively in that he emphatically criticizes the existing Arab regimes. But it also recalls the claim to power characteristic of clerical rule in Shia Iran and demonstrates the limits of

---

[1] Martin Beglinger, Bruder Tariq [Brother Tariq], in: *Das Magazin* 1/2006, http://www.dasmagazin.ch/magazin/magazin.php?MagazinID=GMM4RY (12 January 2007).

Qaradawi's vision of democracy. Religious rule cannot, for example, be squared with the equality of religious minorities before the law inherent in secularism.

Al-Qaradawi sounds almost like Jürgen Habermas and Hannah Arendt, emphasizing that Islamic society must be remade through discourse and social communication (Salvatore 1997, 205 ff.). But he baulks at the prospect of a radically open dialogue for fear that Muslim unity would collapse. He pinpoints 'encrusted' aspects of Islamic law and wishes to carry out reforms, but does not want to lose control and deploy Islamic scholars as the custodians of a new consensus – a markedly different position from that of liberal reformist Islam, which Al-Qaradawi, like Ramadan, rejects as a 'Western' import. Conservative reformers refuse to follow the path of the liberal reformers. For them, this would mean giving up the means of making Islam an agent of social and political renewal. From the point of view of conservative reformers, liberal pluralism and the abandonment of the mobilizing pressure of Islamic law make liberal reform an intellectual movement of great cultural importance over the long term but with negligible short-term political significance.

Whether the desired new Islamic consensus should include the normative supervision of the state and its laws, or is merely a unified but not legally binding moral canon – in other words, a kind of modernized Islamic Catholicism – is unclear. However, Al-Qaradawi seems at least to distinguish between societies with Muslim majorities and minorities. He calls on Muslims to respect French law, which prohibits the wearing of headscarves in schools, because in his view the education of girls takes priority (Gräf 2006, 113). Fahmi Huwaidi takes a similar view, demanding compliance with French laws, despite the fact that wearing the headscarf is a fundamental duty (Baker 2003, 98). It should be emphasized, however, that it remains unclear whether these authors would declare wearing the headscarf a legal obligation in Muslim-majority societies. Such a provision would place religious practice under the dictatorship of the majority, in Al-Qaradawi's case, perhaps even the dictatorship of scholarly opinion alone. The reach of the state would extend into the private sphere beyond any reasonable remit, to say nothing of religious minorities, whose legal equality would not be assured in such a state. At all events, any 'two worlds' doctrine formulated by conservative Islamic reformers (unavoidable adaptation to temporal law in Western democracies, a religious belief-based state in the Islamic world), were it to take hold among conservative reformers, would differ markedly from the Western consensus on political modernity.

Fetullah Gülen, the key Turkish figure in a worldwide movement for educational reform, is generally highly conservative. Influenced by the Turkish tradition of the secular state, however, he highlights the importance of the individual conscience – a motif also present in the work of thinkers such as Tariq Ramadan – and comes close to acceptance of the secular state. The individual Muslim, states Gülen, may not question state law. Islamic activities should be focussed on the improvement of individual rather than state action (Agai 2006, 59). His conservative reformism is coupled with a secular position that seems to lie fully within the Western consensus. But Gülen is not typical of the conservative reformist school in which thinkers such as the Moroccan Nadia Yassine or Egyptian star preacher Amr Khaled exhibit a mode of thought similar to that of Al-Qaradawi or Ramadan. All are prepared to make Islamic law more flexible but shy away from acknowledging the secularism of the law and downgrading the Sharia to the status of moral code. It is this proximity to Islamic fundamentalism that nourishes Western criticism of the centrists. However, when Andreas Jacobs argues that the conservative reformers' main aim is not so much the 'modernization of Islam' but rather the 'Islamization of modernity' (Jacobs 2006, 8), he implies that this school of thought is a case of 'old wine in new bottles', as if the reform and modernization of Islam are merely ploys intended to rescue old Islamic values and concepts of law in the context of modernity. This is wrong, at least in part. Conservative reformers, like their liberal counterparts, are unquestionably concerned with both: Islamization and modernization. More than the liberals, however, conservative reformers continue to assert the unity of Islamic traditions of thought within modernity, avoiding a consistently pluralist credo. Yet they undoubtedly seek modes of transition to, and elements compatible with, Western technological, socioeconomic and political modernity.

It is tempting to compare liberal and conservative reformist Islam with Catholicism and Protestantism. At first glance, the conservatives seem to have much in common with Catholicism and the liberals with Protestantism. While the liberals aim to break radically with the idea of the supreme validity of Islamic law, which has held canonical status since the thirteenth century, the conservatives tread very cautiously here, taking a step-by-step approach. The Catholic Church, too, never entirely stagnated with respect to doctrinal development – it was as a rule merely the last societal force to embrace the social changes brought about by modernity and, thus, proved to be a restraining force. The Catholic Church provided support to many precisely because it became the autonomous stronghold of stocks of tradition. But on closer inspection, such comparisons between developments in Islamic and Christian thought are misleading.

In the West, liberal reformist Islam is often thought to be a carbon copy of the Christian Reformation, an answer to the search for an 'Islamic Luther'. But there are differences as well as common ground. It is true that Martin Luther, like the Islamic liberals, represented a profound challenge to canonical positions, but European Protestantism did not profess a faith in pluralism. On the contrary, it was often highly intolerant and radical. Luther was a confessed opponent of an arbitrary approach to matters of faith and to the humanism exhibited by the likes of Erasmus of Rotterdam, as this humanism was anchored not in faith but human life itself (Gronau 2006). Luther was not the liberal he is often portrayed as, although Protestantism developed a tremendous heterogeneity and variety in the centuries after him, such that today it is indeed pluralist in some ways and gives the impression of being liberal (though in the United States, for example, this has provoked counteracting fundamentalist forces). Luther and the other reformers of his time, such as Calvin, Zwingli and Thomas Müntzer, certainly challenged the omnipotence of the Pope in matters of faith. But they also established new doctrines, which they considered irrefutable and, in the case of Zwingli and Müntzer, disseminated by force or, in the case of Luther, championed in a profoundly radical way. We need think only of the dispute between Zwingli and Luther over communion. How illiberal Protestantism can still be was laid bare by the Protestant Church in Germany, which in 2006 produced a document entitled 'Clarity and Neighbourliness' which asserts that Christianity is superior to Islam (Micksch 2007).

Francis Fukuyama draws direct parallels between the Christian Reformation and Islamic fundamentalism, and his argument can undoubtedly be applied to other illiberal forces, such as the conservative Islamic reformers, as well:

Many Westerners have lamented the absence of a Muslim Luther. But they forget that the historical Luther did not preach pluralism and liberalism but unleashed a wave of religious fanaticism that played out in very intolerant forms such as those found in the Geneva of John Calvin. It was only by smashing the existing connections between traditional religion and political power, and by exercising actual power in a pluralistic political space, that Protestantism laid the groundwork for modern secular politics and the separation of church and state. In Europe, this process took several centuries; we can only hope for a more accelerated timetable for Muslims today (Fukuyama 2006, 78).

Does Islam need its own 'Luther'? This question admits of no easy answers. Contemporary liberal Islamic reformers are often significantly more advanced with respect to the fusion of reformation and humanism than was the historical Luther. Their insistence on the interpretive sovereignty of the individual – which de facto culminates in humanistic-individual solutions, even if they are religiously derived – highlights how processes of modernization occur at different points in history. The liberal Islamic thought of our time is being formulated against the background of worldwide processes of democratization. While Luther and his contemporaries were unfamiliar with concepts of human rights and democracy, this is not true of the Islamic reformers, for whom they serve as a model of a deeply pluralist approach to the interpretation of religion. The question is whether any Muslim liberal reformer would come up with the idea of formulating a new 'catechism' or, like Luther, of going into battle against 'enthusiasts' (*Schwärmer*), spiritualists, Jews, or any other group that might favour a different interpretation than his own.

In many ways, Luther resembles the conservative Islamic reformers more than their liberal counterparts, as the conservatives challenge old certainties but also aspire to produce new collective interpretations. It is this dualism that provides the conservatives' recipe for success, a grouping which in the West – to some extent quite rightly, as we have seen – is lumped together with the fundamentalists. While liberals such as Nasr Hamid Abu Zayd are deconstructivists, who are imparting an approach to the holy texts rather than conceiving a new doctrine, we can discern the outlines of a new doctrinal system among conservative reformers. It is interesting to note that the conservative reformers of Islam draw on models of conservative renewal deployed by the Western world itself when it began to modernize during the Christian Reformation. These helped break through stagnant habits of thinking and feeling and helped people adapt to the changes occurring in a modernizing society without having to abandon everything they had known. Luther, as Fukuyama correctly states, saw that it was essential to do away with the traditional way of thinking. At the same time, he strove to discover new certainties. It is precisely this model of action that characterizes the conservative reformers. If a thinker such as Ramadan is sometimes called an 'Islamic Luther', there is undoubtedly some logic in this. That the principle of illiberal reinterpretation had not only positive but also negative consequences, in the shape of the Thirty Years' War for example, is well-known and should not be forgotten within the context of any comparison with the Islamic world.

Whether we wish to see the Martin Luther of the sixteenth century as a role model for the present Islamic world in the first place is a question of perspective. The liberal reformers seem already to have overtaken him with respect to pluralism, individualism and humanism; conservative reformers are striking a considerable chord with a Lutheran-style combination of reform and intolerance. But Luther is also an exemplary figure in other ways, with respect to his clear profession of faith in secularism for instance. While Tariq Ramadan declares the private and the public, as well as the political and the religious, inseparably linked and leaves open the question of whether a (reformed) Islamic law should have the character of law (Kamrava 2006, 68), Luther submitted to worldly power (Gronau 2006, 74). This he may have done, not out of conviction, but because the authorities protected him from papal attacks. Other reformers, such as the socially revolutionary Thomas Müntzer or Ulrich Zwingli, took a different view. They were frequently ready to use violence and strove to achieve political change. Liberal Islamic reformers have already learnt this lesson. Conservative reformers, who otherwise have so much in common with the basic patterns of Luther's thought, are still wrestling with the idea of the separation of state and religion, though their political intentions remain unclear. (As we shall see, Islamic fundamentalists reject the idea of secularism more firmly than conservative reformers. The fundamentalists also differ from the conservative reformers in rejecting the idea of religious renewal, for which they see no need, though in reality they are no longer traditionalists.)

In making such comparisons it is important to understand the prevailing historical conditions. The liberal Islamic reformers, who often live in the West, all endorse secular law because it protects them. In many cases, they had to flee from persecution in authoritarian Islamic states. Many conservative reformers live in the Islamic world. For reasons of legality, conservative reformers and revivalist preachers steer clear of the fundamentalists' open opposition to the state and instead work within the states' legal framework as supporters of popular mass movements. Returning to the points made above about secular notions of modernization, we should note that the secular state in the Middle East not only had an emancipatory function, but also aided the rise of the authoritarian state. Conservative reformers see themselves as part of a religious mobilization against a state they regard as corrupt. But in contrast to the fundamentalists, they formulate no political programmes, let alone instigate revolutions as in Iran. It must therefore remain an open question whether, despite their professions of faith in the unity of Muslims, in a new orthodoxy, new collectivism and anti-liberalism, they can be more than a straightforward neo-religious revivalist movement and will become politically important or, on the contrary, perpetuate the political status quo (see Chapter 2).

In sum, conservative reformist Islam clearly embodies an interesting synthesis. It underlines the potential for the modernization of Islamic norms while assuaging a widespread fear of social change by proceeding at a slow developmental tempo and calling for a new social unity on values to counter the alleged decline in values in the West. At the same time, this school carries a form of latent political aggression. Though it does not threaten violence, neither does it entirely abandon the notion that Islamic law is the only valid public law, which has a politically challenging effect. Because it pursues no political programmes, however, it exerts no direct pressure on authoritarian regimes, which therefore largely tolerate conservative reformist movements, even as they often make life difficult for the leading figures of these movements. This school maintains an open but ambivalent relationship to the Western consensus on individual autonomy and secular democracy. Only real-world practice will reveal whether it classifies Islamic law as a symbolic moral code or as law, the latter being a sign of fundamentalism.

THE UNINTENTIONAL MODERNITY OF ISLAMIC FUNDAMENTALISM

What is the relationship of Islamic fundamentalism to modernity? Many of the questions posed by fundamentalists are asked in nearly identical ways by Western critics of modernity. The key terms here are anonymization, the decline of community, the decline of values, social justice and the growing chasm between human beings and nature. However, in recent decades at least, a consensus has prevailed in the West that any form of modernity must be democratic and, by and large, secular, which cannot be said of Islamic fundamentalists (see Chapter 3).

Yet, even the relationship of Islamic fundamentalism to Western modernity is multifaceted and often paradoxical. There is unanimity within the scholarly literature that at least the fundamentalist mainstream, in other words the major Islamic fundamentalist organizations, have no objections to the scientific and technological modernity of the West. In the view of Bassam Tibi, what fundamentalists demand is thus 'semi-modernity' (Tibi 1993). Only a vanishingly small minority of fundamentalists envisage a return to the original pre-modern Islamic society of the Prophet

Muhammad. Many opponents of semi-modernity make the standard argument that this is unrealistic because the dynamics of permanent modernization are nourished by social and political freedom. However, examples such as Prussia's development in the nineteenth century and China's present-day path show that social forms that do not dovetail with Western notions of the autonomy of the individual, human rights and democracy may be capable of far-reaching processes of scientific, economic and social modernization. Though 'experiments' such as the Islamic Republic of Iran cannot be considered successful examples of such modernization, Iran has undoubtedly achieved a good deal with respect to the integration and social mobilization of its underprivileged classes (see Chapter 2). Elements identified as central to human well-being in contemporary research on 'happiness' – a modest but reliable income and functioning family and social relationships – are also core features of Islamic fundamentalist ideology (Grimm 2006). The notion that the actions of fundamentalists are directed solely towards the hereafter and that their organizations are indifferent to temporal happiness is wrong, nourished by ideas disseminated at most by small missionary Islamic sects.[2]

But the greatest bone of contention is respect for the individual's pre-state 'human rights'. These seem far from assured in any Islamic state of the kind to which fundamentalists aspire. The price to be paid for Islamic fundamentalist modernity is clearly a kind of 'dictatorship of the commonweal' over individual freedom in both matters of faith and on many other vital issues. What is at issue here is not the procedures of democracy, such as elections, division of powers, parliamentarism and many other aspects, which are often quite acceptable to fundamentalists (see Chapter 3), but the subordination of the individual to the idea of the religious state. This also applies to the state fundamentalism of states such as Saudi Arabia, one of the few countries in the Islamic world, to mention just one example, whose code of journalistic ethics does *not* protect the private sphere; in fact, it does not mention it at all (K. Hafez 2002b).

From the perspective of ideological critique, we might conclude that Islamic fundamentalism is at best compatible with semi-modernity. But there is another way of looking at fundamentalism. Historical comparison reveals that while fundamentalist ideologies certainly preach traditionalism and have no wish to be ideologies of modernity, in reality they are modern ideologies in traditional garb. Classifications of Islamic

---

[2] We shall be examining the division of contemporary Islamism into political, missionary and Jihadist currents throughout the following chapters.

fundamentalism placing it within the spectrum of neo-traditionalism, of the kind so common in the scholarly literature (Bennett 2005), pay no heed to the fact that the political ideology of Islamic fundamentalism is based on elements that arose only in the twentieth century.

The most prominent example in this respect is surely the notion of the hegemony of the supreme spiritual leader over the state in Iran, the principle of *velayat-e faqih*. The origins of this constitutional construct, which grants to this supreme leader the permanent right of veto in all affairs of state, lie in the era of revolutionary leader Ayatollah Khomeini and is unprecedented in Islamic history. Khomeini was as little rooted in the Shia tradition of government as was the late medieval monk Girolamo Savonarola in Catholic traditions when he established his 'divine dictatorship' in the Florence of the late fifteenth century, creating an unprecedented form of theocracy (Piper 1979). This comparison is all the more fruitful given that the Khomeini and Savonarola revolutions were both supported by urban merchant and artisan classes and opposed the profligate tendencies of an authoritarian monarchy (the Shah of Persia and the ruling Medici family). Both figures aimed to further the interests of these classes under the cloak of religion. Savonarola's rule marked a conscious shift from traditional to modern rule at a time when the middle ages was giving way to the Renaissance. Savonarola was at once a reactionary and a social revolutionary, and thus in any case a product of modernity who devised entirely new types of policy (such as a police force consisting of children tasked with monitoring public manners).

A similar role may be ascribed to the Islamic fundamentalists, who are fighting against the Islamic tradition of clerical coexistence with Middle Eastern dynasties of every type rather than consolidating old forms of government. Even in Iran, where theocracy has endured for the last thirty years even as the internal opposition to it has grown, there is a possibility that despite its ambiguous attitude towards democracy (see Chapter 3) fundamentalism may be furthering the 'unintentional modernization' of the Middle East's political foundations. Islamic fundamentalism injects dynamism into societies by throwing social conflicts into relief. This is certainly a dangerous process, entailing the ever-present risk of civil war. However, it also creates the need for a new political consensus that accords with modern Western political thought in the sense that Western democracy facilitates peaceful competition between differing notions of legitimacy. The fundamentalists' modernization of political ideology is a contribution to a new diversity of political thought of the kind that ushered in European modernity.

A COMPARATIVE LOOK AT NOTIONS OF MODERNITY: THE
TIME-LAPSE OF CIVILIZATIONAL PROGRESS

Overall, what stands out when we compare Middle Eastern and Western thought on the political foundations of modernity is that, at present, the greatest disagreement exists at the margins of the ideological spectrum, among secularists and fundamentalists. Islamic fundamentalists do not accept secularism. Secularists accept the equality of religions and genders before the law, but in the Islamic world only some secularists are democrats and many either represent or sympathise with the authoritarian state (see Chapter 3). In reformist religious thought, above all that of the liberal modernizers, and to a certain extent that of conservative modernists as well, there is clear common ground to the extent that both Western and Islamic political thought largely rejects models of authoritarian rule. The reformist project of reinterpreting Islamic sources and legal foundations to modernize Islamic societies does not, therefore, conflict with human rights, the autonomy of the individual and the democratic state any more than – at times authoritarian – Middle Eastern secularism, at least not inevitably.

There is no consensus on individualism, autonomy and democracy among contemporary Islamic religious modernists, but there are numerous points of contact with Western modernity. Can there be multiple modernities in the sphere of political culture? Even Fred Dallmayr rejects this notion, for constitutionally guaranteed pluralism is a key characteristic of modernity that breaks down old ideas before reconciling them again politically. On this view, the repositioning of an Islamic law restored to its former status would be incompatible with the necessary basic consensus, in contrast to a reformist Islamic liberalism, which might, in ideal typical fashion, bridge the gap outlined by Charles Taylor between secular modernity and the religious critique of modernity, which some thinkers believe to exist in the West as well.

Some Western critics expect modernization in the Islamic world to proceed at a tremendous pace. They want a 'fast-forward' version of civilizational progress unprecedented in the West itself; a development in time-lapse. Religious reformation, secularism and humanist enlightenment – all are supposed to occur simultaneously. This is an impossible task. Had the Christian Reformers known about the Reformation's future social marginalization during the Enlightenment, it might never have taken place. It is hard to imagine that any society would take reformation seriously if it failed to do what conservative Islamic reformers have done, namely, place itself at the centre of societal development, 'playing' with ideas of religious legality and maintaining the idea that the new idea of religion reformed by the community enjoys binding force, as did the Christian Reformation. It is culturally paradoxical for Western critics to call for an Islamic Reformation which, before it has even got off the ground, should make way for an Enlightenment.

Conservative Islamic reformers have understood this, and it is they more than any other group who currently embody this paradox. They are a centrist movement important to religious thought in the Middle East, a movement that challenges the ossified dualism of secularists and fundamentalists. Is not Tariq Ramadan – grandson of key early fundamentalist Hassan al-Banna – in effect laying the ground emotionally for an eventual Western-style modernity, not only in terms of science and technology, but also social and political affairs? The conservative reformers certainly imply an adherence to Islamic traditions, but in reality facilitate a process of adaptation to the West with respect to all key values. They cater to an emotional need for an independent identity and a cultural process of coming to terms with social change. In fact, they are transforming Islam into a conservative component – one that is largely unproblematic because it is becoming an object of public discourse – of the 'one modernity', a modernity in which the West and the Islamic Middle East can come to terms with one another.

This modernity certainly entails feelings of independence and Islamic commonality, feelings underpinned by national and religious factors. These are in fact elements in a striving for autonomy which can obviously affect not only individuals but also communities. But temporary processes of decoupling from global trends do not necessarily rule out for ever the possibility of establishing a consensus on modernity. Arab socialists such as Samir Amin, a theorist of dependency very well known in the West, have pointed to the need to facilitate attempts to attain national independence on the periphery of the world system (Amin 1978). Calls for a community with shared Islamic values, one that combines old and new, by no means inevitably contradict the Western minimum consensus on political modernity. Such calls may be constructing a conservatism which is compatible with democracy, as has already occurred in Turkey. Whether Islamic fundamentalism will tread this path of 'Christian democratization' will be discussed later (see Chapter 3).

2

Political Cultures and Social Movements: The Social Rationality of Cultural Change

We would do well to remember that ideologies and political thought do not produce themselves. The Marxist literature has described this as the base-superstructure phenomenon. In *A Contribution to the Critique of Political Economy*, Karl Marx wrote: 'In the social production which men carry on they enter into definite relations that are indispensable and independent of their will; these relations of production correspond to a definite stage of development of their material powers of production. The sum total of these relations of production constitutes the economic structure of society – the real foundation, on which rise legal and political superstructures and to which correspond definite forms of social consciousness' (Marx 1904 [1859], 11). From Marx's point of view, it would be legitimate to regard schools of thought such as secularism or political Islam as codes whose roots are deep in specific socioeconomic structures. We need not share Karl Marx's economic determinism in order to recognize the need to scrutinize the comparative debate on modernity and development in the Islamic and Western worlds with a view to uncovering their foundations in everyday life.

By modernizing the Islamic world, secular state ideologies and political programmes have undoubtedly racked up concrete achievements since the First World War. One example is the abolition of the feudal landowner class in Egypt during the agrarian reforms implemented by President Gamal Abdel Nasser, who placed strict limits on the ownership of land. Arab socialism was never so radical as to carry out a state collectivization of the agricultural economy based on the Soviet model. Apart from a few state-owned enterprises, it left the basic structure of private ownership intact. The abolition of the feudal upper class did not occur in this way in every country, but where it did, this process successfully picked up the thread of village-level traditions of joint ownership which still existed, in Egypt for example, into the nineteenth century. Large estates had first emerged during the colonial period. In this way, Egypt attempted to modernize itself internally while at the same time satisfying Europe's growing need for the commodity of cotton (Baer 1962, 1969; Richards 1982), a development entirely in keeping with Marx's idea that it was necessary to pass through the stages of feudal society and capitalism before achieving communism. The result in Egypt, however, was the opening up of a vast social chasm, which Nasser later corrected in favour of the middle classes. Despite Egypt's authoritarian political traits, it is because of the land reforms carried out in the twentieth century that neither modernization nor the establishment of a democratic-secular order is now hampered by a society ridden with privilege and class divisions, at least not on the classical model found in parts of South America or South Asia (with their vast, privately owned estates), where the benefits of economic growth have been distributed in an extremely unequal way.

At the same time, this path soon led Arab socialism into economic crisis (Waterbury 1983). The potential of the contemporary Islamic secular state to achieve socioeconomic modernization is beset by contradictions. On the one hand, as was clearly demonstrated for the first time in 2002 by the United Nations' Arab Human Development Report (AHDR), the Islamic world's standard of living index is below the global average.[1] The report identifies the key causes as deficiencies in the areas of political freedom, the emancipation of women and the knowledge society. On the other hand – and this is not generally known and was not acknowledged as the AHDR was hailed throughout the world – some progress has been made over the last few decades. Child mortality has declined significantly, and the Arab world features less extreme poverty than any other region of the world. While growth has been slight in the region, it has a certain social depth. Income distribution is more even than in many other countries, where high rates of economic growth primarily benefit specific upper and middle classes while failing to eliminate poverty (LeVine 2005, 133; Zapf 2006, 231). Investment in the educational sector in parts of the Arab world is on a par with that of Eastern Europe and in a far better position than Africa's. What is more, Arab states like Syria which have resisted integration into the world system are now in

---

[1] Arab Human Development Report 2002: Creating Opportunities for Future Generations (2003), New York: United Nations Development Program.

a better economic position than are far more integrated states such as Egypt (LeVine 2005, 137–8).

Are we witnessing the emergence of the Arab-Islamic region's unique contribution to modernization, a synthesis of growth and social justice that has rarely succeeded elsewhere? Is this perhaps even a case of belated justification for the authoritarian model of modernization, the antinomy between freedom and development postulated by German political scientist Richard Löwenthal in the 1960s (Löwenthal 1986) that is now undergoing a renaissance in the form of the Chinese developmental dictatorship (Steinweg 1989)? It is certainly historically correct that modernization may occur under differing conditions and that, at least initially, authoritarian states may foster modernization. Yet the social achievements of most states in the Islamic world, certainly those in the Middle East, rest on shaky foundations. Despite a number of reforms and successes over the last half-century, profound social disparities persist, and many Islamic societies have yet to establish social peace.

WESTERN PARTICIPATION AND ORIENTAL FATALISM?

Islamic political culture can no longer entirely be regarded as a 'parochial culture' in which state subjects are 'apolitical' because they remain enmeshed in feudal and traditional social structures (Pickel and Pickel 2006, 63 f.). The contemporary political culture of the Islamic world is to a large degree a 'subjectivist culture' in which citizens observe and evaluate state actions. Ultimately, there is plenty of evidence that this political culture is to some extent already a 'participatory culture', a central notion for the responsible modern citizen. A number of studies, including those by Gallup, the most famous American polling institute, attest the idea that democracy is widely disseminated among Muslims (Esposito and Mogahed 2007). There is much support in Islamic societies for an enhanced public sphere and pluralism, as is clearly apparent in the popularity television channel *Al-Jazeera* has enjoyed since it was founded in 1996. It has become the expression of a popular televisual democracy, and – before 11 September at least – it won numerous international prizes for taboo-breaking political reporting (K. Hafez 2006). Citizens' interest in participation is also evident in the popularity of political call-in shows on Arab television (Kraidy 2008), though these are admittedly a poor substitute for genuine political activity, which is largely lacking and indeed, scarcely possible given the repressive conditions. In cases where there is a lack of interest in politics, this is plainly not because people are apolitical but because they see no possibility of participation (Zaki 1995, 102–7).

Existing studies on political attitudes do more than confirm a fundamental interest in politics. A majority certainly considers religion important, but not at the expense of democracy (Esposito and Mogahed 2007). Opinion research shows a number of things. The majority of Muslims wants a synthesis of Islam and democracy that brings various ideologies into play. Mark Tessler's finding that the political views of secular and religious individuals do not differ substantially, despite differing ideological points of departure (see Chapter 1), points in the direction of liberal-reformist ideologies. Fundamentally, though, it is unclear which form of religious democracy – liberal or conservative, secular or fundamentalist – people actually want.

Even the fundamentalists may have a role to play within the political culture, as a vehicle of protest for those wanting such a system. This, however, would require that the fundamentalists demonstrate that they are not irreconcilably opposed to democracy. In fact, as we shall see, many fundamentalist organizations have moved closer to democracy on, for example, the division of powers or the prospect of multiple political parties (see Chapter 3).

But we should also keep in mind that a substantial minority of Muslims today does *not* want religion to play a greater role in politics. Only in light of this can we explain the fact that, though criticism of authoritarian systems has increased, secular states such as Algeria, Egypt or Syria are not necessarily ripe for system change for many people are afraid of both Islamic fundamentalist political supremacy and Islamic authoritarianism, next to which the secular authoritarian Arab state is seen as the lesser evil. It is otherwise impossible to understand the relative domestic stability of these countries in recent years.

Irrespective of the difficult questions of what forms the support for secularism, political Islam and democracy take and to what extent it is anchored in the political cultures of the Islamic world, one political model clearly disregards both the people's wishes and political culture: dictatorship, whether secular or Islamic in character. In the context of modernity, it is important to note that theoretical oppositions such as those between 'parochial' and 'participatory' political cultures are problematic, as construction of the category 'parochial' entails a political devaluation of the traditional as narrow-minded, provincial and passive. But does traditional life in agrarian societies really produce apolitical people? Do spheres of subjective political perception truly arise only outside the traditional modes of production and subsequent to the changes in social conditions, social attitudes and ideologies induced by economic changes? What might be possible to justify meaningfully for the steady process of modernization that typified the European Middle Ages is far harder to apply to the formerly colonial world with its multiple economic sectors, side-by-side existence of the most traditional and most modern economic forms, non-mechanized agriculture and high-tech research. Nowadays, families in the developing countries work concurrently in different economic sectors and social conditions, bringing about an intermeshing of 'parochial', 'subjectivist' and 'participatory' political cultures. The deep penetration into rural life of modern mass media, above all radio and television, has also contributed to the changing nature of political communication and the blending of political cultures.

The theory of neo-patrimonialism, which has often been applied to the Middle East, has in many ways renovated Max Weber's theory of political power. It brings out the mixture of old and new, of modern bureaucracy and technocracy and continuing tribal, family and clientelist ties. But in taking its lead from classical institutional politics, political science has so far thought little about political cultures as factors driving political modernity. Rather than specific individuals and institutions within a political system, it is often nearly intangible social attitudes that bring about changes and processes of modernization.

But citizens' desire for participation may be expressed far more directly. The Middle Eastern authoritarian state is in fact rarely 'totalitarian' in the style of the former Union of Soviet Socialist Republics (USSR). Saddam Hussein in Iraq was an exception; he developed his unscrupulous power on the basis of his country's oil wealth. Most other Islamic countries with a secular government, meanwhile, are far from capable of controlling their societies using the Soviet model. This leaves plenty of room for such societies to be organized in unique ways and may have significant political consequences. While the state engenders ambivalent attitudes and garners both acceptance and a great deal of criticism from society, social networks also affect the structure of political attitudes by sowing the seeds of civil society. The Egyptian social networks examined by Diane Singerman reveal astonishing similarities to what Vaclav Havel called the 'parallel polis' in Czechoslovakia before the collapse of real existing socialism: social networks which created parallel societies in areas where the authoritarian state had partially failed, in the labour market, for example (Singerman 1995, 243).

In their similarity to European conditions, such structures belie all notions still captive to a Eurocentric view that there is an uncritical Middle Eastern culture. There are still voices within Western political science who think that the Islamic Middle East lacks cultures of resistance and manifests its frustrations in attempted coups and political murder, whereas the former Soviet states maintained a political culture that made it possible to practice collective insubordination (Hartmann 1995, 185). The central role of Mikhail Gorbachev's 'revolution from above' leaves a question mark over the extent to which the political culture of the USSR was involved in the collapse of communism. Quite apart from this, and in contrast to the work of Singerman, the adherents of the idea of an Islamic 'parochial' political culture often deny the capacity of the Islamic world to produce a political culture that might modernize political systems and ultimately culminate in deep-rooted democratic change.

In sum, the political cultures of the Islamic world are characterized by considerable ambivalence. Alongside a strong subjectivist critique of the prevailing political conditions, these cultures are distinguished by a fear of Islamic fundamentalist coups and violent upheavals. This ambivalence has hindered the development of a secular opposition against the secular authoritarian state but, at the same time, has enabled the rise of a society that increasingly governs itself, a kind of 'civil society in waiting'. The Middle Eastern state often acts with ferocity, but it is essentially weak and losing ever more authority to networks and organizations, often to the Islamic fundamentalists, as is elucidated in the following chapters.

But the parallel Middle Eastern polis is a two-edged sword. An agent of modernization, it contributes at the same time to the further erosion of the state, evades its structures, fosters corruption and threatens the state's monopoly on power, reinforcing the trend towards decline and the creation of so-called 'failed states' such as Afghanistan, Somalia and Sudan (see Chapter 4). It is likely that a solution can be achieved if these states engage in a cautious process of opening up the process of political participation for those who have drifted away from the state to private networks.

RE-ISLAMIZATION: FROM RELIGIOUS STUPOR TO ACTIVE COMMUNITY

The societies of the Islamic world have for a number of decades featured movements that unmistakably link religion and social phenomena, though it is not always clear whether they represent superficial cultural fashions or are far-reaching social movements. Besides the phenomenon of social networks, in other words, the parallel polis, the Islamic world has seen the rise of a large number of movements to which the key thinkers of both liberal and conservative reformist Islam have contributed. Conservative reformist Islam, at least, is not a product of the ivory towers of academe. It entails clearly defined social phenomena.

The neo-religious youth cultures that are common in the middle classes of the Islamic states are a good example (Gerlach 2006). Among the Muslims of Europe and of the Islamic countries themselves, television preachers such as the Egyptian Amr Khaled or the religious singer Sami Yussuf have reached a large number of predominately young, middle-class Muslims with the message that a thoroughly hedonistic youth culture, which satisfies the individual's need for freedom, is compatible with socially conservative, community-based ethics. In this youth culture, modern pop music, music clubs and the like go hand in hand with a 'Catholic' morality that rejects pre-marital sex and drugs. The key thinkers of both liberal and conservative reformist Islam, focussed on reinterpreting the Islamic sources, might be chided for the intricacy of their blueprint for modernity; here, it is replaced by an eclectic religious credo and religious popular cultures.

These young Muslims constitute a genuine lay movement that plainly releases modernist energies by attempting to strike a new balance between the individual's striving for autonomy and a community-oriented religiosity, one that reforms society as a whole rather than merely the private sphere. The values, at once old and new, of this revivalist movement are intended to bring about a social solidarity that supports the shaky integration of Muslims in Europe and the United States and alleviates the social crisis gripping the Islamic world (Roy 2006, 193 ff.). These young Muslims have as little time for the prohibition of music in traditional Islam as for the creed of Western liberalism. This distinguishes them not only from mainstream Western youth but also from Islamic orthodoxy and Islamic fundamentalism with its extreme moral strictness. The main thrust of a 'middle path' between reform and a strict new compliance with Islamic rules, as laid out in the work of Tariq Ramadan for example, is retained here, though Ramadan himself was always a friend of 'decent music', and these young Muslims interpret the idea of conservative reform in their own way. To some extent, the social concretion of conservative reform is taking on a life of its own. It differs from the 'pure teachings' of Ramadan and Al-Qaradawi, which are, in any case, contradictory. This very much suggests that, simply by aspiring to reform Islamic law, the conservative reformers often viewed critically in the West are unleashing social forces which they themselves are no longer able to control, forces that will ultimately result in an Islamic pluralism in line with the Western consensus on modernity as defined by thinkers such as Charles Taylor.

'Online fatwas' are another example of the social resonance of conservative reform. While orthodox scholarly Islam produces a ruling upon request (Arabic *fatwa*), this is increasingly done over the Internet in the Islamic world. People obtain advice on every conceivable everyday issue – undoubtedly another sign of the conservative re-Islamization of societies from which the Islamic fundamentalists have profited over the last few decades. But it is interesting to note that individuals are requesting online fatwas not from traditional scholars but from private firms, another indication that Islamic neo-religiosity entails tendencies towards individualization and pluralization – because the Islamic scholars' monopoly on knowledge is being eroded.

Overall, then, the notion of a conservative Islamic reform is based on a social structure that unites value-based conservatism and modernization in multiple and at times quite paradoxical ways. Andreas Jacobs' notion that conservative reformers are aiming for an 'Islamization of modernity' thus accords only partially with the social realities of this school of thought. The middle class that is so central to the movement is not only Islamizing its lifeworlds; it is at the same time modernizing retrogressive religious dogmas and adapting them to modern needs – a clear case of the 'modernization of Islam'. Here, the young middle class is increasingly expressing itself, and – from the Arab nationalist revolutions to the Iranian Revolution – it has, in fact, been in the vanguard of the social transformations of the last few decades. Conservative reformers occupy the intersection of traditional and modern social structures. They represent a kind of culture of assimilation which at once preaches cohesion, unity *and* progress, very much in line with the approach of Bassam Tibi, who ascribes to Islam the role of 'cultural assimilation of social change' (Tibi 1985).

However, the social reality of conservative reform is also ambivalent. *First*, it is questionable whether these movements really involve the individualization of Muslims, who are no longer willing to be led by the old Islamic authorities and are embracing a commercialized neo-Islamic lifestyle, creating a tailor-made religion compatible with pop music and everyday practices of every kind. Alongside the trend towards individuation, re-Islamization has a strong community-forming tendency. It has produced its own forms of orthodoxy. What are the headscarf fashions characteristic of this movement – sometimes chic, always strictly adhered to – but new orthodoxies? The path typical of Christianity is to cultivate religious community while *at the same time* making space for individual interests, which has fostered the development of a dual morality within society (Bayat 2007, 61). To be Catholic but to have sex before marriage has become the norm in the West, and such a trend towards a post-Islamic culture can also be discerned in the Islamic world (Bayat 2007, 61). In everyday life, the ostensible puritanical stringency rarely reaches as deep as observers believe. Kissing couples on the banks of the Nile, despite social stigmatization, and homosexuals in Damascus and Amman, despite condemnation by the great majority: Islamic societies are by no means free of contradiction and feature a highly fraught relationship between individuality and collectivism.

Second, re-Islamization is often more like an apolitical revivalist movement than a movement for social transformation. Its principle adherents are not the poorest in society, but people who wish to gain both mental and cultural relief. The truly poor do not buy online fatwas. When the poor are involved, as they have been with the increase in mosque attendance over the last few decades, the new religiosity shares some of the same strain-reducing functions as the growing African evangelical movements: here, rather than bolstering social mobilization, religion justifies poverty and injustice, directly or indirectly.[2]

Third, in apparent contrast to this trend, some of the new religious movements maintain close ties with fundamentalist groupings (Gerlach 2006, 209 ff.). Transitions to fundamentalism are thus present in parts of the conservative reformist movement, resulting in the danger that, by overemphasizing community, conservative reform might not only create new dogmas but also make them legally enforceable. Hence, the social forces within Islam that can be assigned to the conservative reformist camp stand at the crossroads between two fundamentally different paths to modernization: the founding of a new conservatism compatible with the Western consensus on modernity or the fundamentalist dissociation of the Islamic world from this consensus. At present, however, alongside the largely secular culture of the new media, such as the popular news channel *Al-Jazeera*, we may regard the existence of conservative reformers, Muslim youth cultures and other revivalist movements as

---

[2] Anouk Batard, Reich und heilig in Uganda [Rich and holy in Uganda], *Le Monde diplomatique* (German edition), January 2008.

guaranteeing that Islamic fundamentalists will not achieve political and cultural hegemony.

Another social dimension of re-Islamization and the neo-religious movements deserves emphasis: the countries of the Islamic world are characterized by tremendous cultural and social differences. Saudi Arabia and Lebanon for instance differ massively with respect to the relative importance of Islamic law, which is the state law in Saudi Arabia but plays only a subordinate role in Lebanon. The astonishing thing about the conservative Islamic reformist school is that there is a real possibility that it might unify the extreme internal cultural differences in the Islamic world, forming an ideological bond that loosely links its different societies, provided, however, that Wahhabism, the predominant Sunnite school in Saudi Arabia and on the Arabian peninsula, proves ready to modernize.

In principle, the Arabian peninsula, which includes Saudi Arabia and the Arab Gulf emirates, is a virtually prototypical example of Bassam Tibi's thesis of 'semi-modernity'. Here, an orientation towards the West in technology, science and economics goes hand in hand with adherence to old and rigid Islamic laws in a way that can be found almost nowhere else, notoriously including medieval penal laws, social banishment of women from the public sphere and feudal-monarchical rule. Saudi Arabia in particular seems to be the realization of these fundamentalist ideals – although its profligate monarchies are offensive to the social justice ideal of fundamentalism, which is why Saudi Arabia tends to be a bogeyman in fundamentalist circles.

What is problematic about this perception is that the monarchies of the Arabian peninsula are *not* absolutist systems of rule in the European sense; rather they are forms of tribal rule extended to the level of state power. Receptions given by the Saudi king immediately lay bare the difference from other Islamic monarchies. In Morocco, for example, the king is a towering, elevated figure, whereas the Saudi monarch consults at 'ground level', surrounded by the major families of the country. Egalitarian Bedouin culture blends with the monarchy in a unique way. Hisham Sharabi has described this form of rule as a 'neo-patriarchy', a seemingly modern state which is nevertheless underpinned by the ethical laws of a tribal culture, whereas other forms of modern government, such as bureaucracy and the state institutions with which Max Weber was concerned, take a back seat to this *Personenverbandsstaat,* or state based on the primacy of personal ties (Sharabi 1988). From this standpoint there can be no modernization of social traditions because it is tradition that unites and legitimizes the government, behind which all class differences must recede: tradition dictates that the Saudi monarch is the custodian of the Arab tribal consensus and the Islamic holy sites of Mecca and Medina.

It is, however, interesting to note that social and political reforms have slowly been introduced on the Arabian Peninsula over the last few decades, set in motion by the inner reaches of the ruling families. The tremendous growth of the Al-Saud royal family, with its hosts of princes, has stimulated internal competition and is one of the key factors driving a shift towards a more broadly based system of rule. In the economic field, countries such as Dubai have successfully left behind the rentist economy and have become modern trading nations, unlike Saudi Arabia. In Saudi Arabia, however, a technophilia has developed that has made the country one of the major regional media providers, despite the fact that, as recently as the 1960s, Saudi scholars often regarded television as an offence against the Islamic prohibition on the depiction of humans and rejected it on principle. In 2005, the first local and city elections were held in Saudi Arabia. Riyadh has a women's university. In the United Arab Emirates, the proportion of women in the parliament-like Federal National Council was a not insignificant 22 percent in 2007.

Unquestionably, and quite understandably, the school of conservative Islamic reformers holds a certain appeal for these states. Yusuf al-Qaradawi, for example, owes his rise to public prominence to the Emir of Qatar, who appointed him dean and made him famous all over the world on the *Al-Jazeera* channel. Despite or precisely because of their criticisms, neo-Islamic thinkers such as the Egyptian journalist Fahmi Huwaidi, who criticizes Saudi Arabia's culture of censorship and calls for the media to be opened up to broad social strata (K. Hafez 1999a), have become role models for the modernizers among the Saudi leadership and are practically revered. It is important to be aware here that the centrists (*Wasatiyya*), unlike many fundamentalists, do not preach any pronounced form of 'class envy' (Baker 2003, 162); they express middle- and upper-class interests, as befits a country such as Saudi Arabia. Hence, it seems that conservative reform, not only makes possible very slow, very 'Catholic' social modernization, staggered over centuries, but also leaves open the possibility of retaining Sharia, albeit a renovated version. It may even enable the rulers to retain their power.

Whether conservative reform will be the Arabian Peninsula's ideal political ideology in the future is not only a question of perspective but also depends on how things develop. From the Western point of view, with its monarchy and Islamic law, even a reformed Saudi Arabia clearly departs from the political consensus on modernity. With its strong emphasis on a new sense of Islamic community, the idea of new orthodoxies, and even with its extensive double standards (it is an open secret that alcohol is consumed on a massive scale in Saudi Arabia when the sun goes down), conservative reformist Islam is very well suited to the Arabian Peninsula. Reformers such as Ramadan or Huwaidi criticize the current regimes, but many conservative reformers could perhaps live with the kind of moderate reforms supported by many young 'royals' in Saudi Arabia and the Gulf states. In addition to religious media, Saudi capital even finances many entertainment channels – a mixture that suits young religious Muslims with a taste for popular culture. And conservative reformers' ambiguous relationship to politics, which is both critical and still adheres to the idea of the Islamic state, and possibly Islamic law, also sounds like a modernity which the established regime of oil billionaires may have little reason to fear. But the situation is quite different with regard to Islamic fundamentalism.

ISLAMIC FUNDAMENTALISM AS 'RADICAL PROTESTANTISM'

Westerners have for the most part got used to viewing Islamic fundamentalism as a movement which wishes to prevent the Islamic world from modernizing itself, at least in a comprehensive sense that encompasses not only the 'semi-modernity' of technological progress but also political and social modernization. It seems quite absurd to regard fundamentalism as a component of any comprehensive attempt at modernization. It is, or so it would appear, an anti-modernity, historically comparable, perhaps, with romantic and *völkisch*-nationalist trends running counter to the French Enlightenment that were popular in the German-speaking world of the nineteenth century, though with a specifically religious tenor that was considered a dead end in the West from the time of Savonarola and the Thirty Years' War at the latest, and which has since come to seem alien there.

Given the development of fundamentalism since its creation by the Egyptian Muslim Brothers and its expansion via the Islamic Revolution in Iran, the question remains: Is the Islamic world headed towards a similar dead end? In this connection one would be forced to hope that fundamentalism will have passed its peak in the foreseeable future and that the Islamic world will return to the path of modernization and democratization and profess its commitment to the minimum consensus on secularism, the autonomy of the individual and the constitutional state. Hope of this kind is common in the work of scholars who, like the French Orientalist Gilles Kepel or the British political scientist Fred Halliday, have an open-minded view of the Islamic world and sometimes criticize culturalists such as their American colleague Samuel Huntington (K. Hafez 1998; Halliday 1996; Kepel 2000). Islam, they state, is internally heterogeneous and quite compatible with Western political traditions, but this, they argue, is not true of Islamic fundamentalism. However, it seems important not to rashly dismiss fundamentalism as 'anti-modernist', viewing it as no more than a 'brake' on the path towards modernity. Such a perspective would be incapable of acknowledging the constitutive role in Europe's history of the dynamics of the Reformation and Counter-Reformation. We cannot, to be sure, equate the Christian Reformation and the contemporary Islamic renaissance, for they are separated by five hundred years, and the conditions in each case are quite different. Yet the key question remains: What social purpose is being served when a movement such as Islamic fundamentalism wishes to turn itself into a virtual state, replacing existing orders with 'Islamic states'?

The case of the Imbaba district in Cairo is illuminating. Here, for several decades, Islamic organizations have made good use of the Egyptian government's inability to cope with the increasing rural exodus and spontaneous settlement of newcomers – Cairo's population has grown from four million to about twenty million from the 1960s to the present day – by taking on key aspects of the municipality's social organization (Ismail 2003). In these irregular settlements, which are lacking in such urban infrastructure as sewerage, roads and transport links, radical Islamic fundamentalist organizations, particularly Al-Jamaa al-Islamiya, have been the guarantors of a social order that was hitherto maintained solely by familial and village ties among rural refugees. Certain mafia-like structures have developed – such as protection rackets and systematic intermarriage among individuals close to the Islamic fundamentalist organizations. At the same time, these organizations are at the core of urban protest movements aiming to mobilize politically new urban groups made up of those leaving the country in response to population pressure. In this sense, besides their religious orientation, fundamentalist organizations were and are also champions of the Middle Eastern *Lumpenproletariat* – Karl Marx's term for the urban poor who exist outside the organized labour movement. In countries such as Pakistan, private Islamic organizations have also taken on functions which the state was incapable of performing, in the educational field, for example.

During the regency of Muhammad Ali (1805–48) in Egypt, the role played by the traditional guilds that organized urban life became increasingly less significant, though they survived in the old urban districts (Ismail 2003, 88). As touched upon earlier, in a parallel process, the village community was also disintegrating within the context of the feudalism that was only then taking off. New housing schemes had to be built in response to the progressive expansion of the urban centres and the rural exodus from the narrow strip of agricultural land around the Nile. But it was from the 1960s on that this development occurred most rapidly, as unauthorized settlements in which neither the state nor other organizations invested sprang up on the urban periphery (Ismail 2003, 90).

With the exception of the Arabian Peninsula, post-war Middle Eastern regimes were secular and nationalist as a result of the colonial era. Islam was thus the most obvious ideological banner around which the new urban poor could rally, and it became a vehicle of protest against the social failure of the secular state. Under the specific developmental conditions of authoritarian secularism in formerly colonial states, Middle Eastern regimes' secular ideologies practically forced parts of society into these religious semantics. We will be looking at this in more detail later on (see Chapter 3). For now, the key point is that every conventional definition of modernity sees social inclusion and mobility as two of its most crucial hallmarks. When, as has happened in a number of urban districts, fundamentalists take on the provisioning function that was originally performed by the state, 'taking the law into their own hands' in order to help advance class interests, it also seems quite reasonable to regard Islamic fundamentalism's state-like claim to power as an element of socioeconomic modernization. If middle-class interests are often prominent in liberal and conservative Islamic-reform ideologies, the associated neo-religious movements are scarcely capable of improving the living conditions of the lower classes. A fundamentalist movement that actively sets about meeting social needs, thus becoming a state within a state, is an almost inevitable accompaniment of an ideology of system change and the foundation of a new statehood that points beyond the kind of nascent reforms described earlier.

But fundamentalism is not merely a social network and protest movement. It also brings together a wide range of discontented groups that rally around a programme of social demands, which on closer inspection, represent quite different interests.

Despite this important function of the Islamic fundamentalists, their religious rigidity in attempting to consistently enforce the segregation of the sexes for example, has also led to numerous conflicts with supporters who are attracted to the socio-political stance of fundamentalist organizations rather than their reactionary and puritanical views (Ismail 2003) – a fraught dynamic also evident in other fundamentalist organizations, such as the Lebanese Hezbollah and Palestinian Hamas. This mixture of longed-for modernization in the absence of a functioning welfare state and resistance to the all-encompassing ideological aspirations of the Islamic fundamentalist leaderships is inherent in Islamic fundamentalist movements, leaving quite open the question of whether, despite all its professions of faith in a quite contrary agenda, fundamentalism will not move over the long term in the direction of recognizing a secular legal framework, the autonomy of the individual and the equality of religions before the law. Islamic fundamentalism is a social movement whose base wishes to change political and social conditions, but a fair number of those who make up this base are a protest clientele who endorse 'Islamic' values merely for strategic reasons.

However, if fundamentalism were to fail to recognize secularism, if in other words, there was no 'Christian democratization' of the movement as there has been in Turkey (see Chapter 3), fundamentalist social mobilization could not aid integration into an overall social order but would instead foster civil war and state disintegration. The question will therefore be: How, despite social and political renewal, can the nation state be saved, a state which is in every model still regarded as the basis of modernization, even that of the fundamentalists (excepting ultra-radical concepts of the caliphate), which now seems to be under threat in many countries in the Islamic world (Algeria, Afghanistan, Iraq, Sudan, etc.)? Diane Singerman has warned against an alarmist view that equates informal networks with organized Islamic fundamentalism, even in cases in which Islamic fundamentalists play a role within those networks (Singerman 1995, 240 f.). We might go further yet and argue that an organized fundamentalist parallel society may be preferable to unrestrained autonomy; the case of Imbaba shows that state collapse is not necessarily the result of the social actions of fundamentalists, as long as they adopt a fundamentally mainstream approach, preaching reform rather than revolution and aiming to achieve integration into the political system, as the Egyptian Muslim Brothers did.

It is not just the fundamentalists' heterogeneous base but also how we assess their leadership that seems key to evaluating developments. It would certainly be wrong to infer the aims of political organizations entirely from the social background of their elites. The potential attainment of power and the social advancement which is bound up with it prevent such a simple equation. But clarifying it is nevertheless important if we wish to understand the preconditions for the rise of Islamic fundamentalism. Two elements are of central importance:

- Sunnite fundamentalists represent a lay movement of the lower-middle and lower classes;
- Shia state fundamentalism (in Iran) was generated by a social coalition consisting of modernity's losers.

In seeking to establish in what sense Islamic fundamentalism is a social movement, it is essential to examine the social constellation, internal structure and agenda of Islamic fundamentalist organizations. Social movements are never created by 'the masses' but are led by elites who create identities and set out a political approach. In general, the social substructure of the Islamic fundamentalist leaderships lies in the lower-middle classes. Denounced by the secular, reform-oriented intelligentsia of the Middle East as 'anti-intellectual', the leadership of many Islamic groups in fact features a fairly large proportion of academics and intellectuals, including: Hasan Turabi and Sadiq al-Mahdi (Sudan); Rashid al-Ghannushi (Tunisia); Ali Abbasi Madani (Algeria); Khurshid Ahmad (Pakistan); Necmettin Erbakan (Turkey); Ishaq Farhan (Jordan); Hasan Hanafi (Egypt); and women such as Zainab al-Ghazali and Hiba Rauf Izzat (Egypt), and Mariam Jameela (Pakistan). In their civilian professions, leading figures are often teachers, engineers, lawyers or journalists, earning Islamic fundamentalism the epithet Revolution of Engineers. Here, education and an aptitude for political thought combine with the lived experience of the wretched social reality of the lower-middle classes, whose jobs barely allow them to feed their families. The leading figures thus embody the aspiration to personal bourgeois advancement.

Furthermore, these leading figures derive Islamic thought from the domain of religious scholarship and, despite their often vehement anti-Western propaganda, integrate elements of Western thought, such as the technophilia that is widespread among Islamic fundamentalists. Although Islamic scholars have also been key thinkers and leaders of Islamic fundamentalist groups (such as Ayatollah Khomeini, Ayatollah Fadlallah of Hezbollah, and Sheikh Yasin of Hamas), Islamic movements, especially Sunnite ones, must generally be considered lay movements that challenge the interpretive monopoly of the orthodox scholars and are in this sense anti-authoritarian in character.

In Shia Islam, scholars have a more prominent position for a number of reasons: the special status of historical Imams as successors to Muhammad, and also the organization of Islamic scholars as a group, which is far more developed than in the case of their Sunnite counterparts (Batatu 1986). Regardless of the leadership of the Iranian legal scholars, the Iranian Revolution may be viewed as a mass protest against an exclusive and elite form of modernization under the Shah. It was *not*, therefore, a countermovement to modernization. The agents of the Iranian Revolution were primarily members of the middle and lower-middle classes who had been sidelined in past attempts at modernization and who, under the banner of an Islamic politics, wished to spread the benefits of modernization more evenly across society.

Iran expert Nikkie Keddie sees the following commonalities in the history of states with strong fundamentalist movements: a break with a past – viewed through the prism of Islamic symbolism – as a result of Western intervention (as in the case of the US-backed overthrow of the Iranian Mosaddeq regime in 1953); rapid economic development and urbanization; and social dislocation and a widening gap between rich and poor (Keddie 1988, 17). In the Iranian Revolution it was mainly sections of the middle classes such as the traditional *bazari* merchants who felt neglected by the modernization unleashed by the Shah, which favoured new technically skilled elites. With the aid of the charismatic Khomeini, who was adept at mobilizing the traditional rural population, these middle classes were for the first time able to win over the masses (Parsa 1984, 24, 34 ff.).

In the Iranian Revolution, political Islam functioned as an ideological articulation of the demand for participation in the modernization process: it served to legitimize political rule and was an independent ideology in the confrontation with major powers and superpowers, particularly the United States, whose client Iran was. Political Islam was an ideology of resistance in the North-South conflict, and it was a consensus-based ideology, straddling the forces of left and right, that aimed to achieve revolutionary mobilization (Benard and Khalilzad 1984; see also Chapter 4 of this book). Against this background it becomes clear why Edmund Burke asks whether organized fundamentalism really involves *Islamic* political movements or, instead, *social* movements in Islamic societies (Burke 1988, 18). It seems right to assume that, rather than representing self-referential phenomena, the religion and ideology of Islam develop through interaction with social processes.

Iranian Nobel Prize winner Shirin Ebadi, attempting to produce a critical evaluation of the Iranian Revolution, points out that it undoubtedly improved the educational opportunities for women from lower social classes, although their prospects of pursuing a career later on are limited (Ebadi 2006, 149). She describes the significant mental upheavals and social tensions as being bound-up with the fact that in the Iran of the Islamic Revolution, the middle classes, who set the tone under the Shah, now had to yield to a revolutionary proletariat, which was frequently a humiliating experience.

Whether Islamic fundamentalism will truly be able to play the role of social mobilizer, which is important to the development of democracy, depends among other things on whether it succeeds in overcoming its evident internal tensions between social and religious motives and, further, whether it will prove capable of resisting the slide into authoritarianism to which many social and revolutionary movements have succumbed. One need think only of the history of the Cuban Revolution. Once the revolutionaries are in power, new cliques often form quickly within their ranks which are primarily concerned with furthering their own interests. Islamic fundamentalism, too, seems to differ markedly in opposition and in power. The Iranian Revolution, for example, certainly helped a new social strata gain influence, but at the same time, it produced nouveau riche elites, such as the family of former President Rafsanjani, while around four million exiles and substantial sections of the middle class have been marginalized. The sansculottic element of Islamic fundamentalism thus leads to new injustices as it expels the old leading classes without forging a viable new social contract (see Chapter 4). The Iranian revolutionary leadership has never managed to fully satisfy the demands for the welfare of even its own clientele, as was clearly apparent in the election of President Khatami as well as in the subsequent election of Ahmadinejad, which were chiefly the outcome of urban poverty and hopes of a revival of a social revolution.

THE SOCIAL RATIONALITY OF CULTURAL CHANGE

All in all, we might put it like this: while liberal reformist Islam incorporates elements of religious reform and even humanistic and Enlightenment-inspired aspects, Islamic fundamentalism embodies a radical Protestantism. It wants to deploy religion as a vehicle of social inclusion. Echoes of European revolutions can be heard in the revolutionary states (Iran, Sudan). The sequence of events in Iran reflects almost perfectly familiar historical patterns of revolution across the globe.[3] Typically, the Iranian Revolution did not occur during a period of material poverty but of intense social change, during which the intelligentsia turned its back on the regime, depriving it of legitimacy. After the fall of the monarchy, there were public demonstrations of support followed by a period of diarchic rule (by Khomeini and Prime Minister Bazargan). Demands for autonomy from ethnic minorities also became vociferous. Further, as Udo Steinbach has pointed out, the Iranian Revolution was the 'first Revolution in the Middle East triggered and supported by the people themselves'. Like other revolutions in world history, the Iranian Revolution was brought about by the lower echelons of society (Steinbach 1979, 311). The assumption, common in the West, that the events of the Iranian Revolution were unique is justifiable only if our comparative system of classification disregards the numerous universals inherent in the Revolution and we narrow our view to include only ideological and religious specifics. Closer inspection reveals that the exceptionality of the Iranian Revolution has been greatly overstated.

But religion was the ideological lodestone of the Revolution, and this peculiarity requires explanation. One of the key factors is the simple fact that, during a period in which the Middle East was under the influence of neo-colonialism, Islam represented a form of cultural independence vis-à-vis the hegemony of Western ideals and demands for modernization. Islamic fundamentalist ideology is at once opposed to ruling secular 'Westernized' elites and a general ideology of resistance. The specifically religious aspect of this mixture of radical Protestantism and anti-colonialism serves a rationally understandable purpose, which may even be interpreted in modernist terms. Francis Fukuyama has described 'jihadism', in other words the terrorist derivative of Islamic fundamentalism, as a by-product of modernity, which, by analogy, also applies to fundamentalism as a whole. According to Fukuyama, the majority of Muslims reject neither the West nor Western modernity, but object to not being included in the Western project of modernization. It is, above all, American policies towards the Middle East that are perceived as governing this strategy of exclusion (Fukuyama 2006, 75 ff.). According to Fukuyama, fundamentalism is a project which, in response to exclusion, set out to radically reform an indigenous tradition and deploy it as political battle-cry. But rather than Martin Luther,

---

[3] Gerhard Schildt, Der Machtkampf in Persien steht erst noch bevor [The power struggle in Persia is yet to come], *Frankfurter Allgemeine Zeitung*, 18 January 1980.

the correct historical parallel of the socially revolutionary goals of a radical religious movement would surely be Thomas Müntzer – or perhaps Savonarola.

The full picture is now beginning to emerge. In light of its claim to broad-based social legitimacy, it is quite possible that fundamentalism, which has broken away from the Western consensus on Western political modernity by preaching collectivism rather than individualism and the dictatorship of religious law rather than secularism, might be capable not only of paving the way for the Islamization of modernity, but also for a socially inclusive overall process of modernization. Against the background of the European Reformation experience, the framework of rationality which is characteristic of a process of *catch-up* modernization may well entail a linkage of religion and politics, a radical Protestantism with social connotations or, as in the case of Iran, even a socially revolutionary radicalism. More than anything else, the diversity of religious and political commitments in the Islamic world demonstrates that the process of modernization and religious reformation has long been underway and that this process is integrating, in a highly accelerated fashion, values that are important in the present era: humanism in the case of the liberal Islamic reformers, middle-class modernization among the conservative reformers and social participation among the fundamentalists. This complexity of historical parallels between Western and Islamic history is due to the fact that Islamic developments are occurring later in history and thus have quite different historical experiences at their disposal than did the European Reformation. Alongside the Western models of Reformation, humanism, democracy and technological modernity, however, the stock of Islamic experiences also includes the neo-colonial realities of limited autonomy within modernity, which on the whole has reinforced the religious element vis-à-vis secular ideologies because it implies independence. The different Islamic schools of thought about modernity represent different social spectra and regionally specific types of society. Taken together, these schools of thought may represent something like a comprehensive leap into modernity.

In any case, the polysemy of the linkage between Islam and modernity shows that we probably must abandon the notion that only a Christian legacy leads to modernity. Whether Middle Eastern societies will join the minimum consensus on modernization, as formulated by Charles Taylor, for example – autonomy and the constitutional safeguarding of the individual and democracy – does not depend on essentialist commitments as suggested by Samuel Huntington's notions of a 'clash of civilizations' between Islam and the West, but on which social set-up becomes politically established. Every part of these multisectoral societies seems to be on a new path or at least set in motion. The variety of motives at play points to the need for a pluralist solution based on the division of powers.

II

DEMOCRACY

A re Islam and democracy incompatible? Can the fact that countries with an Islamic majority lag behind other world regions in
democratization be put down to cultural exceptionalism and a kind of
Islamic 'special way'? In any event, variations on this assumption have
been repeated for decades. On closer inspection, this turns out to be an
Orientalist prejudice (Bayat 2007, 3). Despite the fact that most governments in the Islamic world are still authoritarian (see Chapter 5), we
can already discern many democracy-like processes in the contemporary political practice of most Islamic countries that give the lie to such
sweeping statements. Crucially, we must bear in mind that as recently
as the twentieth century many observers considered the Catholicism of
Europe's Latin states incompatible with democracy – and were spectacu-
larly wrong.

However, in analyzing the relations between Islam and democracy we
must come to terms with a number of key paradoxes. In the contemporary Middle East, there are Islamic fundamentalist groupings in many
states which pay a certain amount of lip service to the idea of democracy
but by no means argue straightforwardly for its establishment, and these
constitute the strongest opposition to existing authoritarian relations of
power. What is the logical outcome of this situation? Could 'democracies
without democrats' arise, as political scientist and former Lebanese minister of culture Ghassan Salamé speculated as long ago as the early 1990s
(Salamé 1994b)? How, he asked, might the oppositional force of Islamic
fundamentalism be used without lapsing into new – fundamentalist –
dictatorships? His answer: by making clear to all political movements
that while democracy may perhaps be only the 'second best' solution for

each of them, it is the only realistic one if they wish to move on from the current state of authoritarian repression. This idea was probably too daring to be taken any further by political scientists with respect to the Islamic world. Yet historical comparison quickly shows that in the West, too, a fair number of democracies have emerged more from complicated struggles between radical forces than from the deliberate reforms of liberal democrats. This fact is widely discussed in functionalist research on political transformation. To this day, however, such findings have not been consistently applied to the Islamic world, and the many parallels between Western processes of democratization and contemporary political developments in the Islamic world have yet to be elaborated.

Is there any prospect of 'democracy without democrats' in the Islamic world? In what follows, we shall see that the ideology of Islamic fundamentalism is highly equivocal about democracy; moreover, it is in competition – a fact rarely appreciated in the West – with a trend towards secular political concepts in Islamic societies, a trend which also has Islamic cultural roots. If resolved peacefully, however, this dualism of ideological superstructure and political culture may also be a driving force for democratization. This insight is reinforced by the fact that the social mainsprings of this conflict resemble the historical development of Western democracies more closely than it may at first appear. As I argued earlier in the discussion of modernization, social conflicts between old and new classes are being carried on here in religious packaging and have set in motion new struggles over power resources. If we view Islamic fundamentalism as the product of both internal and international political conflicts, which characterize the contemporary Islamic states more strongly than other parts of the world, it becomes clear that this is not an irrational political strategy. The unique ideological context, wherein religion is currently more important within the political process than it is in other world regions, becomes understandable and even begins to make sense as a means of mobilizing and rallying social and political forces.

There is certainly a possibility of democratization within the foreseeable future – though there is also a great risk that new dictatorships will emerge. Another country, namely Germany, was long considered to be on a *Sonderweg* or special path, taking longer than other states to become a democracy as the result of a complex, centuries-long interaction between autocracy, enlightened monarchy and political movements of a leftist and Christian conservative complexion that sometimes had little enthusiasm for democracy or republicanism. The worrying thing about this example, of course, is that this very 'democracy without democrats', as the Weimar

Republic was often called, first descended into fascist dictatorship before being re-founded in a new form with outside help.

Is there a chance that the contemporary Islamic world can avoid the intermediate step of 'Islamic fascism' (see Chapter 5)? How do we assess the internal political constellations that might further or impede this outcome? Finally, which strategies of international democracy promotion – in contrast to the belligerent policies of the George W. Bush regime in Afghanistan and Iraq – are best suited to strengthening the opposition forces and enhancing the prospects of successful democratization?

3

The Discourse of Democratization: Grey Zones at the Intersection of Religion and Secularism

What constitutes a democracy? It is important to make clear from the outset that any comparison between the Islamic world and the West must avoid relativizing the concept of democracy, watering it down to the point where we suddenly declare it to be compatible with every conceivable form of political reality. Our task is not to talk up the actual state of democracy in the Islamic world. It is vital that we come up with clear definitions that may serve as criteria for such comparisons. Such a minimum consensus as guided us in exploring the question of modernity (with reference to the work of thinkers such as Taylor) must include the ability to elect a new government and the safeguarding of human rights (Schubert et al. 1994, 32; see also Jahn 2006, 60). It is also essential that electoral democracy go hand in hand with protections for political parties and freedom of political expression.

It is highly questionable whether John Esposito and John Voll are right to characterize democracy as a 'contested concept' (Esposito and Voll 1996, 14). Despite the variety of democratic forms – from American presidential democracy to German party-based democracy – the above criteria apply to all countries which are broadly accepted to be democracies. In what follows, therefore, we take our lead from the key idea that, while the processes of democratization may be shaped by culture in various ways, this does not apply to the core of electoral democracy itself, which is anchored in popular sovereignty (Abootalebi 2000, 36 f.). The idea here is not that only democracy can be seen as a legitimate form of government in every world historical situation. Nor can we overlook the fact that democracy takes different forms across the world. We must, however, work on the assumption that the above-mentioned elements are integral parts of every democracy, and examine whether we can discern ideological and political preconditions in the Islamic world that accord with this democratic minimum consensus in the West and elsewhere.

One further prefatory remark must be made here. In light of the reality of democracy, which we have now defined more precisely, it would make no sense to follow a binary logic according to which entire countries, societies, political systems and cultures are viewed simply as either democratic or undemocratic. If we measure the practice of existing contemporary democracies of Europe and North America against the minimum definition of democracy, we quickly notice the grey zones and setbacks – even with respect to core aspects of the concept of democracy as documented in various measurements and rankings. With his concept of 'polyarchy', Robert A. Dahl has provided us with a preliminary theoretical framework for understanding the incompleteness of all democracies (Dahl 1971). Many emerging economies, such as Brazil and India, feature limitations which are no longer found in the developed democracies of the industrialized West: unstable political parties and flagrant violations of freedom of speech and other civil liberties. Even older democracies have repeatedly seen the imposition of restrictions (often followed by new phases of liberalization). One need think only of the Patriot Act of 2001 in the United States, which limits individual rights in the name of combating terrorism, or the media monopoly enjoyed by Italian Prime Minister Silvio Berlusconi, which, as Immanuel Kant argued, may not limit the 'freedom from' state repression, but certainly limits the 'freedom to' engage in public communication.

As far as the realization of democracy is concerned, the Islamic countries as a whole are currently among the most backward in the world. While Latin America and Southern and Eastern Europe have almost entirely embraced democracy as a political system, only a small number of countries in the Islamic world have done so – though they share this shortcoming with much of Africa and Asia. There is no evidence of clear progress towards democracy in the Islamic world in the twentieth and twenty-first centuries – quite the contrary. A number of democratic experiments, for example, between the world wars in Egypt, after the Second World War in Iran and during the 1980s and 1990s in countries such as Algeria and Pakistan, came to grief. The twentieth century was not only an age of decolonization. In the Islamic world, it also saw the rise of the small authoritarian nation state.

Quantitative comparative research on democratization has developed numerous indices for classifying a country's democratic status with the help of set criteria and generally creates rankings based on surveys of experts, though with very different methods.[1] Among the best known are the Freedom in the World surveys produced by Freedom House and the Bertelsmann Transformation Index. The latter covers only so-called transitional states, not the developed Western democracies, which limits its comparative perspective.[2] On the other hand, the Bertelsmann Index integrates criteria of political, legal and economic development and is thus more comprehensive than the Freedom House surveys, which are limited to the political sphere. But, despite certain differences and divergences in their categorizations, these two reports provide an initial overview of the state of democratization, albeit no more than the beginning of a complex process of interpretation.

The Islamic world can be divided into three groups. Turkey, Bangladesh and Indonesia meet the minimum definition of democracy most fully because they satisfy the core criterion that the government can be voted in and out of office, which fundamentally distinguishes these countries from other states. Despite the many restrictions that exist, the development of civil liberties, including freedom of speech, has advanced to the point that these countries can now be placed on the same level of democratic development as emerging Latin American economies such as Mexico and Brazil. Since the three densely populated states of Turkey, Bangladesh and Indonesia have a combined population of about 430 million people, roughly a third of Muslims worldwide already live in democratic conditions. Much the same is true of the Muslim-majority states of Mali, Niger, Senegal and Albania, which have already completed the transition to formal democracy. It is striking that there are no Arab countries among the democratic Islamic states. The former 'periphery' of the Islamic world, countries such as Indonesia and Bangladesh, along with certain African states, is now among the democratic avant-garde. They are trailblazers for democracy in the Islamic world. It is thus far too sweeping to assume that the Islamic world is entirely authoritarian and undemocratic.

It took a long time for democratic political systems to develop in the West, and both Latin America and Southern and Eastern Europe saw enormous steps forwards and backwards before democracy finally took hold through a series of chain reactions – the famous 'waves of democratization' referred to by Samuel Huntington (Huntington 1991). This turns our attention to another group of Islamic states in which certain aspects of

---

[1] For criticisms of the indices, see Pickel/Pickel 2006.
[2] Freedomhouse.org; Bertelsmann-transformation-index.de.

democracy already exist: Jordan, Kuwait, Lebanon, Morocco, Bahrain, Yemen, Algeria, Egypt, Malaysia and Kyrgyzstan. Measuring these states against the minimum definition of democratization, it must be said that authoritarian systems continue to exist in them, and conditions are unfavourable for political transformation. But these countries can point to some progress over the last few decades. The governments of these states cannot be voted out of office since the presidents or monarchs are not subject to free and fair elections. Elections are pursued, but they are frequently rigged (Hamdy 2004), and real power still lies outside of democratic institutions and processes. As a rule there are political parties, and freedom of speech is developing, although it enjoys few legal safeguards. Liberalism and civil liberties rest on uncertain constitutional ground. In many countries, though, parliaments can be elected. Although they have limited authority, they are to some extent reminiscent of the early European constitutionalism of the nineteenth century, when parliaments and estates' assemblies were not sovereign but often functioned as consultative institutions. The governments in Egypt, Morocco, Jordan and Algeria are authoritarian, but media criticism of the government, though not the head of state, has become par for the course in recent decades, as has a limited amount of discord which is tolerated between parliaments and national leaderships.

These countries can be distinguished from those with basically 'hard-authoritarian' regimes, such as Libya, Syria, Tunisia, Saudi Arabia, Sudan, the United Arab Emirates, Kazakhstan, Uzbekistan, Tajikistan and Azerbaijan.[3] Strikingly, the state ideologies of these countries are partly secular and partly Islamic fundamentalist. Their rulers claim total power; there are virtually no political civil liberties; and elections are rigged or do not occur in the first place. In Saudi Arabia, for example, there are no national elections (in 2005, however, men were allowed to vote in local elections for the first time). But even in these states the first signs of opposition are beginning to emerge. In early 2007, a petition signed by Saudi intellectuals appeared on the Internet, triggering the arrest of many activists. Among other things, it called for the introduction of free parliamentary elections in which both men and women would be allowed to vote.[4]

---

[3] For a more nuanced explanation of the differences between 'hard' and 'soft' authoritarianism' see Chapter 3, the section on 'democratic polyarchies'.

[4] Maalam fi tariq al-malikiya al-dusturiya/daula al-dustur al-islami/daula al-aadal wa-l-schura [Signposts on the way to constitutional monarchy/a state based on an Islamic constitution/a state characterized by justice and consultation], http://www.dostor-islami. com (24 February 2007).

Certain states of the Islamic world, such as Pakistan, Iran, Iraq and Afghanistan, present classificatory difficulties. Should they be placed within the democratic or the 'soft' or 'hard' authoritarian camp? Following the American invasions of 2001 and 2003 and subsequent 'low intensity' wars, Iraq and Afghanistan currently lack key prerequisites for a democratic transition, such as a state monopoly on power, legal security and stable political parties and institutions. As a result, both countries lag far behind in the indices of democracy. However, within the context of the occupations, progress has been made in key areas of electoral democracy, although conditions for the formation of political parties and the holding of free elections to choose the head of state continue to be difficult. In these areas, however, Iraq and Afghanistan are generally more advanced than other countries within the Islamic world. The American invasions have engendered progress with respect to the so-called 'procedures' of democracy, though at the cost of a vast number of victims and impending state disintegration; this shows once again that democratization is a complex process that includes social and cultural factors. It may be successfully steered from outside only following a total collapse of the state and large-scale social devastation, as was seen in Germany and Japan after the Second World War.

It is at least partially misleading to classify Iran as authoritarian. The term may be correctly applied to the policy-making powers of the supreme Islamic scholar (*velayat-e faqih*). Revolutionary leaders such as Ayatollah Khomeini or his successor, Khamenei, cannot be elected, yet they enjoy a right of veto with respect to all political issues. But we must also take account of the dualism of the revolutionary leader and the president. The presidents steer the day-to-day politics of the executive (government) and are the product of elections which are considered, by and large, free and fair by international observers, include women's suffrage, and have produced unexpected results such as the election of reformist President Mohammad Khatami (although the manipulated election of President Mahmud Ahmadinejad in 2009 was a clear setback). Remove the institution of the revolutionary leader and the supreme legal scholar, and Iran would be a democracy with embedded democratic institutions on the same level as newly industrialising countries (NICs) such as Turkey, though there would be a lot of legal catching up to do, especially in the area of civil liberties. Even in this area, however, the 1990s saw extensive progress with respect to freedom of speech and of the press in Iran. As far as most of the procedures of democracy are concerned, Iran is actually fairly progressive, despite its fundamental problems with secularism and the concepts of civil liberties and human rights independent of religion. Were these obstacles to be eliminated, Iran would take a great democratic leap forward overnight.

Finally, Pakistan is another state it is difficult to categorize. Here, too, there exists a dual power structure, though one which recalls the self-styled 'custodianship' of the Turkish armed forces. Like Turkey, Pakistan has experienced an alternation between democratic practice (in the era of Zulfikar Ali Bhutto and Benazir Bhutto, for example) and military dictatorship (under Zia ul-Haq and Pervez Musharraf), with the difference that Turkey seems largely to have left the era of military rule behind, while it is the present-day reality in Pakistan. Further, in Pakistan the role of custodian is less clearly associated with the secular legacy of state founder Ali Jinnah than are the Turkish armed forces with the laicist legacy of Kemal Atatürk. Jinnah wished to create a state for the Muslims of the Indian subcontinent but not an Islamic state (Ziring 2003). Under the military regime of Zia ul-Haq in the 1970s, however, the first elements of Sharia law were introduced into the Pakistani legal system. Nonetheless, over the last few decades, Pakistani political culture as a whole has shown the first signs of democracy, placing it close to Bangladesh and Indonesia.

If we look at the Bertelsmann Transformation Index for states' level of secularization, the incompatibility of Islam and democracy appears to be borne out. Countries in which Islam functions as the state doctrine, that is, Pakistan, Saudi Arabia and Iran, do not meet with the minimum requirements of democracy. In fact, though, the figures also tell us something else: in cases in which Islamic fundamentalist regimes came to power, not as a result of elections, but through coups and revolutions, these regimes have a tendency, with the aid of Islam, to legitimize themselves in an 'absolutist' manner. But this does not inevitably mean that Islamic governments that come to power without revolution and through elections must automatically be authoritarian. The case of Turkey, where Recep Tayyip Erdogan, a follower of political Islam, has been prime minister for years, proves the point. The connection between Islam and democracy thus remains initially unclear.

There does seem to be a certain correlation between democracy and secularism to the extent that democracy has, as yet, never been introduced in a non-secular state. But other dimensions must also be taken into account. A number of hard authoritarian states consist of secular political systems in which Islam functions in part as the 'state religion', but the religious institutions are controlled by the state. Countries such as Syria, Libya and Tunisia, which basically have secular authoritarian systems of rule, are on the same level as the Islamic dictatorships of Saudi Arabia and Iran with respect to restrictions on political and civil rights.

Overall, the Islamic world is clearly far from uniform in its degree of democratization. Given these realities on the ground, Daniel Brumberg and Larry Diamond suggest that it is highly questionable that Islam is an obstacle on the path to democratization (Brumberg and Diamond 2003, XI). Overall, the thesis that the Islamic world is resistant to democracy and exceptional fails to take into account significant differences between political systems and political cultures – transitions to electoral democracy in some states, pre-democratic development and heterogeneous ideologies in others.

THE 'CHRISTIAN DEMOCRATIZATION' OF ISLAM?

If we consider political Islam in light of a structuralist theory that takes into account the interactions among social conditions, political ideologies and both domestic and international processes, it quickly emerges that the notion that Islam and democracy are incompatible is misleading (Bromley 1997, 321). An integrated analysis of objective structural and subjective action-related factors is capable of uncovering universal social and political processes behind particular ideological manifestations – such as political Islam. Questions relating to the distribution of economic and political resources are certainly taken up in a culturally specific way in the process of political change. But the formulation and interpretation of ideologies is a constant process (Hall 1980) in which countless actors, both elites and the 'masses' are involved, making it hard to produce clear-cut ideological critiques. Rather than ideology, it is often more helpful to refer to a complex societal discourse that molds the subjective side of events (see, for example, Salvatore 1997). But the reconstruction and critique of a discourse and its ideological components is no more than a fleeting snapshot of contemporary thinking, one always beset by great uncertainty.

This sense of uncertainty also quickly sets in if we examine the relationship of Islamic thought to democracy. Some modern ideologies of Islam comply straightforwardly with the minimum consensus of democracy. Others seem entirely at variance with it. But, as we shall see, the most interesting perspectives lie between these extremes – in the 'grey zones' opened up time and again by pragmatic political actors.

It is crucial to acknowledge that the institutionalization of power is still one of the greatest problems of Islamic doctrine. There exist numerous interpretations. The Iranian Shia concept of the *velayat-e faqih*, for example, which legitimizes theocracy and clerical rule in Iran, plays no role in the majority Sunnite school of Islam and is rejected as a universal model of Islamic rule by all forces, from the scholarly hub of Azhar University in Cairo to the various reformist schools to both moderate and extremist Islamic fundamentalists. In the Sunnite world, too, the caliphate model followed by the successors of the Prophet Muhammad, the supposedly ideal symbiosis of power and law, has taken on a powerful normative charge. But only a vanishingly small minority calls for the restoration of the caliphate, abolished in 1924 following the disintegration of the Ottoman empire. The contemporary discourse of political Islam is thus vague about the correct form of rule (*hukm*).

The classical principle of *tauhid* (the oneness of God) is often interpreted as divine sovereignty, in contradistinction to the popular sovereignty that is the hallmark of democracy. Yet, as a practical matter, this principle is relativized by the fact that *tauhid* does not include rule by a religious class (Esposito and Voll 1996, 23 f.), which in principle, shifts the question of rule away from the discourse of Islamic scholars and back to society as a whole. Classical Islamic jurisprudence also recognizes the concept of *shura* (consultation), according to which the ruler must consult with others when exercising power. It is unclear, however, whether *shura* implies a panel of experts made up of legal scholars or the entire community of Muslims, though the concept of *ijma* (consensus), generated within the Islamic legal tradition, seems to speak in favour of the latter (Esposito and Voll 1996, 28). Further, the term 'monarchy' has negative connotations in modern Arabic. It is therefore now generally accepted that, however unclear they may be, the principles of Islamic constitutional law can be interpreted to mean that an 'Islamic order' is potentially compatible with the principles of division of power and parliamentary democracy. Certain elements of the Western minimum consensus of democracy could thus be fulfilled in light of Islamic teachings: elections, electable governments, and even freedom of speech, as required by the Islamic concepts of consultation and consensus building.

The early European constitutionalism of the nineteenth century (as exemplified by the *Vormärz*, the period of German history from 1815 to the revolution in March 1848) also rested predominantly on constructions in which 'popular sovereignty' was still regarded as 'mob rule' (Boldt 1975; Sheehan 1978). It is true that the constitutionalists moved away from the concept of the 'divine right' of the monarch. But the latter's authority was to be largely retained as long as he or she took advice and, in certain areas, allowed others a supervisory role (through estates' assemblies, for example). The claim to such supervisory rights was traced back to 'state sovereignty', a transitional concept falling between 'divine right' and 'popular sovereignty' in European constitutional law. But because the above-mentioned principles mean that Islamic law is already equipped with proto-democratic legal constructions, *tauhid* (the oneness of God) must not be confused with the favour and arbitrary rule of a divinely legitimized monarch; *tauhid* legitimizes *all* Muslims. *Shura* is an embryonic form of parliamentarism and *ijma*, a prototype of 'public opinion'. (We should bear in mind that the idea of a new consensus within the Muslim community currently plays a major role in the thinking of the conservative Islamic reformers around Tariq Ramadan and Yusuf al-Qaradawi, for instance; however, with respect to the *shura*, in other words, to the question of *who* is to establish this consensus, Al-Qaradawi ascribes greater significance to the scholars than Ramadan [see Chapter 1]). Overall, then, it could be argued that there is a marked similarity between Islamic constitutional law and early European constitutionalism. Islamic law does not equate with the idea of popular sovereignty and secularism, which explicitly state that all power emanates from a national community of equal individuals. But it at least points to the idea that a division of powers and political participation are desirable.

The concept that Islamic legal thought is compatible with a parliamentary system is also characteristic of Shia Islam, which, in Iran for example, has institutionalized the procedures of political modernity – parliament, constitution, elections – albeit with the proviso that God is the ultimate sovereign. This is expressed in the veto power enjoyed by the supreme legal scholar, a result of Shiism's uniquely strong focus on the successor caliphs to Muhammad.

The question of how to interpret Islamic thought in relation to democracy has been the subject of constant and ongoing debate, some of which points beyond early Western constitutionalism and implies genuine republican parliamentary government and division of power. For example, for the Muslim Brothers of Egypt, the prototype Islamic fundamentalist organization in the Islamic world, struggling against the multi-party system was the top priority during the country's 'liberal era' (1919–52), a fight for which the term *hizbiya* (Arabic *hizb*: party) was coined, translatable as 'party strife' and the corruption of reverent governance. Into the era of Anwar al-Sadat, the dominant idea was to establish a one-party system after getting rid of the old system. However, when Umar al-Tilimsani took over the leadership of the Muslim Brothers, the organization took a pragmatic, non-violent and moderate course, while the meaning of the term *hizbiyya* changed fundamentally. *Hizbiya* now implies a positive commitment to party pluralism, elections, alliances and parliamentarism (Farshid 1989). The multi-party system is no longer merely regarded as compatible with the principle of consultation (*shura*), but also explicitly with *hukm*, in other words with the system of rule. The dispute within Islamic fundamentalist circles about what constitutes 'just rule' is so firmly established, at least within Sunnite Islam, that it seems to represent the best guarantor of participative forms of governance and the pluralism of political views. Thus, the main problem with the compatibility of Islamic legal discourse with democracy lies less in the area of democratic procedures (such as parliamentarism, elections, division of power and the formation of political parties), than in the area of the 'values of democracy': popular sovereignty and secularism continue to be contested, creating human rights problems for all (see also Krämer 1987–8).

A recent analysis by American policy research institute the Carnegie Endowment for Peace provides instructive evidence of overlaps and differences between Islam and democracy. In their paper 'Islamist Movements and the Democratic Process in the Arab World: Exploring the Grey Zones', Nathan J. Brown, Amr Hamzawy and Marina Ottaway explore the question of the compatibility of Islamic fundamentalism and democracy. They begin their analysis with the premise that the radical Islamic fundamentalists who are demanding the revival of the caliphate are a peripheral phenomenon within the contemporary Islamic fundamentalist movement (Brown et al. 2006, 3). This assessment is correct in that, more than eighty years after the disintegration of the caliphate in 1924, it is no longer possible to speak of a unified Islamic world. The Islamic umbrella group Organization of the Islamic Conference (OIC), which is made up of representatives from Islamic countries, is a loose association whose resolutions are about as binding as those of the Socialist International. The Islamic world now consists of separate nation states, and the cohesion of the Islamic community (*umma*) is a pipe dream of internationalist radical Islamic fundamentalists that is quite out of touch with reality (Roy 2007). Even among violent Islamic fundamentalists, there is a strong current of nationally oriented organizations such as the Lebanese Hezbollah or the Palestinian Hamas, whose goals differ substantially from those of globally active terrorists aspiring to unify the Islamic world (see Chapter 7).

The Carnegie study categorizes as 'moderate Islamic fundamentalists' Morocco's Parti de la Justice et du Developpement (PJD); Egypt's Muslim Brothers and the Al-Wasat party (Centrists); Yemen's Islah (Reform Party); Jordan's Islamic Action Front; Kuwait's Islamic Constitutional Movement and Bahrain's Al-Wifaq (National Accord) (Brown et al. 2006, 4). The study takes it as read that the political programmes of these groups have become increasingly pragmatic over the last decades, bringing them close to compatibility with Western-style democracy, though there remain a number of open questions. The authors call these 'grey zones'.

As a result of the splintering of extremist forces, these mass organizations as a rule express at least rhetorical approval for 'democracy' and 'human rights'. But the meanings behind these concepts are often problematic. The Muslim Brothers, for example, are certainly credible supporters of the division of power, a multi-party system, transparent elections and the rotation of power, political freedoms, and the like. But they oppose equal rights, for the Coptic Christians, for example, who make up 10 percent of the Egyptian population, a clear break with the above-defined minimum consensus of democracy (Brown et al. 2006, 6, 13).

What tends to go largely unnoticed is that the Muslim Brothers' notion of the Islamic nature of society discriminates not only against non-Muslim minorities, but also against Muslims. As the fundamentalists see things, even Muslims can become politically active only as 'believers'. Converts, atheists, agnostics and the great army of secularists who, even in 'Islamic societies', consider religion a private matter that belongs outside the political domain, are discriminated against in the moderate Islamic fundamentalist organizations' political approach. This is a fundamental problem with pre-state human rights. It cannot be alleviated by the fact that, in the view of the moderate Islamic fundamentalists, a Muslim should be a member of a community that participates in politics, that elects, argues and discusses – but that may never attack the fundamental Islamic character of politics.

The authors of the Carnegie paper note that most Islamic groupings refuse to tolerate foundations of political groups other than Islamic ones. It is hard to resist the suspicion that the Islamic fundamentalist understanding of democracy is basically that of a participative, conviction-based dictatorship. It is not the individual, but the Muslim that is a member of the political community (Brown et al. 2006, 14). One example is the rights of women. Both active and passive female suffrage are fundamentally uncontested outside of the Arabian peninsula, even in Iran, and especially in the non-Arab world, in states such as Indonesia, Bangladesh, Pakistan and Turkey, where it is quite normal for women to be national leaders. More problematic for the Islamic fundamentalists, however, is the recognition of equal *civil rights* in the area of marital law, in other words, with respect to marriage, divorce, child custody laws, inheritance, citizenship, and the like (Brown et al. 2006, 15). In assessing these issues we should certainly take into account the fact that in Europe, too, equal rights in many of these areas were achieved only during 1970s and 1980s. Before then, a married woman could function as an equal legal entity only to a very limited degree in many European states. It is possible to conceive of equality between men and women in a reformed Islamic fundamentalist democracy, but currently fundamentalists are dyed-in-the-wool traditionalists, teaching gender-specific inequality in civil law despite granting political rights for women. Hence, Islamic fundamentalists continue to discriminate, not only against religious minorities, but also secularist sections of the majority Islamic society and women. Women in fact face discrimination on several fronts: as members of religious minorities, as culturally Muslim secularists and as individuals with respect to the exercise of civil rights.

While classical Islamic fundamentalism has undoubtedly made much progress, the justification for continuing to describe most Islamic groupings as 'fundamentalist' is that they insist on the primacy of religious affiliation and on placing a large number of restrictions, familiar from the Sharia, on the civil liberties of women, minorities and secularists. At the same time – and frequently bound-up with a particular individual, as was evident in the case of the preacher Yusuf al-Qaradawi – a comprehensively reformed political understanding is gradually taking hold within the practice of political Islam. It is interesting to note that the Egyptian Wasat party now accepts Copts as members and is even open to the use of quotas (Brown et al. 2006, 16). On questions of human rights and democracy, a distinction is rapidly emerging within the Islamic fundamentalist camp of the kind also found in the contemporary intellectual discourse on modernity. Alongside a fundamentalist political understanding of Islam, there also exists a reformed conception. Here, Islam remains a key source of inspiration but – akin to European Christian democracy – it is no longer the foundation of law, which would call into question equality before the law.

In view of this potential for ideological development, we should take heed of Simon Bromley's warning not to underestimate Islam. Even in the twentieth century, Spain's traditionally Catholic culture was often blamed for its enduring dictatorship: a view which seems quite laughable in retrospect (Bromley 1997, 333). In fact, the first signs of something of a 'Christian democratization' of Islam, which has gained a firm foothold in countries such as Turkey and Indonesia, are already beginning to emerge in the Arab world. The significant differences among fundamentalist political movements, which also exist within Christianity, particularly in the United States, and Christian democracy lie in the fact that the latter represents a form of ideological conservatism that derives its political values from Christian thought but accepts a secular constitutional framework in attempting to realize its goals. It is true that, even today, European Christian democrats advocate *cultural* and *social* discrimination between men and women and between majorities and immigrant minorities; but they put forward no *legal* arguments with respect to the granting of full political and legal freedoms for citizens, regardless of their gender or origin.

Christian democracy is an element of the transformation of European conservatism from a structural conservatism seeking to safeguard authoritarian monarchical rule based on a Christian view of the human being to a value-based conservatism which seeks to realize Christian values within a secular democratic order. It took a long time for this to happen, and it did so via a highly circuitous route from unconditional support for the principle of monarchical rule in Prussia, Austria-Hungary and the later German empire, for example, in contrast to the emerging democracies in Britain, the United States and to some extent France as well, to the internal cordoning off of denominations in the Weimar Republic (only Catholics could become members of the Catholic Centre Party) to support for the Nazi Party in the German Reichstag by the Christian conservative parties – in opposition to social democrats and communists. In fact, European Christian democracy has illiberal and anti-Enlightenment roots hard to imagine today. As late as 1884, a Catholic party which called openly for the abolition of secularism and the liberal constitution and the establishment of a Christian monarchy attained a parliamentary majority in the young Belgian democracy (Kylvas 2000). Only after the Second World War did European conservatism finally bid farewell to its unconditional loyalty to monarchy, dictatorship and clergy.

In comparison, the beliefs of the moderate Islamic fundamentalists, termed 'political Islamists' by the International Crisis Group[5] and studied

[5] Understanding Islamism, International Crisis Group, Middle East/North Africa Report, no. 37, 2 March 2005, n.p.

by the Carnegie Endowment, are already far more compatible with democracy, although the secularist process of opening to non-Muslims has yet to be completed. The possible objection that the European conservatism of the nineteenth and twentieth centuries never demanded a 'theocracy' fails to take account of the fact that, through the notion of divine right, the monarchies of Russia and Prussia were also given religious absolution, and this occurred centuries after the Thirty Years' War and the secularization of European governance, which at the time was nominally complete but far from truly embedded. Classical Islamic constitutional law and the evolution of political Islamic thought in the twentieth century suggest that, in their recognition of *democracy within the Islamic world* and in their anti-authoritarian creed that embraces the division of powers, mainstream Islamic fundamentalism may now be significantly further advanced than was monarchist European conservatism for much of the nineteenth and early twentieth centuries.

By the 'establishment of Sharia law', these mainstream Islamic fundamentalists mean nothing more than the highly selective religious legitimation of a values-based conservatism in the form of a morally rigid law, as was supported for centuries in a similar way by European conservatives, with respect to the curtailment of women's civil rights, for example. Gender-based guardianship, in which the husband was the guardian of his wife, was abolished in Europe only in the nineteenth century, and key aspects of the material power of disposal only in the second half of the twentieth century (Duncker 2003). Whether the putative compulsory veiling of women in Islam would be something categorically different is well worth discussing. Of course, such measures are in principle just as incompatible with a secular constitutional state – which must treat genders and minorities equally, and to which conservatives, too, professed their commitment after the Second World War – as was gendered guardianship with the German basic law, which is why such provisions have now disappeared from European laws.

It is true that Islamic fundamentalists are yet to engage in such processes of recognition, but certain reformist tendencies are already beginning to emerge. Is it conceivable, then, that Islamic fundamentalism will undergo 'Christian democratization'? A comparison with European history at least shows that internal paradoxes and ideological hostilities to the democratic state, even if entrenched over centuries, may be swept away by a major political rupture (such as the Second World War), which allows us to hope that an Islamic fundamentalist transformation may occur in the wake of a change of political system.

It is tempting to compare Islamic fundamentalism with the Protestant fundamentalism found in the USA. Do these movements not exhibit a far greater degree of overlap? Over the last few years, a number of US states have, after all, enhanced the legal status of 'creationism', that is, the Biblical teaching on the creation of the world in Genesis, vis-à-vis Darwinism. A similar pattern seems to be emerging here as with Islamic fundamentalism: a Christian majority wishes, through entirely demo-cratic electoral and legislative procedures, to raise a religious worldview to the status of universal law. In an article on Protestant fundamentalism, Martin Riesenbrodt goes further still, casting doubt on the fundamental loyalty to democracy characteristic of American fundamentalists: 'Some fundamentalists' commitment to democracy is far from unconditional. Particularly at times when their political and moral ideas are unable to command majority support, they face a dilemma: on the one hand, they approve of the constitution and the democratic process, on the other they cannot live with their results' (Riesenbrodt 1987, 17).

Can we infer from this comparison with Protestant fundamental-ism that democracy would present Islamic fundamentalism, too, with a permanent dilemma? This is possible but by no means certain, for two reasons. First, American Protestant fundamentalism is not entirely anti-democratic. For the most part, it is a religious revivalist movement within the bounds of democracy – at least, as long as it does not call for religious laws. In this sense, it would be a good role model for the evolu-tion of Islamic fundamentalism towards compatibility with democracy. Second, however obvious it may appear, the comparison is contested in part – and experts on the various hues of Islam have for decades resisted any equation of the two phenomena – because programmatically, the attention of Islamic fundamentalism is *not* focussed on theological issues but on political ones. It is true that Christian communities in the United States have always had a socially integrative function, particularly for the immigrant population, very much like the function of modern-day Islamic fundamentalist groups in the urban centres of the Middle East (Hefner 2005, 19). But they have never become established in the form of a political party. Meanwhile, the organizational form of the major Islamic fundamentalist organizations is party-like, and it is this political character that points to a comparison with phenomena like European Christian democracy rather than with American fundamentalism.

Islamic fundamentalists, however, again with the exception of Saudi Arabia, play an oppositional role of a predominantly political nature and do not stabilize the existing authoritarian forms of rule as did European conservatives for hundreds of years. Thus, alongside the development of European Christian democracy, another comparative perspective suggests itself. This is what renowned specialist in the economics and politics of the Middle East John Waterbury is referring to when he asserts that political Islam faces the challenge of Eurocommunism (Waterbury 1994, 40). The remarkable social flexibility of Islamic fundamentalism, which supports an absolutist hereditary monarchy in Saudi Arabia, whereas other Islamic fundamentalists in Saudi Arabia and elsewhere in the Islamic world take action against authoritarian regimes, rules out any simple identification with the historical phenomenon of European conservatism or American Protestant fundamentalism. In its support for the Republican Party, the latter possesses a certain middle- and upper-class character that distinguishes it from Islamic fundamentalism.

At first glance, comparisons such as those between Islamic fundamentalism and 'Eurocommunism' or social democracy seem difficult to justify. The Eurocommunism metaphor, which alludes to the history of Western European communist parties' gradual break with dictatorial Marxism-Leninism, particularly in the 1970s (Kellermann 1984; Richter and Trautmann 1979), seems to lend itself to comparisons with the undemocratic forces across the secular political spectrum in Islamic countries but not to Islamic fundamentalists, with their specific problems in recognizing secularism. But in view of European Christian democracy's strong roots in the bourgeoisie and middle classes more generally and the significantly greater presence of Islamic fundamentalism among middle *and* lower classes, the question arises, which is the more useful comparative level: European socialism or European Christian conservatism?

If the former, it is plain that the communist current of the European labour movement, but also its socialist counterpart, required more than a century – from the mid-nineteenth to the latter stages of the mid-twentieth century – to finally accept the subordination of the socialist/communist utopia to the democratic state and its particular form of political organization. In the case of social democracy, this process occurred significantly faster and led – in Germany the key term was 'Bernstein' socialism – to abandonment of the maximalist objective of realizing the specific demands of the lower classes through revolutionary means and the exclusion of the rest of society ('dictatorship of the proletariat'), if necessary (Meyer 1977).

As yet, the moderate Islamic fundamentalists have fully repeated neither the developmental processes of European Christian democracy nor those of the Social Democrats or Eurocommunists. However, to use the terminology of the Carnegie study, they find themselves in a 'grey area' of open developmental processes, in which some of the developmental stages of the comparative models already seem to have occurred. In particular, the idea of an 'avant-garde', perverted by Lenin in order to establish an absolute party dictatorship over the people, has already been shelved by moderate Islamic fundamentalists. Believing it their mission to liberate the people, the Islamic extremist groups and terrorists resemble the Cambodian Khmer Rouge, taking action if need be against their own compatriots in order to 're-educate' them (see Chapter 7). In contrast, the moderate groupings have long since turned pluralist – at least as long as the polity remains within an 'Islamic' framework.

The Carnegie study points to uncertainties in another area as well, and here again there are parallels with the above-mentioned European political currents. This is the marked gap between political programmes and political practice. It is true that all Islamic fundamentalist organizations theoretically call for the reintroduction of Sharia. Yet so far the Islamic parties have launched very few concrete legal initiatives and – in cases where this was possible in the first place – introduced virtually no parliamentary bills to this end. The authors see the key reason for this hesitation as lying in the complex character of the Sharia. As a legal corpus, the Sharia defies straightforward and uniform interpretation. In most countries, it has in any case become so closely interwoven with secular legal norms over the centuries that any radical switch to the Sharia would be impossible – simply because it does not address numerous problems of modern society (Brown et al. 2006, 9 f.). As a result, these organizations deal with the Sharia in a highly selective fashion. The Islamic fundamentalists cannot give up the goal of introducing Islamic law without losing face, but in practice they by no means demand its consistent reestablishment.

This simply means that the substance of the putative 'Islamic state' is becoming increasingly blurred as a consequence of the pluralism within Muslim societies. The key criterion distinguishing conservative reformist Islam and fundamentalism (see Chapter 1) is beginning to erode, making way for a situation in which conservative reform is viewed as the most valid goal. Even the final bastion distinguishing fundamentalism from liberal reform – equal treatment of Muslims and non-Muslims – is tending to disappear, as in the case of the Wasat party in Egypt for example (Norton 2005, 144). Thus, across the entire spectrum of the practice of political Islam there are now real signs that it may *in future* be entirely compatible with democracy, as with the Turkish model, for example.

The theory that Christian democratization is a singular process that cannot be re-enacted in the Islamic countries crops up again and again in the scholarly literature and in the media.[6] Reference is made to the supposedly unique separation of Christendom from papal dogmatism in the modern era and the impact of external impulses, such as the American and French revolutions. Such arguments overlook the fact that, in the shape of Atatürk's reforms, Turkey responded vigorously to European influences and that, as we have seen, Islam has long featured major reformist tendencies. The notion that Islam lacks a definitional centre because there is no equivalent of the papacy, supposedly making it incapable of development, is quite outdated and not without a certain irony: the papacy's interpretive monopoly, lamented by Christian reformers generally and Protestants in particular, which impeded social progress for centuries, is now belatedly declared the sine qua non for the renewal of religion and politics across the globe.

We should resist both such comparative historical determinism and rash claims that the way is clear for democracy. The Carnegie Endowment's concept of 'grey zones' is appealing and helpful because some scholars – who made such a signal contribution by correctly pointing to the democratic potential of Islamic fundamentalism as early as the 1990s – were overly optimistic. Francois Burgat is a French expert on Algeria and Islam who, in his famous book *Face to Face with Islam,* attempted to determine the Islamic fundamentalists' capacity for political integration in an interesting and incisive way. Burgat makes numerous comparisons between Islamic fundamentalism and contemporary practice in Western states, simply denying extant differences. He sees references to God in the American and certain European constitutions as contradicting the principle of secularism (Burgat 2003, 133), and equates the principle of citizenship, which 'discriminates' against non-citizens, with Islamic fundamentalists' unequal treatment of non-Muslims (Burgat 2003, 135).

These are untenable comparisons, which nonetheless crop up repeatedly in the debate. Despite their symbolic references to God, the American and European constitutions grant each citizen the same rights and by no means favour Christianity over other religions. The notion that citizenship in the Western nation state is a form of 'group membership' on the same level as affiliation to Islam among the fundamentalists – that is, a Frenchman cannot become chancellor of Germany – is also unconvincing

---

[6] See for example Jan-Werner Müller, Mit Gott und Menschenrechten [With God and human rights], *die tageszeitung*, 1 July 2008.

because, firstly, universal human rights are considered *pre-state* rights independent of citizenship, even for the stateless, while the fundamentalists link human rights to religious affiliation, and secondly, no Islamic fundamentalist has yet managed to explain how nation states might be abolished. Hence, in addition to discrimination by Muslims against non-Muslims, there exists in practice the discriminatory criterion of nationality, even within the Islamic world. A Turk will probably never become king of Saudi Arabia: this represents a form of dual discrimination within the Islamic fundamentalist state with respect to both human rights *and* nationality.

The problem with simplistic comparisons of this kind is that they tend to obstruct rather than illuminate our view of real commonalities and differences. They work on the dubious assumption that Islamic fundamentalist and secular democratic orders enjoy a similar degree of legitimacy with respect to human rights, which may lead to dangerous strategic errors. As we shall see, it may be possible and necessary to cooperate with Islamic fundamentalism even during periods when it remains within the grey zones of democratic compatibility. Yet, this in itself would force all truly democratic forces and even reformist Islamic politicians to position themselves strategically with much care, for Islamic fundamentalism still has some way to go before it is entirely compatible with democracy. The opportunities for democracy that might arise from its current radicalism and the circumstances under which we might expect further moderation are discussed later on (see Chapter 4).

MUSLIM WORLD: SECULAR DEMOCRACY ON THE MARGINS
OF GLOBAL SOCIETY

It is extremely difficult to bring the contemporary secular modernism of the Islamic world down to a satisfactory common denominator. As a group, secular modernists include the broadest range of personalities and views on desirable forms of political structure. Because of their secular orientation, they often take on an air of 'commonality' only when differentiated from Islamic thinkers. Such diverse thinkers as contemporary Syrian philosopher Sadiq al-Azm, Egyptian sociologist Saad Eddin Ibrahim, Franco-Algerian philosopher Mohamed Arkoun, such key thinkers of the revolutionary post-war period as the founder of the Syrian Baath party Michel Aflaq and Taha Hussein, leading intellectual of the liberal interwar period in Egypt, are considered secular modernists of the twentieth and twenty-first centuries – and this is just a brief selection. What these intellectuals have in common is that they reject the use of Islam as an element in the development of political ideologies and see secular alignment as a more direct route to the modernization of Arab societies.

What makes this current difficult to describe is that secularism constitutes a residual category uniting quite different, even opposing, political ideologies. Secularism is a negative categorization. It dissociates itself from religion, but has developed no positive homogeneity, and this is one of its key weaknesses in the Middle East. Secular modernism unites the representatives of the revolutionary developmental dictatorships of the post-war era in countries such as Algeria, Tunisia, Libya, Egypt and Syria, whose political systems are to this day predominantly secular in character, and includes democratic opposition forces that wish to change the authoritarian status quo and promote a democratic system. Time and again, however, the champions of authoritarianism manage to highlight their secularism in the struggle against the threat of Islamic fundamentalism – in such a way that even many democrats are prepared to embrace 'standstill alliances', in line with the principle that when considered alongside fundamentalism, the authoritarian revolutionary state is the lesser of two evils. In this way, such phenomena as authoritarian Egyptian Nasserism regularly experience renaissances.[7] In Syria, a large section of the middle class rallies around the dictatorship of the Asad family. In Algeria in the early 1990s, the FLN (National Liberation Front) government managed to cut the burgeoning secular opposition down to size by raising the menacing prospect of a fundamentalist regime.

The secularism of various political forces in the Middle East certainly matches the Western notion of religion forced into the private sphere. In contemporary practice, however, it has become the subject of political sloganeering and has led to an impasse of modernism. It seems as though one may be liberated from religion only at the price of giving up on *other* promises of autonomy proffered by Western modernity, namely the democratic constitutional state. That things could come to such a hopeless pass has nothing to do with unchanging cultural deficiencies of the Islamic world, but with a historical development quite different from anything seen in the West. The Middle Eastern authoritarian state is *not*, like the European state, the successor to a feudal and monarchical state based on the divine right of kings, which had to be done away with because it stood in the way of bourgeois notions of freedom that entailed

---

[7] Richard Jaquemont, Rückkehr zu Nasser [A return to Nasser], *Le Monde Diplomatique* (German edition), July 1997.

a hunger for modernity. The authoritarian Middle Eastern nation state was in fact an *instrument of this modernity* on the margins of global society. Following a brief interlude in the interwar period, it rapidly rose to prominence because it combined two things: the battle against domestic and external injustice, that is, against the feudal classes, which were dispossessed in the course of the agrarian reforms implemented by the Egyptian President Gamal Abdel Nasser, and against the external enemy of neo-colonialism, symbolized by Israel or by Britain and France in the Suez war of 1956.

Hence, the Middle Eastern authoritarian state of the last half-century was certainly no parasitical state on the model of French absolutism, but rather a trans-historical mixture of the Prussian developmental and Soviet redistributive state. On the periphery of the West, the political system developed in a quite different way, sometimes in fact more rapidly, but also in more unstable fashion because, in addition to domestic developmental needs, the state systems tailor made by the colonial powers, in Iraq, Lebanon or Jordan for example, were constantly threatening to collapse. The Middle Eastern state also began to totter as a result of growing economic problems. Secularism, national stability, modernization and authoritarianism entered into an understandable but precarious alliance. The Islamic fundamentalist opposition to authoritarianism, which had been growing since the 1970s, was now directed against one of the last ideological pillars of those in power: secularism. After the political failure of the Arab states, in their opposition to Israel for example, and economic breakdown, adherence to the secular state and opposition to the Islamic fundamentalists is now the only source of legitimacy enjoyed by the authoritarian state, from Algeria to Cairo to Pakistan.

This conflict includes secular supporters of democratization in the Arab world, such as Syrian philosopher Sadiq Jalal al-Azm. He rejects the view that the problems of the Arab world point to a permanent gulf between Islam and the West.[8] As Al-Azm sees things, the West's democratic lead over the Arab world is no culturally-rooted inevitability, and the Arab countries are quite capable of developing democratic values and procedures. Al-Azm sees this as the only way of overcoming the current social crisis, a significant component of which is the schism between secular and Islamic fundamentalist forces.

---

[8] Democratization Is a Gradual Process, Interview with Sadiq al-Azm, 2003, http://www. qantara.de (18 November 2006).

As we have seen, supporters of democracy are very much in accordance with the political cultures of the Islamic world, where there is majority support for democracy. So far, the Islamic world includes only a small number of democracies, but public attitudes seem to reflect a more positive view of democracy than might appear at first sight. Independently of the Gallup study (Esposito and Mogahed 2007; see also Chapter 2 of this book), in their comparative empirical analysis of attitudes towards democracy across the world, Pippa Norris and Ronald Inglehart conclude that, in principle, democracy enjoys as much support in the Islamic world as in the West – greater support, in fact, than in some post-communist countries in Eastern Europe (Norris and Inglehart 2004, 133 ff.).

Overall, though, a mixed picture emerges with respect to secular political thought in the Middle East. Numerous intellectual voices share the Western minimum consensus, according to which societies can develop meaningfully only on the basis of the constitutionally guaranteed autonomy of the individual, human rights and democracy. In the Islamic world, however, secular thought is not necessarily republican but has a strong authoritarian undercurrent arising from its specific history. Unlike secularism during the European Reformation, secularism in the Muslim world was not something people fought for. In several countries it was 'granted' by the state, which thereby justifies its reform projects, legitimizes its continued existence and misuses secularism as an authoritarian state ideology to oppose democratization. Secularism used to be a progressive idea characteristic of the Middle Eastern state. After the First World War Turkey and after the Second World War countries like Pakistan, Egypt, Algeria, Tunisia, Syria or Iraq were run by secular nationalist regimes. Nowadays, however, secularism is increasingly degenerating into a retrograde ideology that impedes the advancement of political modernity and, ultimately, the consensus on democracy. Today, it is not just secular democrats who oppose this authoritarian misuse of secularism but also various Islamic schools of thought.

4

Political System Change: The Radicals' Democracy

Is democracy the result of a planned process in which, from deep within an authoritarian political system, perhaps with a little help from outside, democratic forces bring about a democratic transformation? For a number of reasons, this idea is highly simplistic. For many of those living in an autocracy, it is hard to develop a pro-democratic attitude and outlook without having experienced democracy first-hand. It often takes some time after a formal democratic framework is established for a civic culture to take hold. Oppositional elites and parties, should any exist, may of course profess their belief in democracy. But an opposition can survive in an authoritarian state only if it refrains from clearly raising the prospect of system change – which is precisely what calling for democracy would entail. Even if the opposition has produced a democratic vision, doubts often remain about the seriousness of such aspirations. Is the commitment to democracy merely a means to an end, the opposition's way of blinding political opponents and the international community to their true intentions, namely to abolish democracy once in power and replace it with a new dictatorship?

Despite the doubts that inevitably remain for the ideological critic, it is reassuring to note that there is another quite different perspective on political change. Rather than a process that opposition forces consciously aim to set in motion, democratization may be viewed as a kind of historical accident. Dankwart Rustow and Adam Przeworksi note that democracy may be regarded, even by opposition forces with questionable democratic credentials or of an unambiguously authoritarian character – from dogmatic leftists to Islamic fundamentalists – as the 'second-best solution' should all other political strategies risk achieving nothing at all, if the opposition risks ongoing repression or complete destruction (Przeworski 1991; Rustow 1970). This view of things, which is influenced by game theory, assumes that political actors' thought and action is rational and pragmatic rather than ideological.

Can democracy be regarded as a kind of constitutionally fixed snapshot of a specific constellation of historical forces that is anything but the result of a culturally-rooted commitment to democracy? It seems very likely that the majority of democracies in the world came about in precisely this way. Without this perspective, it is quite impossible to adequately explain the political upheavals in Southern Europe, Latin America and Eastern Europe over the last few decades of the twentieth century. The major historical waves of democratization did not involve a uniform process (Karl and Schmitter 1991).

Why, then, would anyone claim, as many commentators and even some scholars have done, that such a development can be entirely ruled out in the Islamic world, regardless of the current state of its political systems and opposition forces?[1] It is time we consider adopting a revised and more differentiated view of the processes of democratization in the Islamic world. A number of theorists of political transformation, political scientists with a focus on the Middle East and Islamic studies scholars have already pointed out that in the West, too, democratization was a historically slow and contradictory process. Alongside committed democrats, the broadest range of political forces, demagogues and ideologues were involved. It often proved possible to integrate them into a democratic system only after revolutionary and armed conflicts (Esposito and Voll 1996, 193). Often, democracy developed out of tricky situations rather than conviction. It was and is the political system in which the rationality of avoiding civil war prevails, without this necessarily being due to republican motives on the part of political actors. The role of democratic thought in a society or culture cannot be denied. But in line with the relative strengths of various political forces, the way in which this stock of ideas has been implemented and given legal force has never simply mirrored specific party programmes.

Does such a perspective open up new intellectual spaces in which to view political development in the Islamic world? Or is it sheer historical cynicism that puts an end to theorizing? After all, comparison with European developments may lead us to conclude that democracy will become established in the Islamic world only after more bloody conflicts

---

[1] For example, Huntington 1984; see also the critics mentioned in Esposito 1995, p. 214 ff.

and wars. But a comparison should not be rejected because we are dissatisfied with the result. What we need is a new realism that highlights the prospects of democratic development in the Middle East as they are at present, without denying the risks involved. The fact that democracy has often been a 'daughter of crisis' (Salamé 1994, 16) in European history does not mean that all crises must take a violent course. It does, however, underline that democratization may be associated with human costs which may, at times, make the continued existence of contemporary autocracies seem the lesser of two evils.

A functionalist explanation of political transformations in the Islamic world provides a more comprehensive picture of the opportunities as well as dangers arising from any putative process of democratization, particularly during transitional phases. Such an approach is a good way of breaking through Samuel Huntington's culturalist political science of the 'clash of civilizations' without merely replacing it with new monocausal interpretations. It reveals the ways in which, in the foreseeable future, Islamic societies might even develop by leaps and bounds, in much the same way as the West has done, while taking into account the 'grey zones' and political risks that emerge as soon as we include Islamic fundamentalism in our simulated plan for ending the present dictatorships.

STABILITY AND STATE COLLAPSE IN THE TWENTY-FIRST CENTURY: THE MIDDLE EASTERN LEVIATHAN

What, then, are the key components of any process of political transformation culminating in democracy? Wolfgang Merkel distinguishes between a number of ways in which transformation can come about (Merkel 1999, 129 ff.), including:

- *gradual evolution* – basically the British model of advancing democratization over several centuries;
- *change initiated by regimes* – the classic 'reform from above' in the style of Gorbachev;
- *forced system change* – on the French or Iranian model of world historical revolutions;
- *regime collapse* – often following wars, as in Iraq in 2003;
- *negotiated system change* – on the model of numerous processes of democratization in Southern Europe or Latin America.

In many countries, rather than a straightforward process corresponding precisely to one of these models, the shift to democracy occurred in hybrid form. The background to Gorbachev's *Perestroika* was the threat of state collapse that the bankrupt USSR was facing. Perhaps the most challenging scenario for political theory is 'negotiated system change', as seen in Germany after the First World War, and later in Poland, Czechoslovakia and Yugoslavia. The processes of democracy in Turkey, Brazil and Ecuador, meanwhile, were examples of reforms from above as in the Soviet Union. Negotiated democracy, based on a combination of strong pressure from the 'streets' and a political transformation supported by a robust opposition, will be the focus of our attention in what follows, in part because all other forms of change depend largely on chance occurrences: on a reforming of individuals and a revolutionary dynamic that are scarcely amenable to planning; both factors are highly resistant to theorization. If it is to be successful, however, negotiated democracy must integrate elements of both revolution and reform from above.

In addition to these routes to transformation, we can distinguish a number of important factors that foster political system change. These are our focus in the following sections.

- *The stabilization of the nation state.* If the state has not already undergone a process of consolidation during the phase of authoritarian rule, it may collapse in the course of rapid transformation.
- *The worsening of social inequalities.* Experience has shown that political transformations get off the ground only when social shifts have occurred that necessitate renegotiation of the political order. It is not a country's economic level and wealth that are decisive here, but the fragmentation of the middle classes into 'winners' and 'losers' in the existing system.
- *The opposition's capacity to engage in political combat.* For democratic change to succeed, it is important that social movements and civil society bring forth political actors, groups and parties that embody political alternatives and therefore possess great potential for mobilization. This potential cannot simply be suppressed by the authoritarian state – if events such as the crushing of the Tiananmen uprising of 1989 are to be avoided.
- *The opposition's capacity to network and form alliances.* Strong, all-embracing anti-authoritarian movements may strengthen the opposition's capacity to engage in political combat and establish democracy as a long-term compromise between the state and the various oppositional forces, such that the risk of lapsing back into authoritarian conditions can at least be lessened.

- *Favourable international conditions.* Democratization from outside, in other words, through foreign military occupation, has only rarely succeeded (Germany, Italy and Japan after the Second World War). Yet support for democratization by the international community may be extremely helpful in the context of dynamic processes of political transformation, particularly in the so-called 'transitional phases', as developments in Eastern Europe since 1989 have shown.

The process of democratization in the West began with the disarming of the religious parties that were engaged in civil war through the Peace of Westphalia of 1648 and the firm establishment of a state monopoly on violence and the constitutional state (Schubert et al. 1994, 22). This process, which ultimately extended across three to four centuries, roughly entailed the following stages: Reformation, religious wars, authoritarian constitutional state, liberal authoritarian constitutional state, democratic constitutional state and social free-market state. Identifying which stage the countries of the Islamic world are in at present is no easy task. Religious wars such as in Sudan seem to point to stages of as yet unconsolidated statehood. Iraq and Afghanistan on the other hand were for many decades stable nation states that are nonetheless at risk of collapsing today. Helmut Hubel has good reasons for describing the 'application of basic principles of the "Peace of Westphalia" to the contemporary Middle East as one of the key challenges of the present era' (Hubel 2005, 190).

The reasons for this lapse into internal conflict are highly complex in each individual case. Religious rivalries seem to be the source of unrest in Iraq, but it is very difficult to place the rivalry between Kurds, Sunnites and Shiites within a scheme of cause and effect. Iraq is a relatively artificial state entity, created after the First World War from the outside by the colonial power of Britain (Fürtig 2000). However, the notion that the various ethnic and religious groups challenged the power monopoly of the state and pushed for the country's partition after the toppling of Saddam Hussein is by no means uncontested. The Iraqi nationalism that had developed in the decades before the regime was brought down in 2003 (Rohde 2003) was, however, repeatedly undermined by systematic discrimination against Kurds and Shiites by the ruling Sunnites. Genuine democratization entailing the disarming of militias, the re-establishment of sovereignty and a federal financial settlement of some kind might be a possible solution for Iraq. In light of the civil war between Shiites and Sunnites in 2006–7, however, Iraq's continued existence is more than uncertain and its disintegration into three constituent states remains a possibility.

Afghanistan appears superficially similar to Iraq. The country's problems are nonetheless different in that the collapse of state power – in a country that for decades following the Second World War was regarded as a stable constitutional monarchy and that represents a venerable historical entity – was initiated by external intervention by the USSR and the United States. From Iraq's foundation as a state onwards, there were warnings that it faced disintegration. While the problems of Afghanistan are partly determined by ethnic divisions, these would not have erupted but for the imperial interests of the major powers (see Chapter 6).

The Islamic world of today cannot be fitted into the above sequential scheme of Western state development. Ancient and stable states such as Egypt and Iran, which unproblematically meet the nation-state-based requirements for democratic transformation, exist alongside unstable ones. The fact that, since the 1980s, an armed militia, the Hezbollah, has again established a 'state within a state' in Lebanon was a response to the displacement of Palestinians caused by Israel, which triggered the civil war in Lebanon and the Israeli invasion of 1982. It is hard to say at what developmental stage of statehood the Islamic world would be without the massive interventions from outside. In any case, the constant threat of nation-state collapse is not a problem exclusive to the Islamic world, as is evident from comparisons with Africa and Asia. Rather, as a result of the colonial period and of the neo-imperialist behaviour patterns of the major Western powers, which extend into the present, the Islamic world has frequently been robbed of any basis for positive democratic development.

DEMOCRACY AND A NEW SOCIAL CONTRACT IN THE MIDDLE EAST

Seymour Lipset's old dictum that the introduction of democracy is possible only with advanced socioeconomic development and a degree of modernization comparable to that of the Western industrialized countries is outdated (Lipset 1960). The economic dimension is unquestionably a key factor in the progress of democracy, but in a different way than has been long assumed by Lipset and many others. The relative democratic lag in much of the Islamic world can hardly be satisfactorily explained by the region's socioeconomic backwardness. The social indicators and economic conditions in the Middle East do not differ significantly from those in countries such as the Philippines, Brazil or Mexico, which have completed the transition to democracy in recent decades (Waterbury 1994, 25). There are enough examples of relatively poor countries in Asia, Africa and Latin America – we need only think of India – which, despite the many limitations that the under-financing of democratic institutions may entail, have at least introduced functioning electoral democracies and generally respect freedom of speech. In other words, they correspond to our limited, basic definition of what constitutes a democracy (see Chapter 3). Democracy can therefore become established even in comparatively underdeveloped economies. As the experiences in Bangladesh and Indonesia show, it may do so even in relatively poor Muslim states – and by no means does it take off in every *rich* country.

There is another flaw in Lipset's equation, namely, the idea that national wealth inevitably leads to the development of democracy. The countries of the Arabian peninsula have impressively refuted this assumption. The gross national product (GNP) and per capita income of these countries are on a par with those of Western industrialized countries. Clearly, though, the *type of wealth* and its distribution plays a more decisive role than the absolute level of prosperity. As a result of their oil revenues, the Arabian Gulf states and Saudi Arabia have become so-called 'rentier economies', in other words, they live less from productive capital than from resources which the state redistributes to its citizens in such a way as to ensure a sufficient income. Simon Bromley neatly captures this idea: if the slogan coined in the American struggle for independence 'No taxation without representation' is correct, so his argument goes, than perhaps states which raise no taxes have no need for democracy. No representation without taxation? (Bromley 1997, 334).

But what evidently matters more than wealth and economic growth is social mobility, the formation of social strata and diverging class interests, in other words, a social shift that creates pressure for a new political consensus. As Barrington Moore has already recognized, democracy is, above all, a political system designed to pacify any conflicts over resources that have flared up within a society (Moore 1966). Industrialization, multi-sectoral economic development, in other words, the presence of both agriculture and industry, together with processes of education, are indeed important parameters for the development of democracy. But more important is the presence of a virulent social conflict sparked by the question of wealth distribution (Abootalebi 2000, 6, 46). Fundamentally, with the exception of the Arabian peninsula, the Arab world is the epitome of this constellation. Multi-sectoral economies and a pronounced contrast between city and country coexist with a level of education which is statistically higher than that of the Indian subcontinent, especially at university level, though it is hindered by the relatively high rates of illiteracy in some countries. There therefore exists a highly dynamic mixture of educational mobility, an awakening, new middle-class consciousness and a socially distressed lower-middle class that is denied a share in the country's wealth. Educated proletariats, as in Egypt, where a vast army of highly trained students and teachers live in a state of structural unemployment, lead to social and political tensions on a large scale. Here, the opposition not only makes social demands but, because of its high educational level, is able to articulate them, organize and engage in meaningful political combat.

In the case of the Middle East, it is striking that middle-class interests took on political force once before, after the Second World War. The national revolutions in the Arab countries were directed *against* burgeoning democracy because it was seen as the political vehicle of a feudal upper class that was closely aligned with the West and exploited the people. Both the early constitutionalist movement in Iran at the beginning of the twentieth century and Mohammad Reza Shah Pahlavi (1953–78) came to grief because their base was too narrow. And Egypt's early experience of electoral democracy between 1919 and 1952 (see Hottinger 2000), in an era classed as 'liberal' in intellectual-history terms by Albert Hourani (Hourani 1983), saw feudal lords and urban notables abuse democracy to their own ends, thus playing a role in their own decline (Tehranian 2003, 92). After Gamal Abdel Nasser came to power in a military coup in 1952, he never failed to point out that Egyptian democracy was a clientelist system of the upper classes in which the people's social dependency was used to get them to the ballot boxes. The social prerequisites for democracy were not yet in place.

Though the question of secularism or Islamization is a problem that divides the Islamic world and the West in the present era, the social failure of early attempts at democracy and the relapses into authoritarian models of government is something that European countries have in common with the Islamic world. While it is true that Germany was no longer a feudal state during the Weimar Republic, east of the Elbe at least the old landed gentry of the Junkers resisted abolition of their privileges and exercised a pernicious influence on President Hindenburg, particularly during Hitler's assumption of power (Engelmann 1977). Arthur Rosenberg, who wrote the earliest assessment of the Weimar Republic, blamed its collapse on the failure to resolve the 'socialization question' through the revolution of 1918–9 (Rosenberg 1983). In other words, even as early attempts at democracy came to grief as a result of politically instrumentalized social conflicts in Egypt and Iran, the Weimar Republic was suffering similar upheavals. Shortly after Germany's supposed social saviours, the Nazis, had moved to destroy democracy, nationalist officers revolted in the Islamic world, abolishing liberal democracy in favour of experiments in Middle Eastern socialism.

Socially speaking, the Arab 'democracy of notables' of the inter-war period rested on an overly narrow base and had to make way for the enforcement of middle-class interests in the new autocracies (Bayat 2007, 35). Removing the feudal lords entailed great costs, ushering in a dictatorship of the new middle classes, who kicked off industrialization but developed into new upper classes in the process, giving rise to new social tensions that brought Islamic fundamentalism into the picture. Modern-day Islamic fundamentalists are the inheritors of these unfinished social reforms. In the West, the issue of secularism has long since been resolved in favour of bourgeois democracy. Fundamentalists, meanwhile, are by no means fighting against the system of democracy as a whole but, like the secular revolutionaries before them, they reject liberalism. At the same time, they are using Islam as both an 'ideology of difference', marking their opposition to society's winners, and an 'ideology of integration' that aims to unite the people across class boundaries.

It is surely due to a profound lack of knowledge that at every available opportunity a broad coalition of Western politicians, intellectuals and academics calls for the catch-up democratization of the Middle East – without coming to grips with the problematic social experiences of the early democratic experiments in the region, whose effects are being felt to this day. Bangladesh, for example, is certainly an established electoral democracy, but it is dominated by a small number of (corrupt?) families close to the leading figures Khalida Zia and Sheika Hasina, who make up an elite that keeps the country in poverty. The example of Bangladesh highlights a reality experienced by Egypt in the inter-war period, namely that, while democracy is capable of resolving social problems, whenever influential families hold sway over democracy rather than dynamic social movements and parties, it may also worsen them. Albert Hourani's *Arabic Thought in the Liberal Age* (Hourani 1983), which has been read at Western universities for decades, is often revered as a manifesto of the 'liberal era' of Arab democracy and of a 'vanished' democratic culture – while the basically aristocratic rule of the period is readily left out of account.

The Islamic fundamentalists are one of the key contemporary forces expressing social discontent. They by no means simply represent 'the lower classes' but rather a coalition of lower, middle and even upper classes who wish to curb the prevailing influence of the state and of the strata and groups on whom it depends. The Islamic fundamentalists' social base came into being against the background of two key factors: unfulfilled promises of education and unfulfilled promises of urbanization (Ayubi 1991, 162). The authoritarian state established after the Second World War brought about a growth in education and created a new lower-middle class that never got to enjoy the mobility it had been promised because of a lack of suitable and well-paid jobs. At the same time there developed enormous metropolises consisting of rural incomers. These formed an urban *Lumpenproletariat* mired in structural poverty. It is in the fusion of these two clienteles that the secret of Islamic fundamentalist success lies. The downward social and economic spiral that took hold in many states from the late 1960s at the latest drove ever greater numbers into the arms of the Islamic fundamentalists.

It has occassionally been asserted that the Middle Eastern bourgeoisie is sated and self-satisfied, entwined with the existing dictatorships and ill-prepared to take on a political role (Waterbury 1994, 28). But we should be careful not to generalize, for the existing economic bourgeoisie is also characterized by constant movement, new co-optations and internal struggles. In the 1970s, for example, Egyptian president Anwar Sadat initiated his policy of economic opening (*infitah*) and created a nouveau riche class, enraging the traditional middle classes (Heikal 1984). Frictions within ruling classes have undermined a fair number of political systems. Though this is difficult to gauge through independent opinion polls, dissatisfaction with poorly functioning economic systems, increasing corruption and legal uncertainty, etc. also seems to have taken hold among those forces and strata hitherto among the winners of the authoritarian state. The Arab developmental dictatorship, which was quite successful for a number of decades, has certainly redistributed wealth, but it has since the 1970s increasingly been gripped by crisis (Waterbury 1983). Comparative studies of Iran, Egypt, Malaysia and the Philippines have shown that, increasingly let down by the authoritarian welfare states in which they had placed their hopes, those classes which have long undergirded the political system are drifting towards the opposition in ever greater numbers (Brownlee 2007).

It would be wrong to assume that the Islamic fundamentalists can claim a political monopoly on the socially dissatisfied of the Islamic world. But they have undoubtedly attracted a portion of the strata on whose support the contemporary authoritarian states depend – those who hope to benefit from an 'Islamic economy' based on conservative values. Islamic fundamentalists, moreover, are often considered incorrupt (Baumgarten 2006, 132). At the same time, we should bear in mind that a portion of the secularist middle classes and elites are critical not only of the state but of the Islamic fundamentalists as well. They, too, are suffering social stress, but the 'two cultures' of secularism and Islamicization exercise an influence here, making them potential supporters of a non-Islamic fundamentalist social critique. The prospect of a process of democratization in which social rights are renegotiated politically and a new social contract agreed to lie, not in any Islamic fundamentalist monopoly on representation, but in a new socio-political diversity, provided that this new dispensation is supported by strong political organizations and institutions (rather than families, etc.).

The dissatisfaction felt by a chunk of the upper, middle and lower classes might create a social constellation in which different professional and social groups, both separately and in tandem, oppose the current state, triggering a cross-class movement for social and political change. We should bear in mind that, while the bourgeoisie may have been the key underpinning of democratization in the old Western democracies of the USA, Britain and France, a different social situation applied in Germany. Germany's proclamation democracy in 1919 occurred with the crucial involvement of the social democrats, who by no means represented the bourgeoisie per se but, at most, the 'workers' bourgeoisie'. The transitions to democracy in Latin America over the last decades would have been quite inconceivable without the participation of rural strata, movements and parties, from the Nicaraguan Sandinistas to the Mexican Zapatistas. With respect to the Islamic world, it is therefore legitimate to ask whether, alongside those parts of the middle classes ready to embrace change, other sections of the populace would also have to be politically mobilized for there to be any prospect of democracy. It may be that the wellspring of democratization is the mobilization of the working class (Abootalebi 2000, 45), though we may question the Marxian notion that this must be limited to the industrial workforce – the only group capable of organizing the class struggle in Marx's view. The Islamic fundamentalists have so far been remarkably successful in activating the kind of heterogeneous clientele typical of developing countries and NICs.

In most Islamic countries, with the exception of the Arabian peninsula, the political frustration felt by different social strata is so widespread that the social preconditions for negotiated democratization 'from below' are in place, and merely await historical momentum. But the combination of social circumstances alone is not enough in itself to produce political change, and the same goes for a 'civil society' whose development is in any case seriously hampered by most governments. Social strata are the expression of differing social interests, and these can be enforced politically only by robust political actors.

THE OPPOSITION'S CAPACITY FOR POLITICAL STRUGGLE: THE CRUCIAL ROLE OF THE ISLAMIC FUNDAMENTALISTS

If we take a closer look at the different paths of structural change, we find that some are highly resistant to theorizing. The 'gradual evolution' of a classic democracy such as Britain's, which took centuries to mature, presents insurmountable difficulties for any political scientist analyzing the processes of democracy. Meanwhile, given the excessive human costs, 'regime collapse' of the kind seen in Iraq in 2003 is impossible to justify on ethical grounds. Reforms from above require reasonable autocrats, but hopes that the young successors to the throne in Syria, Morocco and Jordan would bolster reform have for the most part long since faded. In the twenty-first century, the rulers of these countries have proved to be the trustees of their fathers' policies. They are willing to permit a few liberal reforms, but these have amounted to mere democratic window-dressing.

In view of the failure of other experiments, the remaining routes to political change revolve around two core concepts: system change through 'revolution' or through 'negotiation'. In cases where political pressure from outside (from the USA) and the will to reform from above (indigenous autocrats) have stalled, only massive pressure from the opposition and populace will produce system change in the foreseeable future. If one wishes to avoid violent revolutionary eruptions, it is essential to scrutinize the conditions under which the opposition's capacity for political combat can be enhanced without unleashing a reign of violence.

Unfortunately, violence has been a frequent accompaniment to democratization. Only rarely has it ever been achieved through the peaceful transfer of power, and it was often a violent, and, in any event, 'unintended result of group conflicts' (Schubert et al. 1994, 17, 18, 19, 41). Portugal's transition to democracy between 1976 and 1986 (the year of its EU accession), which came about as a result of a military coup and was constantly threatened by anti-democratic forces, is an example of the historically common form of contested system change in which democracy is nothing less than a compromise solution accepted by radical forces in government and the opposition, who realize, at literally the last moment, that they lack the power to take revolutionary action. Democracy, at least, opens up the prospect of participation and involvement and of implementing at least some political goals.

In their comparison of democratic transformations in Latin America and Southern and Eastern Europe in the second half of the twentieth century, Terry Lynn Karl and Philippe C. Schmitter arrive at the conclusion that, while there is no uniform route to democracy, many democracies arise from messy political situations that seem far from likely to result in such a transformation. The authors call for a radical reorientation of research on democratization, which in their view has for far too long seen revolutions or the famous 'reforms from above' as the only routes to democracy. Karl and Schmitter do consider reform from above the most successful model – though closely followed by democratic system changes in which parties and political groups come together to form a broad oppositional base, expressly including all potentially threatening interests (Karl and Schmitter 1991, 281).

Relatively early democracies, such as Germany's, are in many respects evidence that democracy is rarely the result of a systematic development that instigates a democratic civil society from within. As touched on earlier, the German constitutionalist movement of the nineteenth century featured only a small number of republicans. Most of its key intellectual figures called for a restricted monarchy. But whether liberal or conservative, they were much afraid of government by the people (Boldt 1970, 1975; Gall and Koch 1981). The gradually evolving social movement of German industrial workers was led by a labour movement whose mainstream declared its belief in democratic socialism only at a very late stage – in the context of the First World War. It is therefore no surprise that the first German democracy, the Weimar Republic established in 1919, was a chance historical result of an anarchic post-war predicament, described by many as a 'democracy without democrats'. This first German democracy came about despite widespread hostility within society and among the elites, but against the background of a strong social movement which was forced by the enduring forces of conservatism to embrace a historical compromise. In the end, none of these groups got what it wanted, but they all got a little of what they needed. The workers got the eight-hour day while the old elites held on to their property, which was quite something in view of the threat of 'Bolshevism'.

But can a democracy that has come about in this way endure? The Weimar Republic did not. But there are other examples that give us greater grounds for optimism. Experiences in other countries show that it is not necessary, and after long periods of authoritarian rule quite unrealistic, to expect that political forces exhibit a clear democratic outlook in the early stages of democratization (Pridham 2000, 145 f., 157). Democratization is not a feat of strength performed by a democratic camp. Authoritarian rule often results in a dearth of 'cultural democrats' who fully support democracy, while radical views proliferate. It may therefore be enough for the opposition, and for the elites willing to embrace change, to behave as 'functional democrats' (Pridham) who accept democratic rules of play on rational grounds, in other words, because their political survival is at stake and because there is no feasible political alternative. An example of such a development is Spain, where democratization was driven primarily by Communists and Falangists, political groupings that were by no means made-up of perfect democrats.

The shift towards democracy in the southern European countries had little to do with the efforts of a pro-democratic civil society. In most countries, such forces were only just beginning to get off the ground during the period of transition. Rather than democracy being the product of democrats, it was the democrats that were the product of democratization. As Mehran Kamrava writes:

In some democratisation processes civil society either does not initially play a determining role or emerges only later on, or it does not appear at all, even well into the life of the supposedly democratic country. Examples from Southern Europe are most instructive in this respect. In Greece, Portugal and Spain during the mid-1970s, when each country witnessed a democratic transition, civil society was only nascent at the time of the change-over and was caught largely off guard by the collapse of the old order and its reconstitution into a democratic one. Today, however, by most accounts democracy appears to be on a solid social and cultural footing in each of these countries and is built on a strong foundation of civil society (Kamrava 2000, 198).

You would think that the commentators who never miss a chance to underline the Islamic world's supposedly exceptional cultural resistance to democracy might also have examined the cultural ties that have existed between the countries of the Mediterranean region for thousands of years. Is it not possible that the neighbouring areas of the southern and eastern Mediterranean will develop in a similar way to the southern

European states? Tellingly, no one has as yet explored this idea in any depth. Culturalist arguments are always put forward when the aim is to establish a difference, but rarely when cultural commonalities are at issue – those between Greece under military dictatorship and contemporary Syria for example. That the stability of the southern European democracies is due in no small measure to their rapid integration into the European Union is beyond doubt. This immediately leads to the thought that a close association between the EU and the North African states might strengthen internal processes of democracy. The so-called 'Barcelona Process', which has been up and running since 1995, and whose aim is to enhance Euro-Mediterranean relations, incorporated this idea from the outset. Unfortunately, however, the concrete processes of implementation in subsequent years have shown that the EU is concerned first and foremost with security. It is on this that most of the money has been spent, ultimately strengthening the existing authoritarian regimes (Jünemann 2000) (see below). Nonetheless, the rest of the money went and continues to go to projects intended to strengthen civil societies.

While the Europeans' efforts in the south were half-hearted, in 2007 the potential for externally supported 'unintended democratization' and the associated opportunities became apparent in the west, in Northern Ireland, the main actors being Ireland, Britain and the EU. The devolved power-sharing government formed by Protestants and Catholics after decades of civil war was described in the German media as a coalition of 'preachers of hate' and 'former terrorists' – and evaluated positively as such.[2] Ian Paisley of the Democratic Unionist Party (DUP) and Martin McGuinness of Sinn Féin formed a democratic government, a typical case of 'democratization without democrats' or 'democracy as second-best option'.

Against the background of these contemporary historical processes in Europe, would a southern Mediterranean region in close partnership with Europe have no prospect of democratic development? Alongside Ghassan Salamé, Najib Ghadbian was one of the first scholars to attempt to apply to the Middle East the notion of an unintended democratization that comes about, not as an idealistic endeavour, but as a result of a last-minute rational insight on the part of autocrats and a radical opposition

---

[2] Peter Nonnenmacher, Der Hassprediger und der Papist regieren Nordirland [Preacher of hate and papist in power in Northern Ireland], *Frankfurter Rundschau*, 9 May 2007; Ralf Sotschek, Alter Hassprediger koaliert mit Exterrorist [Former preacher of hate in coalition with ex-terrorist], *die tageszeitung*, 9 May 2007.

(Ghadbian 1997, 12, 142 f.). According to Ghadbian, democracy comes about in the following way: None of the significant political forces engaged in social conflict, whether secular or Islamic fundamentalist, are able to wipe out the other. Yet the costs of the authoritarian status quo become intolerably high because the regime can suppress the opposition only by means which are perilous to both the opposition and itself.

In this sense, the Islamic world is not unusual in its resistance to democracy, and the Islamic fundamentalists are in fact an important component of the opposition's capacity for political combat. They are, without doubt, the most influential forces opposing the ruling authoritarian governments in most Islamic countries (Antar 2007, 63) because they increase the costs of autocracy – though they are too weak to bring about system change on their own. Precisely because of this relative strength, which is not, however, a position of omnipotence, there is the possibility that the Islamic fundamentalists' still dubious ideological compatibility with democracy might be improved through compromise with other opposition forces – and that they will emerge in this sense as 'functional democrats'. They are relatively strong and capable of doing political battle with existing regimes. Much like the Falangists and communists in Spain or the radical Protestant and Catholic forces in Northern Ireland, they might sooner or later contribute to democratic structural change in collaboration with other social forces.

The value of a capacity for political combat on the part of a well-organized opposition, conscious of its power, was laid bare by the crushing of the student uprising in Beijing's Tiananmen Square in 1989 and by events in Burma in 2007 and Tibet in 2008. Opposition forces that had emerged out of civil society but which lacked political leadership were quickly and brutally repressed by the ruling dictatorships. Over the last few decades, in the Middle East and the Islamic world as well, the opposition's weakness has created many problems. In hard authoritarian states such as Iraq (under Saddam Hussein), Syria, Libya or Tunisia, it was and is impossible for an opposition to take shape in the first place, unless it moves abroad. So far, though, no successful opposition has emerged in exile. The only groups who make their presence felt as opposition forces in these states are Islamic fundamentalist organizations. But Islamic fundamentalists are, to put it mildly, highly 'controversial', particularly in the West, because in many respects they seem to be the polar opposite of the West's political aspirations. Yet even their opponents rarely dispute that Islamic fundamentalists are the strongest opposition forces. Even short-term setbacks in elections, which are in any case generally rigged, or internal ideological disputes have done nothing to change this status (Alterman 2007).

What does the Islamic fundamentalists' capacity to engage in political combat consist of? So far, no one has really systematically discussed this question. It thus seems essential to assess Islamic fundamentalism in light of the capacity-for-political-combat criteria developed by the theoretical research on political transformation. The concept of 'strategic and conflict-capable groups' (SCOG) identifies the following as significant to the strength of the opposition (Schubert et al. 1994, 69): the degree of formal institutionalization (Does the opposition exist in the form of a dispersed social movement or as a stable organization and party?); ideological coherence (Is the opposition pro-democratic? Above all, does it represent an alternative to the authoritarian status quo?); the opposition's legitimacy and credibility; and the opposition's potential for social mobilization, which is partly the result of the other factors, but also of its communication skills and media strategies.

We may question how compatible the doctrines of political Islam are with democracy. But why is religion so popular as an ideology of political resistance in the Islamic world? And why does it play this role to a greater extent than in many other parts of the world? Is it really because of the undemocratic nature of Islam, as suggested by the thesis of exceptionalism that has been discussed for so many decades? Or is it because many of those involved believe that religion is the only way to effectively articulate and organize political resistance?

As far as the first criterion of capacity for political combat is concerned, the *degree of formal institutionalization*, in the Islamic world religion ensures that the opposition survives, at least in a minimal form, as it confronts the ruling dictatorships. Like the churches of the former Eastern Bloc, Islam, as an anchoring ground for the political opposition, offers a certain protection against state repression. In Egypt, for example, tens of thousands of Islamic fundamentalists are behind bars. Yet political preachers always manage to stir up popular resistance because the state cannot entirely prevent religious gatherings, especially in 'unofficial' mosques not sanctioned by the state. In contrast to the secular opposition, whose political parties, media and gatherings may be prohibited as subversive without further ado, this is not so easy to achieve with respect to religious practices, as religion enjoys greater legitimacy than any state. What is more, as history has shown, the traditional organizational forms of Islam – mosques, the legal scholars, religious endowments, etc. – function as effective networks for the development of modern Islamic fundamentalist parties that can survive underground even during periods of formal prohibition, such as in Egypt under the rule of Gamal Abdel Nasser. There are, however, often major differences between countries in this regard. The Syrian state was on the whole more successful than Egypt in repressing Islamic fundamentalists. Yet even this hard authoritarian state has never managed to keep them entirely in check. The same is true in Tunisia. Despite its authoritarian style of politics, it is home to a number of well-known Islamic fundamentalists, most notably Rashid al-Ghannushi.

Islamic fundamentalism's suitability as an anti-authoritarian force is rooted in the fact that even the most rigid regimes cannot challenge Islam's right to exist (Tessler 2000, 271). What better parallel could there be here than the role of the Catholic Church, in Poland for example? The Christian opposition, of course, never wished to establish a 'Catholic state', while references to an 'Islamic state' are key for Islamic fundamentalists. An Islamic fundamentalist-style relapse into religious authoritarianism was never a danger for the Catholic Church. The Church's struggles with modernization and secularization lay too far in the past for that. At the same time, though, the Catholic Church never had to organize resistance to the authoritarian state. The church was less a driving force for change than a place where the opposition could take a breather and occasionally meet – no more and no less (more detailed research would be required to determine whether, as a number of authors believe, this also applies to Latin American 'liberation theology', a theology for the poor that raised the social question but saw itself primarily as a movement for reform within the church rather than a political opposition [see for example Bayat 2007, 8]).

The Islamic fundamentalists, of course, are involved, not only in the anti-authoritarian struggle, but also in the confrontation with secularization, which prevents us from viewing them solely in terms of their anti-authoritarian function. At the same time it is analytically vital that we avoid looking at Islamic fundamentalists *solely* in anti-Enlightenment terms. We must place their development in the context of Islamic societies' capacity for political combat with the authoritarian state. That these two aspects may even be two sides of the same coin and that the illiberalism of Islamic fundamentalism is therefore not necessarily a historical accident, but part of its anti-authoritarian capacity for protest, emerges as a tricky problem for any theory of democracy. The SCOG model regards *ideological coherence* as a key factor in the opposition's capacity for political combat. Underpinning this is the idea that an oppositional grouping can make its mark as an umbrella movement for protest within a society only if it develops clear, unambiguous, generally understandable and perhaps even radical political positions. As in the era of Christian Reformation, when Luther and other reformers, taking radical and often intolerant counter positions, fought against the supreme authority of the Pope, the Islamic fundamentalists for the most part appear uncompromisingly opposed to the principle of secularism. They present their supporters with an ideological clarity supposedly rooted in the purity of the period of Muhammadan rule – a traditionalist claim they by no means live up to on closer inspection (see Chapter 1), but one which is intended to signal ideological coherence and an unqualified desire for system change.

The relative weakness of the secular camp is due, among other things, to its lack of ideological superstructure. Communists and liberals often have little in common and are seldom prepared to join forces against authoritarian rule. It is no coincidence that in Iran the archaic and intolerant Muslim Ayatollah Khomeini was able to unite behind him a broad coalition comprising world views of every kind in order to topple the Shah. Khomeini allowed no ideological uncertainty regarding his objective of ending the Shah's 'godless' rule. His guiding political principles were radical but had the advantage of being incorruptible. The Iranian example reveals the opportunities that are bound up with Islamic fundamentalism, as well as the risk of lapsing into authoritarianism.

Legitimacy is another criterion closely connected with ideology. The SCOG concept ascribes great significance to the credibility of traditional and religious leaders, such as the Egyptian Muslim Brothers (Schubert et al. 1994, 95). This is probably linked to the simple historical fact that, at times when contemporary authoritarian power is being critiqued, those forces claiming to represent the rule of earlier heroic periods become highly popular. Examples from other world regions lend support to this thesis, such as the Tibetan liberation struggle, which following the Chinese invasion, was based on the Lamaist priesthood and the Dalai Lama. Whereas ideological coherence, with its promise of clear solutions, thus seems directed primarily towards the future, legitimacy arises from the successful reactivation of traditional ideals of government.

When actors have to deal with current political issues, ideology and legitimacy are fused together. The Islamic fundamentalists make clear to their supporters and sympathizers their aim of fundamentally revising undesirable trends begun in the past. Secularization, for example, is characterized as a break, imposed by the colonial powers, with the tradition of the Ottoman Empire and with the caliphate, which had existed since

the time of Muhammad. For tactical reasons, namely, to avoid diluting
the clarity of the notion of the 'West as the enemy', Islamic fundamentalists as a rule keep quiet about the fact that the decline of the Islamic
empire was in part due to an internal process of decay that necessitated
secular reforms a century before its collapse (see Chapter 3).

If we seek to understand why Islamic fundamentalism enjoys such
widespread support in Arab countries while it is less prominent in the
non-Arab Islamic world (Turkey, Bangladesh, Indonesia), we are confronted with the fact that most of the world's oil reserves are found in the
Arab world (and Iran). The Western notion that Arab oil belongs to the
world and cannot simply be left to the Arabs has motivated an unusual
degree of interventionism in these states by Western powers,[3] in the form
of wars (as in Iraq in 2003), various kinds of intervention and the presence of Western military bases scattered throughout the states bordering
the Persian Gulf, things which do not exist on this scale and with this
degree of intensity outside the region (see Chapter 6). As the supporters
of Islamic fundamentalism see it, these exceptional regional conditions
justify exceptional countermeasures of which Islamic fundamentalism is
a good example: it is an ideology of struggle aimed at restoring justice
to North-South relations. 'Stay away, no more imported solutions!' is
the Islamic fundamentalists' subliminal but powerful political message
to Western countries. As the indigenous religion, Islam symbolizes this
hostility towards external influences in a particularly emphatic way.

Thus, if there is a reason the Arab world lags behind in the process of
democratization, it certainly lies less in its Islamic character than in the
Middle East's incomparable economic and strategic importance in the world.
Emad Shahin of Harvard University comments on the special structural
position of the Arab world and the Middle East: 'This is where Middle
Eastern exceptionalism comes in. The Middle East is not Eastern Europe.
Eastern Europe was ruled by an anti-western dictatorship, the Middle East
is ruled by pro-western autocrats. In Eastern Europe the opposition was
pro-western; in the Middle East, the opposition is feared to be anti-western
and Islamist. Most outside aid is being channeled through state institutions, which only enhances the power of authoritarian actors.'[4]

---

[3] Henry Kissinger: 'Oil is much too important a commodity to be left in the hands of the
Arabs.' Quoted in Hans von Sponeck/Denis Halliday, The Hostage Nation, *The Guardian*,
29 November 2001.
[4] Transitions to Democracy in the Middle East and North Africa: Lessons from other
Regions, American University, Center for Democracy, 9 March 2007, http://www.ccd21.
org/pdf/TransitionstoDemocracyminutes.pdf (20 August 2007).

As far as the final criterion of capacity for political combat is concerned, the *potential for mobilization* of a group or movement, Islamic fundamentalism's greatest attribute is probably its social multifunctionality. As a religion of the lower classes Islam offers no advantages compared with other ideologies, for the role of religion can be played more effectively by communism. With the exception of such cases as Iraq in the 1950s, communism has occupied a marginal position within the Islamic countries. The widespread aversion felt towards it, which is often explained in terms of its atheism, is due in significant part to the fact that Islamic fundamentalism advocates a doctrine of social integration that attempts to do justice to all social strata. Islamic fundamentalists criticize the ruling classes, which they reproach for social injustice and for offending God, thus mobilizing the lower and lower-middle classes. At the same time, Islamic fundamentalism also wins supporters and sponsors in the upper-middle and upper classes, whose livelihood the Islamic fundamentalist organizations ensure under the cloak of a generally very liberal 'Islamic economy'. A crucial element of Islamic fundamentalism's capacity for political combat consists of its potential, not only to turn the opposition into a group capable of engaging in conflict, but also to incorporate elites as groups of strategic importance to political change in a way that transcends class and other social divisions.

To sum up, there are a number of rational and understandable reasons that Islamic fundamentalism is a widespread oppositional ideology in the contemporary Islamic world. Mark Tessler, an expert on political culture, describes the contrast between the adherence to Islamic fundamentalism and an interest in democracy as only apparently paradoxical:

> It is important to recognize the commonalities that underlie the Islamic resurgence and the concern for democracy in the present-day Arab world. Each trend has for the most part been driven forward by the same underlying stimulus, namely a deep dissatisfaction among ordinary citizens with established patterns of governance and prevailing political and economic relationships. (…) (A)lthough it might appear as a contradiction to those unfamiliar with the Arab world, a desire for economic and above all political change is producing both support for democratization and support for political Islam (Tessler 2000, 269 f.).

Fundamentalist Islam has become an umbrella movement for political protest (Takeyh and Gvosdev 2004, 14 ff.). Once it has achieved its aims, however, this movement may also develop the kind of post-Islamic fundamentalist critical features (Bayat 2007) that would be appropriate to a democratic public sphere. If we want evidence, against the background of current social conflicts, that Islamic fundamentalism represents a vehicle for political opening and participation, we may consider the fact that when Islamic fundamentalist governments assume power they are subject to critical scrutiny by the people. In Iran, the elections of presidents Khatami (1997–2005) and Ahmadinejad (2005) were clear evidence of the growing internal criticisms of Islamic fundamentalism (Abootalebi 2000, 131). If democracy in Iran was not restricted in an artificial, authoritarian way by the office of the supreme Ayatollah, with his political veto powers, Iran would in all probability be an example of a vital democratic system in which, alongside Islamic fundamentalists, a large number of secular parties – including Marxists and communists – would also be active. Turkey already embodies this reality. In 2007, millions of demonstrators protested against certain political decisions (concerning the presidency) by the Islamic Erdogan government, which shows how participatory the political system has already become – and how stable. In earlier decades, mass assemblies would have been banned by the government.

Islamic fundamentalists can be said to occupy an extreme position within the debate on modernity and modern politics. From the perspective of ideological critique, they must be placed outside of the minimum consensus of democracy, above all, because of their hard-line stance on secularism. From the point of view of democratic transformation theory, however, Islamic fundamentalists may represent the crucial force that societies need in order to establish democratic conditions and reach a new democratic consensus. The democratic orientation of Islamic fundamentalists might be suspect – yet they may nonetheless be indispensible to democratization. This is the core paradox of any attempt to assess the relationship between Islamic fundamentalism and democracy.

It is of course important to underline that evaluations of Islamic fundamentalists are theory dependent. While many theorists now regard democracy as the unintended outcome of group conflicts, that is, a process in which non-democratic or questionably democratic groups often play a decisive role, most theorists of civil society view Islamic fundamentalists as opponents rather than supporters of democratization because of their demands for ethno-religious privileges and failure to embrace universal human rights (Croissant et al. 2000, 18). This position is undoubtedly legitimate. Islamic fundamentalists cannot automatically be considered part of civil society. It must be said, however, given their often heterogeneous objectives and 'schizophrenic' attitude towards democracy (Hamzawy 2005, 19), that it now seems just as impossible to clearly exclude these forces from civil society.

The weakness of civil-society theory, however, is that it is a 'pure theory' of democratic change supposedly brought about exclusively or predominantly *by* and *through* democratic forces. Some theorists concede that 'a vibrant pluralism of civil-society organizations is by no means sufficient for the emergence of a democracy' (Croissant et al. 2000, 20). But it is unclear whether this leads to the necessary step of including society as a whole in the transformation process. Otherwise, the theory of civil society remains an unintegrated component of transformation theory (Wiktorowicz 2004a, 3). Ultimately, there is absolutely no evidence that a functioning process of democratization is driven by civil society alone, quite apart from the question of whether a civil society can emerge under authoritarian conditions in the first place. Even in Eastern Europe and the German Democratic Republic (GDR), where the forces of civil society were significant drivers of system change, the political sea-change would have been almost inconceivable in the absence of Gorbachev-style reformed communism, in other words, reform from above.

Classical Western civil-society theory is open to the criticism that, by excluding the Islamic fundamentalists, it theoretically accepts the weakening of the opposition. Indirectly, this results in the permanent self-exclusion of all 'genuine' democrats. The theory of civil society thus tends to think past the realities on the ground. In view of the weakness of the secular democratic forces of civil society in many Islamic states, we would be more or less forced to wait for the next regime collapse or 'reform from above'. To ask a deliberately provocative question, how many more generations do we want to sacrifice to this vague hope of the democratic evolution of a civil society, leaving them with no alternative but to live under authoritarian conditions? Would it not be at least worth considering whether democratic forces of civil society should not enter into coalitions with Islamic fundamentalists in order to promote system change, ideally supported by the West?

Numerous alternatives to the classical exclusion of the Islamic fundamentalists from civil society have been put forward over the last few years. These represent attempts to close the theoretical gap between the theory of civil society and the theory of democracy. Robert W. Hefner shows that in Indonesia, the Islam-oriented opposition played a significant role in bringing down the Suharto dictatorship (Hefner 2000). Social science having long ignored religion, has in a general sense rediscovered it as a social organizer, mobilizer and ideology of resistance (Heft 2004;

Herbert 2001). However Volker Stahr, who makes similar arguments, points out that, in contrast to much of the Arab world, leading Islamic fundamentalists such as Nurcholis Majid are syncretically inclined, in other words, are liberal or conservative reformers with no fundamentalist aspirations (Stahr 1997, 140). We might attempt to explain the difference as follows: in the Arab world, authoritarian regimes are better able to resist change because oil ensures them an exceptional degree of support from the West, while Western interest in Indonesia faded away in the 1990s.

Because of the national and regional differences among the cultures of political Islam, Carrie Rosefsky Wickham's study of one of the core countries of Arab Islam – Egypt – is of particular significance. Wickham argues that so far, unfortunately, researchers studying Islam and those concerned with civil society have generally worked in isolation from one another. As a result, Islamic movements have hardly been studied as social movements and, as the author notes, the theory of social movements is based almost entirely on Western experiences (Wickham 2002, 4 f.). Wickham asks why Islamic social movements were able to have a mobilizing effect which neither President Sadat nor Mubarak could do anything to counter (Wickham 2002, 11). Wickham sees it as a specific feature of Islamic fundamentalists in Egypt that they enhanced their capacity for political combat, outside of the zone of the established parties, by mutating chameleon-like into a religio-political party movement, one that has eluded clear-cut institutional categorization and proved strategically adaptable. Countless Islamic study groups and networks reach a clientele made up of the lower-middle classes in a haven that is safe from authoritarian rule, while the hard organizational core of the movement, above all the Muslim Brothers, plays the role of political force (Wickham 2002, 16). The state has thus never managed to get at the entire movement. Over the years, it has opted to view the Muslim Brothers as a point of contact within an otherwise uncontrollable movement and to accept their existence.

We might describe as a counterpart, and to some extent a tribute, to this organizational flexibility and network-like character the fact that the Islamic fundamentalists unite the widest range of forces – democrats as well as professed radicals – and remain doctrinaire, particularly with respect to secularism, in order to provide the movement with a clear profile. The leading figures of the Black civil rights movement in the USA, such as Malcolm X and Martin Luther King, also combined extreme differences, not all of which were lawful, and in accord with the rules of democracy. But while Malcolm X has now become a Hollywood icon, Wickham laments the fact that the diversity and strategic dexterity of the Islamic fundamentalists, who are part of society and are struggling against authoritarian power structures, has so far scarcely been acknowledged in the West: 'Rather than conceptualizing the Islamists as protagonists in some dichotomous battle between authoritarianism and democracy, I propose that we take more seriously their creative – and thus both liberating and coercive – powers. Just as authoritarian regimes can assume many forms, so too can the alternatives that surface in their midst. (…) The degree to which Islamists incorporate such priorities [as human rights and democracy] into their political practice will depend less on fixed doctrinal imperatives than on their evolving relationship with other social and political forces' (Wickham 2000, 213).

PACTS AMONG OPPOSITION GROUPS: FUNDAMENTALISTS AS (IN-)CALCULABLE RISK

Islamic fundamentalists should not be excluded from reflections on democratization. The question, however, is how best to integrate them in such an enduring way that even when they win electoral majorities and form governments, they cannot simply abolish democracy once more. Ultimately, it is the risk of a double system change – first to democracy, and then to religious dictatorship – that has not only alarmed theorists but also engendered widespread scepticism about fundamentalist majorities among Middle Eastern publics (see Chapter 2). Choosing between old (secular) and new (Islamic fundamentalist) authoritarianism seems like a 'choice between the devil and the deep blue sea', leaving many societies in the contemporary Islamic world 'rigid with shock', in other words, politically stagnant. Few have any interest in increasing the existing repression to the point of religious fascism, which is, nevertheless, conceivable. The prevailing uncertainty contributes to exclusivist reflexes, as in Algeria in 1991–2, when a silent majority tacitly condoned the abandonment of the 1991 elections out of fear of an Islamic fundamentalist government, which culminated in a civil war (Brumberg 2003, 268–75). This underlines the importance of integrating the Islamic fundamentalists politically but in such a way that the risks of their involvement are minimized.

Hitler's assumption of power has taken hold as *the* historical metaphor for the possible dangers entailed in the integration of Islamic fundamentalists into the political system. The legal seizure of power – the preferred term these days is *Machtübertragung* or 'transfer of power' – was used by the National Socialists to put an end to democracy. It is, however essential that we scrutinize and relativize this historical experience so often used as a parallel, because it took place under specific conditions, which also offer pointers to key fields of action for democratization theory with respect to the Islamic fundamentalists. On seizing power, Hitler did not enjoy a parliamentary majority, and both John Esposito and John Voll, along with Etel Solingen, have correctly pointed out that Islamic fundamentalists, too, have never managed to obtain absolute majorities in democratic elections (Solingen 2003, 48 f.). Even in Algeria where the Islamic Front Islamique du Salut (FIS) managed to come out on top in the first ballot in late 1991, this happened only because turn-out was extremely low. Its true level of electoral support was probably no more than 30 percent. Sudan's National Islamic Front (NIF) never achieved a larger share of the vote than this. Hitler's seizure of power was no legal walkover on the back of a democratic vote. He made use of the structural faults of the Weimar constitution, which conferred excep-tional status on a popularly elected president, an office occupied by the anti-democratic First World War admiral Paul von Hindenburg in 1933. It was he who helped Hitler become Reich Chancellor, disregarding the Reichstag. Applied to the situation in the Islamic world, this means that the risks of a dictatorial usurpation of power by the Islamic fundamental-ists can at least be significantly reduced through a carefully chosen consti-tutional framework. Legal checks and balances are needed to ensure that a mandate for government cannot be used to destroy the political system. Ultimately, though, legal provisions alone will not prevent a government using 'emergency powers' to annul the democratic system – and this is another lesson of the Nazi seizure of power.

The Iranian Revolution is in many respects an example of how Islamic fundamentalists ought *not* to come to power if we wish to ensure that democracy remains undamaged. Let us disregard for the moment the fact that the Islamic fundamentalists in Iran, Sudan and Afghanistan super-seded dictatorships rather than democracies. More important is the fact that Ayatollah Khomeini came to power through a revolution, enabling him to shape political conditions entirely according to his own inter-ests and to dominate the revolutionary forces of Islamic fundamentalists, nationalists and communists, who were disunited politically, and impose a theocratic system on society. Political forces and sections of society who could not be counted among the Islamic fundamentalists, that is, perhaps half of Iranian society, were in no way prepared for the Islamic fundamentalists' new claim to political power.

Under what conditions, then, can negotiated system change, which avoids the unpredictability of revolutions, come about? According to Wolfgang Merkel, a specialist in political transformation, it may occur in the following situation: 'If a stalemate develops between regime elites and the opposition and both sides lack the power to define unilaterally the terms of the future political system – provided that both sides act "rationally" – there will be negotiations on a new form of political rule. Through a series of negotiated compromises and pacts, access to power, the structure of power, claims to power and mode of power are then redefined' (Merkel 1999, 131). The key factor is the relative strengths of both government and opposition, as well as of groups within the opposition. 'Negotiated system change' is decided through compromise and pacts. Merkel has described this as *one* among a number of routes to political transformation, while Karl and Schmitter characterize it as one of the most successful routes to democracy in recent world history.

Turning first to conditions within the opposition, it is of particular importance to democratic development that the Islamic fundamentalists are induced to make a political arrangement with secular forces. At least three things, however, are necessary if this is to happen: the development of strong secular parties which the authoritarian state is unable to suppress and which do not degenerate into mere client parties of the ruling classes; the promotion of internal alliances among the secularists, who must not allow their ideological differences to come between them; and, finally, constitutionally relevant pacts between Islamic fundamentalists and secularists, which not only strengthen their shared capacity to engage in political combat but also clarify in advance the democratic constitutional guarantees for the period subsequent to the democratic transition.

The specific reasons that secular parties are so often weak cannot be examined in depth here, as they differ greatly from one country to another. In Egypt, for example, the authoritarian state for many years systematically bolstered the Islamic fundamentalists vis-à-vis other political forces before gradually realizing the danger of this as the Islamic fundamentalists went from strength to strength. Apart from the opposition of the authoritarian state, however, the problems are often homemade (Koszinowski 1999). Experts refer constantly to the self-imposed weakness of a secular opposition that often consists of isolated campaigners.[5]

---

[5] See Reformen im Mittleren Osten. Was können Europa und die USA beitragen? [Reforms in the Middle East. How can Europe and America help?], 133. Bergedorfer Gesprächskreis, 17–19 March 2006, Washington DC, p. 64 f., http://www.koerber-stiftung.de (10 March 2007).

It does not embody a common political goal. Rather, nationalists, socialists and liberals often maintain as much distance from one another as from the state they oppose. This is one of the main problems of many secular forces: their inability to form alliances, which weakens tremendously their capacity to engage in political combat and protest. Here, 'secularism' is really an artificial label. The separation of religion and politics may indeed be a goal that sets this opposition apart from the Islamic fundamentalists and may unite it. But secularism is a secondary virtue that cannot make up for the fact that its exponents often advocate very limited interests. Secular parties in the Islamic world are often not people's parties with a broad social base. Only a group such as the Palestinian Liberation Organization (PLO), within the specific context of its resistance against Israel, has consistently managed to forge alliances made up of different factions, from Marxists to economic liberals. It has nonetheless often been tested by ideological divisions.

It is only in recent years that secular parties, socialists and communists have regained some degree of popularity. This is the result of neo-liberal economic policies and the rising cost of bread and other foodstuffs, which led to demonstrations in many countries in 2008.[6] However, it is generally the weakness of secular parties that has sunk attempts to forge alliances with the Islamic fundamentalists. Attempts by various Egyptian parties in the 1980s to form electoral pacts and coalitions failed (Harders 1998) because secularists were afraid of being the junior partner in a coalition with the Muslim Brothers, whose strength meant they were likely to hog the limelight. What this shows is that internal reform, restructuring and improved mobilization based on a stable organizational structure are probably vital if a secularist coalition with the Islamic fundamentalists is to stand any chance of success. What we have seen in the Arab countries over the last few years, in Lebanon for example, is an increasing tendency for Islamic fundamentalists to form coalitions with non-Islamic fundamentalist groups (Schwedler 2007) and to agree to take part in Arab 'parliaments'. Even in Syria, efforts appear to have been made in this direction.[7] The Egyptian Kifaya movement, which consists primarily of secular forces, also contains some Islamic fundamentalist groupings (Schäfer 2008).

---

[6] Joel Beinin, Hunger und Zorn in Ägypten [Hunger and rage in Egypt], *Le Monde diplomatique* (German edition), May 2008.
[7] Nicholas Blanford, Syria's Secular and Islamist Opposition Unite against Baathists, in: *Christian Science Monitor*, 10 June 2005.

For secular opposition forces, history shows that an important pre-condition for a viable coalition across factional boundaries is that they first of all preserve and sharpen their ideological profiles and do not allow themselves to be 'Islamicized' by the fundamentalists, which would threaten their internal cohesion. Internal party tensions on both sides can be countered with self-confident ideological profiles, which each party must strive to turn into concrete policy achievements. Second, it is essential to establish a minimum consensus between Islamic fundamentalists and secularists that gears the coalition towards a common goal. This does not require a comprehensive ideological reconstruction for the different political factions can largely stand by their aims, with one exception: each must guaranty the 'other' side its political survival after system change has occurred. In other words, a secular system must be agreed upon that facilitates the political participation of non-Islamic fundamentalist forces which is at the same time not so strictly laicist that the Islamic fundamentalists have reason to fear for their survival.

When such attempts to form alliances are unsuccessful, Islamic fundamentalist groupings quickly develop into umbrella movements for protest voters. Central Asia, for example, reveals the typical consequences of a crippled secular opposition. Many citizens of the Central Asian states have a choice between no opposition or an Islamic fundamentalist opposition. As a result, the latter attracts protest voters who are far from committed supporters of religion-based politics.[8]

But this one-sided political dynamic by no means makes the Islamic fundamentalists omnipotent. However strong they may be, they, too, generally lack the support of other forces that they would need to bring about political change. The Islamic fundamentalists are either too weak to engender revolutionary ruptures or they are largely unsuccessful, as in Algeria and Sudan. Another possible trajectory for Islamic fundamentalist politics would be withdrawal from the political sphere. This would, in a sense, mean returning to the era prior to the emergence of Islamic fundamentalist political movements in the 1920s, which would certainly dovetail with the long tradition of de-facto secular official Islam (see Chapter 1). Such a renunciation of politics would meet the expectations of French Middle East scholar Gilles Kepel, who predicted at the beginning of the

---

[8] On Central Asia, see Ulrich Schwerin, 'Tiananmen' in Usbekistan ['Tiananmen' in Uzbekistan], 2005, http://www.qantara.de (21 March 2007); 'If Secular Opposition Fails, Religious Opponents Come to Power', APEHA Committee for Freedom of Speech and Expression, 2005, http://www.freeuz.org (21 March 2007).

millennium that political Islam would go into decline (Kepel 2000). But it is more probable that the Islamic fundamentalists will pursue two further options: the formation of broader political coalitions with non-Islamic fundamentalist forces or even the reworking of Islamist positions with a view to a process of 'Christian democratization' – on the model of the Turkish Justice and Development Party (AKP) of Prime Minister Recep Tayyip Erdogan (El-Affendi 2006, 12 ff.).

Coalition forming and ideological renovation among the Islamists would have the great advantage of being moves towards conformity with democracy. The establishment of such a democratic minimum consensus would, however, spark internal ideological struggles within the various Islamist groupings (El-Affendi 2006, 13 f.). The very character of Islamic fundamentalist organizations as rallying points for protest has brought together very different interests, as we saw in the case of the Islamic fundamentalists in the suburbs of Cairo (see Chapter 2). Not all factions within the Islamic fundamentalist groups view the hegemony of an Islamic agenda merely as a symbolic political expression of political and social protest. Core supporters, in particular, would probably refuse to accept a secular order. We can not rule out the possibility that the Islamic fundamentalists will be thwarted by their insistence on a particular milieu (Wickham 2002, 210): alone they are ultimately too weak, but they are incapable of achieving a rapprochement with other opposition forces. Tensions grow when coalition partners begin to doubt that the Islamic fundamentalists take political compromise seriously and confront them with the challenge of the final developmental step, the process of 'Christian democratic' restructuring. Even in coalitions, most Islamic fundamentalist groups are not prepared to unambiguously commit to a secular order. Hence, as necessary as it is for all opposition forces to cooperate with one another, it is just as crucial that they firmly commit to a new political framework if a lapse into dictatorship is to be avoided. It is hard to say *when* Islamic fundamentalists might be prepared to abandon their radical anti-secularism, which they regard as an ideological strength, in favour of coalition proposals and, above all, guarantees for secular forces, which Islamic fundamentalists, too, must pursue. But the *search* for historical compromises, such as took place in Northern Ireland, is the only way to go if we wish to democratize the existing systems.

The consolidation of the opposition camp depends crucially on the right conditions at the level of the state. Non-Islamic fundamentalist forces, in particular, would have to wake up to the fact that it is vital to form coalitions with Islamic fundamentalists if they wish to be effective.

At the same time, there is a need for a strategy of alliance that prompts the state to collaborate with the Islamic fundamentalists, while making concessions to and obtaining concessions from the Islamic fundamentalists – before a democratic political system can be established (through free elections).

We should recall at this juncture that the SCOG concept identifies *two types* of actor. Alongside the conflict-capable groups within society sit the strategic reformist groups, which exist within many authoritarian regimes. Although the hardliners and softliners that are usually present within a government cannot initially bring themselves to pursue reform from above because they generally try to hold on to their power – as is presently the case almost everywhere in the Arab world – an authoritarian government can play an important role in the process of democratic transformation. It sounds absurd, but the repressive authoritarian state may help force the Islamic fundamentalist opposition to embrace democracy. In Turkey, for example, it is hard to imagine how the Islamic fundamentalist AKP could have developed into a democratic party without the supervision of the Turkish armed forces.

Such insights into the paradoxical necessities of coalition building have yet to take hold in the specialist literature. Most commentators either reject entirely the hazards of cooperation or recommend trial-and-error strategies (Hamzawy 2005, 17). It is undoubtedly true that politics always entails risks, uncertainties and even social fears, none of which can be controlled, and that every political development – outside of theoretical reflections – thus has its own unique dynamic. The American intervention in Iraq showed with particular clarity that political system change is anything but risk free. Years after the 2003 war, the country's political system has failed to stabilize.

But a political 'mistake' in dealing with Islamic fundamentalists may have serious consequences, and it is therefore essential to sharpen strategic options and avoid those mistakes that are in fact avoidable. Democratic elections should not be a case of Russian roulette in which no one knows which form of government is being selected and whether one authoritarian government is not ultimately being replaced by another, perhaps worse, one. One of the few scholars who has attempted to analyze the potential for cooperation with Islamic fundamentalists is Michael Hudson. Alongside the usual extreme positions, which aim either to include or exclude the Islamic fundamentalists, he describes an approach that he calls *limited accommodation* (Hudson 1995). One of the key conditions for such a strategy would be the forming of pacts which go beyond loose alliances and bindingly regulate essential political developments. This would have to occur before the protracted process of drawing up a common constitution, a process which, in any case, only gets off the ground once a democratic mandate has been obtained – in other words, far too late, as the very different cases of Iraq and Iran have shown so strikingly.

Classical views on the formation of pacts are expressed, for instance, in the work of Karl and Schmitter, who refer to the examples of Venezuela, Uruguay, Columbia and Spain as successful models (Karl and Schmitter 1991, 280 f.). Guillermo O'Donnell and Philippe C. Schmitter recommend a combination of military, political and economic pacts. The political aspect entails all actors assuring themselves that they will be able to participate politically, while the military aspect guarantees to the state and its armed forces a monopoly on violence, conceiving of the new state as a custodian of democracy (O'Donnell and Schmitter 1986, 37 ff.).

The Aspen Institute in the United States proposes a strategy for dealing with Islamic fundamentalists that includes the following elements: a willingness to form secularist-Islamic fundamentalist alliances; the working out of 'red lines' for a future constitution; and as a final step following free elections, the development of a system of checks and balances.[9] Clearly, this model can succeed only if the political system is marked by a willingness to cooperate, the secularists qualify their aversion to the Islamic fundamentalists and the latter overcome their internal cleavages by signing on to the fundamentals of democracy. But what is important for all involved is that this model at least provides a possible timetable for political developments, one which reduces the political risks of system change.

Ideally, it may be important for non-Islamic forces to develop a multi-stage strategy in which they would first pursue a democratic alliance with the Islamic fundamentalists to bolster the opposition's capacity for political combat, prompting a division of the state into hardliners and reformers. The secular opposition would then have to exploit this division in order to demand security guarantees from the state. It is entirely possible, after decades of revolution and civil war, most recently in Algeria, that such a development will eventually occur in one country or another. However, Arab regimes have so far always broken their promises, as in Jordan, where the king unilaterally abandoned the pact

[9] Mona Yacoubian, Democracy and Islamist Parties: The Arab Experience, http://www.aspeninstitute.org (27 March 2007).

with the opposition he forged in the early 1990s, which provided for the development of a constitutional monarchy based on the British model (Dieterich 1998; Ghadbian 1997, 132 f.). No one can say under precisely what circumstances democratization will be set in motion and a balance achieved between the forces of the secular and Islamic fundamentalist opposition, on the one hand, and the ruling regimes, on the other, which have thus far been polarized within an authoritarian context. But the important thing is to encourage strategic thinking about this framework of democracy – which is quite conceivable in principle – as the 'second-best option' for all political forces.

There are authors who have long since discerned the beginnings of such a development in the Arab world. Daniel Brumberg considers the Lebanese model, often described as untypical, to be a positive example, as Islamic groupings such as Hezbollah are politically integrated but show no eagerness to establish a dictatorship (Brumberg 2003, 271). In this view, integrative and participatory politics would be a key structural means of reducing the risk of an Islamic take-over. This is evident in the case of Lebanon, where, according to a constitutional agreement between confessional groups, the posts of prime minister and president are filled proportionally, or in Turkey, where the voter is able to elect a secular president (through the parliament) and an Islamic prime minister. It should be pointed out, however, that in the case of Hezbollah, the crucial disarming of all parties and the conferment on the state armed forces of the monopoly of violence has not taken place, which may trigger major setbacks such as the 2006 war in Lebanon.

THE INTERNATIONAL DIMENSION OF DEMOCRATIZATION

Although most of the problems relating to the formation of oppositional alliances are similar throughout the world, there is one factor that makes the Islamic world seem exceptional: the outstanding importance of a political-religious movement. Islamic fundamentalism is to a significant degree a reaction to constant Western interference in the Islamic world, where most of the opposition groups espouse an anti-Western worldview. This is understandable in view of the US and European support of authoritarian governments over the last few decades, from Morocco to Saudi Arabia and from Baghdad to Jakarta, which has blocked political development (see Chapter 6). This should be borne in mind when we discuss the Western approach to Islamic fundamentalism.

Contrary to the hopes of some observers,[10] the Eastern European policy of *Perestroika* and the political sea-change that took place in 1989 failed to spread to the Islamic world. From a global perspective, it is in any case rare for events in one location to help spread democracy elsewhere over the short-term. The 'waves of democratization' to which Samuel Huntington referred are testimony to the fact that, after Western and Southern Europe, first South America and then Eastern Europe saw *regionally specific* chain reactions of democratic development which were clearly separate from one another, at least in a temporal sense (Huntington 1991). Among other things, geographical, linguistic and cultural proximity may have played a role in each case, strengthening public awareness of political developments in neighbouring countries.

Alongside this factor, often referred to in the literature as a 'demonstration effect' (Schubert et al. 1994, 26), the politics of democratization is also a component of international politics. Political pressure applied from outside may help bring about changes in a given country. The fate of the Apartheid regime in South Africa, for example, was closely bound up with the country's international isolation and support for the opposition. But even in South Africa, the key movements for system change came from within the country. In recent years, the examples of Afghanistan and Iraq have made it very clear that, in the field of democratization, external factors can play a supporting role but cannot force democratic system change.

Exceptions include Germany and Italy after the Second World War. As a kind of world historical rule, it is very difficult to create democracy under an occupation regime. In Germany, defeat was total and the armed forces were disarmed. The Western powers were welcomed following this catastrophe, for Germany was treated as a partner by the USA, and it was in the American strategic and economic interest that Europe regain its strength. Things were different in Afghanistan and Iraq: as strategic bargaining chips in the context of the Cold War and later, of competition with China, both countries were conquered and destabilized by the USA. The differing position of Europe and the Middle East, respectively at the centre and on the periphery of the American imperium, is clearly apparent here.

If comparison with democratic developments elsewhere in the world is to be fruitful in analyzing the Islamic world, it must be acknowledged that Southern and Eastern Europe, not to mention South America, underwent

---

[10] See, for example, Betz/Matthies 1990, p. 39 f.

democratic transformation during periods in which the West exercised, at most, political and economic but not military pressure. Conversely, as a result of military pressure from a global imperially inclined power such as the USA, even hostile social forces, in other words, governments and oppositions of various kinds, often establish a national consensus because to do so becomes essential. Time and again, when America has threatened war and intervention, Iran has been a prime example of this, States on the periphery of global power often react differently than those at its centre.

In the Arab world, the most promising campaign for more open political systems – the famous 'bread riots' in countries such as Tunisia, Algeria and Jordan in the late 1980s and early 1990s – were sparked by socioeconomic crises rather than external intervention (Tessler 2000, 266). That they collapsed and failed to achieve their aims despite forcing a number of elections has something to do with the weakness of secular and Islamic fundamentalist opposition forces.

Is there a 'third way' for Western foreign policy? Can Western countries escape the dilemma of having either to ingratiate themselves to the autocrats of the Islamic world or fight them militarily, courses of action which have proved far from helpful accompaniments to democratization? Can sustainable political change be supported from outside? Since the attacks of 11 September 2001, these questions have found no real answers in Western foreign policy. Quite the opposite. Notably, after 9/11, Western intellectuals called for a shift away from the developmental goal of democratization of the Islamic world for the first time since the end of the old colonial era (see Chapter 6). The key factors here are the fear that Islamic fundamentalists might gain parliamentary majorities and visions of Islamic fundamentalist dictatorships. This is precisely what Fareed Zakaria, editor of *Newsweek International*, fears might happen. Authoritarian states such as Tito's Yugoslavia and Suharto's Indonesia receive retrospective praise as strongholds of stability (Zakaria 2004, 17 f.). Zakaria calls for the abandonment of democracy as a foreign policy goal and for a distinction to be made between 'liberalization' and 'democratization': 'At the start the West must recognize that it does not seek democracy in the Middle East – at least not yet. We seek first constitutional liberalism, which is very different. Clarifying our immediate goals actually makes them more easily attainable. The regimes in the Middle East will be delighted to learn that we will not try to force them to hold elections tomorrow. They will be less pleased to know that we continually press them on a whole array of other issues' (Zakaria 2004, 151).

Zakaria is certainly correct to point out that improvements in human rights can be achieved within the framework of authoritarian systems. There are many historical examples of this. We need only think of the profound difference between the totalitarian or fascist systems of Hitler, Stalin and Pol Pot, which annihilated staggering numbers of people, and dictatorships such as that of Cuba under Fidel Castro, where state repression occurs within certain limits, or Egypt where, notwithstanding the authoritarian conditions, a significant degree of freedom of expression has taken hold (see Chapter 5). European history, too, has seen a large number of enlightened monarchies, such as in nineteenth-century Prussia. We may, however, identify just as many cases where any move away from the ultimate goal of democracy seems ethically bankrupt. Czarist Russia left the path of reform following the death of Czar Alexander I (1801–25), ultimately paving the way for the October Revolution of 1917, and reform-minded Prussia, renowned across the world for the reforms of Stein and Humboldt, culminated in the Wilhelmine police state.

The examples of Tito and Suharto, whom Zakaria praises as developmental role models, illustrate the ultimate absurdity of any human rights policy that abandons the idea of democracy. Tito's Yugoslav dictatorship culminated in the disaster of the Balkan wars, while the Indonesian dictator Suharto – with the assent of the USA – murdered hundreds of thousands of people in East Timor in the 1970s (see Chapter 6). Dictatorships are unpredictable. To secure their power, dictators tend to respond to social pressures with violence. Only in a very limited sense can they be viewed as partners with whom it is possible to pursue a legitimate foreign policy. The paradigm shift which leading American thinkers such as Zakaria would like to usher in is thus really no more than a covert means of justifying the power-political status quo and the failures of American and European policies on democratization. At least so far, the policies on the Middle East and Islam pursued by the USA and Europe have failed to foster the development of democracy. In all probability, the democratization of the Islamic world has been hampered by international power relations. Without extensive US economic aid many of the dictatorships in the region would have long since come to grief as a result of their economic and social incompetence.

From the perspective of our own political values, there is really no alternative to democracy as our foreign policy lodestone. Only if we advocate the establishment of popular sovereignty can we claim to be acting in the interests of the people of the Islamic world – for in the absence of independent elections, the true interests of the people will never become visible. Democracy, moreover, is by no means a story of failure across the world, as Zakaria claims, but has become established on every continent and in parts of the Islamic world (Turkey, Indonesia, Bangladesh). But if democratic policies are not to be imposed by war, as in the era of George W. Bush, the question we must answer is: What might it mean to constructively promote democracy in the Islamic world?

A key problem here is recognition of the moderate, non-violent Islamic fundamentalists and cooperation with the major mass organizations such as Morocco's Parti de la Justice et du Developpement (PJD), Egypt's Muslim Brothers and the Al-Wasat Party (Centrists), Yemen's Islah (Reform Party), Jordan's Islamic Action Front, Kuwait's Islamic Constitutional Movement and Bahrain's Al-Wifaq (National Accord). Neo-realist approaches like Zakaria's are not the only ones up for discussion in the United States. In the American political think tanks based in Washington DC, very different views have taken hold over the last few years. The Council on Foreign Relations and the Aspen Institute, for example, have often called for the taboo on contact with Islamic fundamentalists to be dropped, as democratic progress is inconceivable without it.[11] Aspen proposes that the American government engage in intensive dialogue with moderate Islamic fundamentalists and promote a civil-society-based dialogue on democracy and legal projects between Islamic fundamentalists and secularists.

In a publication produced by the German foreign ministry's special representative on Islam, Amr Hamzawy of America's Carnegie Endowment for International Peace calls for a cautious reorientation towards cooperation with Islamic fundamentalists:

A second viable strategy is to engage democratic Islamists primarily at the local level and in less politicized realms. In a first phase of collaboration it might be easier for both parties to leave aside the explosive terrains of national and regional politics and adopt a low-profile approach. Different joint projects designed to promote mutual trust and moderation within the Islamist spectrum can be envisaged for example in the fields of civic education, women's empowerment, and local capacity building. In fact, a number of European donor states have already started to allocate significant tranches of their developmental aid to Arab countries for this purpose. Identifying potential Islamist partners cannot but follow a minimalist, more pragmatic and less normative, approach. Provided that the respective movement or organization clearly and generally renounces violence and is willing to collaborate with the West it becomes eligible. Engaging Islamists at the grassroots should be understood as a result-oriented experiment in which

[11] Ibid.

Western governments assess the impacts of the new policy on their partners within the initial period of two years, depending on concrete results and trend developments within the Islamist spectrum. In the last few years, Arab liberals have been gradually reaching out to democratic Islamists and engaging them in campaigns calling for reforms. Secular-religious national alliances for democracy are instrumental in contesting the authoritarian state power and articulating popular consensus over the need for political transformation. Islamists, on their side, have seized the integration opportunity and positioned themselves at the heart of growing opposition movements across the region. In Morocco, Lebanon, and Egypt differences between liberals and Islamists remain relevant, but the degree of their convergence over national priorities is systematically growing. These are steps in the right direction. Democratic opposition platforms are by far more effective with Islamist participation than without it. The cause of political transformation in the region is best served by bringing in Islamist movements and their popular constituencies. The United States and Europe should move forward in the same direction of engaging democratic Islamists. Inviting Islamist politicians to dialogue conferences in Europe or getting American diplomats in the Arab world to set up regular consultations with their movements are, although indicating openness towards Islamists, not enough. (…) [Western and US pressure on] Arab regimes to ease their repressive measures against democratic Islamists and to grant them access to the political sphere might represent a good starting point that is badly needed (Hamzawy 2005, 18; see Youngs 2004 for similar points).

According to this view, to enhance the opposition's capacity for political combat and increase the chances of bringing about system change in the Islamic world, it is vitally important that the United States, Europe and the international community nurture incipient efforts to create cross-factional alliances. Think tanks such as Aspen or Carnegie demand far more than the traditional American Middle East policy that President Bill Clinton, for example, was prepared to contemplate – to say nothing of President George W. Bush. The Greater or Broader Middle East and North Africa Initiative produced by the Bush administration in 2004 after the Iraq war was supposed to help deepen relations and promote democratization. However, because of America's close cooperation with Arab monarchies such as Jordan and its continued adherence to militaristic policies, this initiative has rightly been criticized as a cover for the maintenance of American interests, quite incapable of achieving any democratic breakthrough.[12]

Yet the United States has by no means generally eschewed contact with Islamic fundamentalists in recent years, as one might have assumed, but has in fact displayed an astonishing flexibility in whom it is willing to

[12] Gilbert Achcar, Greater Middle East: the US Plan, *Le Monde Diplomatique* (English edition), April 2004.

talk to. The US government has been in contact with moderate Islamic fundamentalists in many Islamic states, such as the Egyptian Muslim Brothers. When the Islamic fundamentalist Turkish Prime Minister Necmettin Erbakan came to power in 1995, the American government took a pragmatic approach and even viewed the good relations taking shape with him and his Refah Party as a way to improve its relationship with the Islamic fundamentalist movement (Gerges 1999, 202 f.). The USA's flexible approach to dealing with moderate Islamic fundamentalists has always been moulded by the desire to safeguard American national interests despite changes of government. Relations with Egypt's Muslim Brothers, for example, were intended to create an authoritarian alternative in case the Mubarak administration fell, in line with the motto: If one Middle Eastern dictatorship is to be replaced by another, what matters is that it is on good terms with the USA. No serious attempt has ever been made to prompt the Egyptian or any other government to integrate the Islamic fundamentalists more tightly into the democratic process. Even in the case of Erbakan, the United States merely sat and watched as the Turkish armed forces drove him from office.

This tradition of American dialogue with moderate Islamic fundamentalists never entirely ceased, even during the administration of George W. Bush. In 2007, for example, the Democratic majority leader in Congress, Steny Hoyer, made personal contact with the Muslim Brothers in Egypt. Because they felt that a rapprochement with the Islamic fundamentalists made sense in terms of the development of democracy, Egyptian intellectuals welcomed Hoyer's visit, pointing out that Islamic fundamentalists had long since involved themselves in democratic discourse and ruled the streets.[13] Other observers, meanwhile, remarked critically that the USA's shift away from an anti-Islamic fundamentalist, militaristic policy towards one based on political dialogue was merely a change of strategy aimed at warding off Islamic fundamentalist aggression against the United States and increasing its influence on the movement. Hoyer's visit by no means reflected an active policy of democracy promotion that included the Islamic fundamentalists.

Initially, America's integration of the Islamic fundamentalists into its foreign policy strategies would unsettle the secular opposition, which was already far from enthusiastic about highly sporadic contact such as

---

[13] MB Meeting with Congressmen Raises Controversy in Egypt, 30 May, http://www.aljazeera.net/NR/exeres/0D509A04-E226–469D-AEE3-CBC7C6AFE270.htm (21 August 2007).

Hoyer's. It would be a bitter blow if Western foreign policy moved closer to certain Islamic fundamentalists only to ignore those forces which, though often in a weaker position, have a clear programmatic orientation towards secular democracy. But secularism cannot be equated with a democratic mentality, a point made adequately by others. A shift in American foreign policy towards the Islamic fundamentalists may be more than strategically important. It would also put additional pressure on the secular camp to sharpen its democratic profile. In return, American foreign policy would have to make more of an effort to persuade the governments of the Islamic world not to harass the secular opposition.

A constructive American policy on democratization in the Islamic world would carry a political price. Meaningful strategies on democracy incorporating Islamic fundamentalists can be produced only if key regional conflicts can be solved with American involvement. Within the ranks of the Muslim Brothers, any dialogue with the USA provokes criticism of possible rapprochement because Islamic fundamentalists reject the USA's imperialist policies in Iraq and Afghanistan and its decades-long unilateral support for Israel. For the Islamic fundamentalists as well as the USA, more intensive cooperation would put internal cohesion to the test.

Overall, the outlines of a new and desirable American foreign policy strategy on democratization fit neatly within a logical plan of action: an American policy towards the Middle East reformed in light of realpolitik, one that convincingly pursued the resolution of the Israeli-Palestinian conflict, Afghanistan and Iraq would, through cooperation and dialogue with both secularists and Islamic fundamentalists, be in a position to increase the political and economic pressure on the authoritarian regimes of the Islamic world and thus stimulate the process of democratization. The autocrats' common tactic of using the fear of Islam as a means of countering Western calls for democracy would be ineffective in such a situation.

European countries have often found it easier than the United States to informally approach the Islamic fundamentalists. Because Europe's Middle East policies are less influential than America's, it is easier to establish contacts – but these involve less commitment. Whether Europe is generally more tolerant towards Islamic fundamentalist movements (El-Affendi 2006, 41), is not yet clear. European countries take different approaches to dealing with Islamic fundamentalists; the core states of France and Germany differ markedly. Anti-Islamic fundamentalist foreign-policy reflexes are rarer in Germany than in France, as is evident in the fact that the German state granted political asylum to many high-ranking supporters of the Algerian FIS in the 1990s, while France supported the abandonment of the Algerian national elections of 1991–2 that would have brought the FIS to power (Salamé 1998, 40). Because of its strict commitment to laicism, France has always had a harder time dealing with Islamic fundamentalists than many other European countries, and perhaps even the United States. However, France has long vehemently criticized Israel for the occupation of Palestinian territories and has distinguished itself as a pro-Arab force in this regard, in opposition to the USA. As a result, Nicolas Sarkozy endorsed talks with the Islamic fundamentalist Hamas in 2008.[14] Meanwhile, immediately after the resignation of Tony Blair, the United Kingdom, under Prime Minister Gordon Brown, encouraged new thinking on cooperation with fundamentalist organizations such as Palestinian Hamas and even the Afghan Taliban.[15]

Germany's dialogue with Islamic fundamentalists, like that of other European countries (Silvestri 2007), has so far, however, shown little political depth. Beyond sporadic contact, there is no common European policy on democratization. In the efforts of so-called Second Track diplomacy and among German political think tanks relevant ideas have repeatedly been put forward – such as calls to recognize Islam as a partner in dialogue.[16] But neither the Social Democrat-Green Schröder government (1998–2005) nor the conservative Merkel administration (2005–) vigorously pursued these goals, chiefly because they would require the United States, Germany's ally, to rethink its foreign policy, including forging a new relationship with the autocrats of the Islamic world. Against the background of widespread criticism of Islam in the European media and public, any political attempt to move closer to the Islamic fundamentalists would also be unpopular and hard to enforce within the domestic political context. In 2007, for example, when the then chairman of the Social Democratic Party (SPD), Kurt Beck, demanded that the German government attempt to cooperate with the reinvigorated Islamic fundamentalist Taliban in rebuilding Afghanistan, which was at risk of descending into civil war, he faced strong public criticism. Few were willing to back him. The Merkel government was also very quick to

---

[14] Steven Erlanger, France Acknowledges Contacts with Hamas Leaders, *The New York Times*, 20 May 2008.

[15] Peter Nonnemacher, Grossbritanien will seine Außenpolitik neu gewichten, [Great Britain wants to reassess its foreign policy], *Tages-Anzeiger*, 26 September 2007.

[16] Inga Börjesson, Jenseits von Irak, 2004, [Beyond Iraq, 2004], http://www.bildung-gegen-antisemitismus.de (15 March 2007).

withdraw economic aid from the Hamas government in the autonomous Palestinian areas. German foreign policy cannot, therefore, be viewed as a straightforwardly pro-Islamic force within Europe. There is no consensus that Islamic fundamentalists ought to be integrated.

It remains to be seen whether the West will change its foreign policy, adopting a new approach to the promotion of democracy that might endanger its own strategic and economic goals and frighten autocratic governments and elites in the Middle East and North Africa. There is of course a possibility that any serious reorientation of Western foreign policy in favour of democratization might tempt some dictators in the region to sell their countries' oil to the Western powers' resource-poor competitors, particularly China. The Chinese economic boom may therefore be politically damaging to the Islamic world. In light of global financial interdependencies, however, there is no real prospect of a serious slump in the oil markets. Ultimately, the question is whether the West wishes to actively promote its own ideals of human rights and democracy or whether safeguarding its own interests will continue to be its sole concern. Should this be the case, then the affected regions' oil wealth would itself have become a curse, as it seems to be economic interests that cause the West to baulk at genuine efforts to promote democracy.

EURO-ISLAM OR ISLAM-ORIENTED OSTPOLITIK: TWO MODELS OF TRANSFORMATION

Those in contemporary Europe, the USA or elsewhere in the West who want to see the enduring and comprehensive democratization of the Islamic world are faced with two basic strategic alternatives. They may, as is generally socially acceptable in the West, foster those political forces which may be seen as arousing no suspicions of pursuing anything other than perfect democracy, in other words, free elections and secular freedoms. But it quickly becomes apparent that the number of those who can be unambiguously ascribed to this camp is very small. As a rule, it is Middle Eastern intellectuals, often educated or even living in the West, who come to embrace the idea of 'Euro-Islam' or an 'American Islam' that is decidedly non-violent and secular in orientation.

At present, only a small number of oppositional forces in the Middle East, let alone within the predominantly authoritarian governments, are prepared to embrace democratization. In the secular and Islamic fundamentalist camps, and in numerous transitional reformist milieux featuring a mixture of worldviews, within both the approved parties and

the wider civil society, numerous agents clearly renounce political violence. But we often find no more than vague statements on issues such
as free elections, the separation of powers and the observance of equal
basic and civil rights regardless of gender, religion and ethnic origin.
Authoritarian systems severely hinder the development of such moderate
political views. Regime critics wish to force political changes with the
kind of ideological 'sledgehammer' represented by fundamentalist slogans, through the introduction of Islamic law for example. Yet Islamic
law is no monolith, but rather a – frequently inconsistent – corpus of
case law built up over centuries. Sharia in Saudi Arabia takes a different form than it would in Turkey, where, for example, harsh corporal
punishment for theft has never existed. But political watchwords such
as 'Islamic law' and 'Islamic state' exclude non-Muslims and represent
artificial attempts to wrap Muslims in a collectivizing cloak. By no means
all Muslims approve of the idea that religious affiliation should function as a key criterion of citizenship or political action. A solid minority,
clearly discernible in opinion polls, wants neither a dictatorship nor an
'Islamic democracy' that would permit the separation of powers and legal
provisions only within the framework of the Sharia. All we know about
the majority is that it would like to reconcile religion and democracy.
It is unclear whether it supports a reformed 'Christian democratic' or
fundamentalist anti-secular creed.

But it is easy for radical political demands to emerge in an authoritarian
milieu in which the opposition appeals to, and wishes to mobilize, different social strata, not least those at the lower end of the social scale.
The probability of bringing about political changes in the contemporary
Middle East by means of an unambiguously reformed Islam based on
the model of a constitutionally loyal Euro-Islam is thus extremely low.
Societies that permit almost no political participation do not produce a
favourable climate for liberal democrats.

Is the West thus incapable of taking action with respect to democratization? Does it have no other option than to come to terms with authoritarian national leaders? Far from it. A growing number of voices suggests
that Western foreign policy should embrace a new accomodationism that
no longer shies away from dialogue and cooperation – even with certain
groups and parties of a near-radical character. To wait until Catholics and
Protestants in Northern Ireland had changed into peaceable democrats
would have meant abandoning any attempt to bring them together in a
shared parliament and thus 'civilizing' them. From a historical point of
view, as one influential group of democracy theorists now argues, some

degree of democratic change has been accepted as the 'second-best option' even by radical forces, after which stable democracies have developed.

We should not forget that this approach of actively supporting secularist and Islamic-fundamentalist opposition forces entails risks. It would mean forging political alliances that might cause instability. The alternative to the active promotion of democracy, however, is to continue to do nothing. This would mean passing up the chance of promoting democracy within a global framework, with future generations abandoned to despotism. On the margins of global society, military intervention based on the Second World War model takes a devastating humanitarian toll and provokes nationalist resistance. What we need is an approach that applies Willy Brandt's successful Ostpolitik, which played a crucial role in bringing down the Eastern Bloc regimes through a strategy of diplomatic 'embrace', to the Islamic world. Talking to anti-democratic forces, even supporting them to some extent, while at the same time pushing for human rights and limiting the military threat, played a significant role in ensuring that the people of the Soviet Union stopped seeing the West as The Enemy. Western policy on Islam now stands at a crossroads very similar to the one it faced at the end of the Cold War.

III

POLITICAL VIOLENCE

If, then, as this book asserts, the Islamic world and the West are far from being radically distinct with respect to political modernity and the emergence of democracy, there is one dimension that has consistently been regarded as insurmountably different, namely, attitudes towards political violence. Pope Benedict XVI's controversial 2006 speech at the University of Regensburg exemplified the still widespread idea that the Islamic Middle East is the violent opposite pole to a West that has embraced peace as a result of Enlightenment, democracy and the painful experience of war. The Pope set out his view that Christianity has long since reconciled itself to the rationality of non-violence, while Islam, at least according to the implicit message of the speech, still subscribes to the idea that faith can be spread by violent means.[1]

Pope Benedict is by no means alone. Influential intellectuals, authors and academics such as Samuel Huntington, Benjamin Barber, Bernard Lewis and Daniel Pipes have advocated variations on the same thesis over the last few decades, namely, that Islam is more violent and dangerous than other religions. The points of reference here vary widely. Huntington's main emphasis is on critical internal factors such as demographic pressures and the role of Islam in the formation of political identity ('Islam has bloody borders') (Huntington 1993, 1996). Barber on the other hand sees the readiness to use violence as caused by the shock effect of Western

---

[1] Address by Pope Benedict XVI at the University of Regensburg on 12 September 2006: 'Glaube, Vernunft und Universität. Erinnerungen und Reflexionen', [Faith, rationality and the university. Memories and reflections], http://www.benedikt-in-bayern.de/EMF244/EMF024339.asp (17 February 2008).

cultural globalization in the Islamic world (Barber 1993). For Middle East specialist Lewis, it is the sheer incompatibility of Western values and Islam that arouses hatred for Western civilization among many Muslims (Lewis 2003a).

For Mark B. Salter, the idea that the Islamic world, in contrast to the West, is characterized by an anti-systemic open or latent tendency towards violence is the revival of the old categories of 'civilization' and 'barbarism' (Salter 2002). According to Salter, the West 'barbarizes' the non-Western and, in particular, the Islamic world. It is of secondary importance here whether Islam is truly taking on the old function of 'barbarians' during the colonial period or in fact that of a 'counter-civilization'. In any event, the noteworthy thing is Salter's argument that just a few decades after the West was compelled to ask critical questions about the naive notion that Western modernity is peaceful in light of two world wars and the Holocaust, this cultural humility has given way to a new sense of civilizational superiority in much of Western society. The Holocaust is declared a historical mistake, an exception, one that poses no questions about the pacifying effect of the Western project of Enlightenment and modernity. What is more, for many authors, the annihilation of the German Jews is viewed as a warning against taking a non-aggressive approach to an aggressive and at times neo-fascist Islam – thus helping lay the ground for further violence.

The idea that a cultural faultline divides the civilized West from uncontrolled, terrorist and aggressive Islamic political violence did not begin to take hold only after the attacks of 11 September 2001 on the World Trade Center and the Pentagon. Authors such as Huntington, Barber and Lewis, who published their basic positions in the 1990s, demonstrate that events such as the Iranian Revolution of 1978–9 and the ideological vacuum that arose once the East-West conflict had come to an end required a revival of the idea of an Islamic-Western civilizational rupture within international politics. Yet the attacks of 11 September have left their mark on Western thinking. The severity and media presence of the events triggered major intellectual departures, as is evident, for example, in the contemporary renaissance of a neo-imperialist school in mainstream Western political thought. Far beyond the neo-conservative current in the United States, there is great enthusiasm for the idea of pacifying the world through a 'humanitarian imperialism' that will curb the inner- and outer-directed political violence of the Islamic world (see Chapter 6).

While there is a strong tendency in the West to regard the Islamic Middle East, perhaps alongside China and parts of Africa, as one of the last refuges of political violence, violence coming from the West itself is often overlooked. In reality, the difference between Islam and the West with respect to the use of violence has more to do with form than substance: both sides have killed huge numbers of people over the last few decades. Pope Benedict XVI has been heavily criticized from a theological point of view because ideas on violence within the main theological currents of Christianity and Islam are basically very similar (see Chapter 7). From a social scientific perspective, the dichotomy of 'peace-loving West versus violent Islam' is open to attack from various angles. The idea that state or privatized forms of political violence are the exclusive domain of Middle Eastern despots or anarchist Islamic fundamentalists is extravagantly wrong. The use and deployment of political violence are also fundamental features of the West's capacity to wage war and its pursuit of power-political hegemony.

Jochen Hippler argues that in view of the realities of political violence we cannot declare our own civilized peaceableness the rule, and barbarism the exception, while doing the opposite in the case of the Islamic world (Hippler 2006, 7). Hippler is implicitly referring to a problem that might be described as the asymmetry of hermeneutics and comparative political analysis. Violence was and is a reality on all sides, but it takes different forms, and often occurs at different times or even in different epochs. This is why the violence of the 'Other' appears more clearly and more sharply outlined as an unusual and prohibited form of violence than that produced by one's own social system, which is regarded as 'normal'.

To put it very simplistically, but in line with the findings of comparative research on violence, we might say that the main problem of the Islamic world lies in the violence carried out by the authoritarian state and the suppression of freedoms, which occasionally bring about the collapse of the state's monopoly on violence. These problems generate a terrorism that is by no means directed only against the West but, first and foremost, against regional political orders regarded as unjust (see Chapter 5). The West, which finds itself in a historically unique period characterized by internal civil liberties, left such problems behind decades or even centuries ago. Though certain authoritarian temptations – Guantánamo being a case in point – as well as various forms of so-called 'modern slavery' are blots on the copybook, Western democracies have warded off the great fascist danger and now reject utterly the authoritarian and crypto-fascist politics found in Islamic countries and movements. At the same time, weak and in a state of long-term crisis, the predominantly authoritarian

Islamic world has generally had to bid farewell to its imperialist history in the present era, though the West, led by the USA, has now filled this gap. The expansionist violence of the West, which has never consistently broken with its colonial history and now has a military presence in the Middle East on a scale not seen for a century, receives more attention in the Islamic world than in the West. Here, it is seen either as a neo-conservative exception or as humanitarian intervention, but rarely for what it is: a continued tradition of military interference intended to secure Western interests, a phenomenon far distant from the policy of world peace anticipated by Immanuel Kant as the logical consequence of democratization (see Chapter 6). At present, both the Islamic and Western worlds are having to deal with Islamic terrorism – but this does not mean that they do so in the same way. Terrorism is generally regarded by the West as a consequence of religiously, culturally or politically induced internal failings of the Islamic world. In the Islamic world, on the other hand, it is often viewed as a reaction to imperialism (see Chapter 7).

In terms of systematic comparison, such 'economies of attention' prove highly prone to error. It is not only that there is evidence of political violence in both the Islamic world and the West, though it may occur at different points in history. We can also make out a superordinate structure of Islamic-Western interaction, what we might call a Middle Eastern–Western system of violence generation. Acts of violence occur at different times because they are mutually dependent. The countries of the Islamic world no longer constitute empires because the West has won the race for the world, its resources and its political domination. This crisis of the Islamic world has in turn given rise to the modern authoritarian state, which either continues to practice political violence or produces zones of state collapse in which terrorism holds sway; this in turn produces asymmetrical wars with the West. By comparing different forms of political violence, we can bring out how violence interacts in the Islamic-Western context.

5

Authoritarianism: Dictatorship Between Fascism and Modernization

We can approach the task of locating the political systems of the Islamic world within a comparative international framework from various perspectives. Theories of civil society, of social movements and of political transformation have grown out of democratic theory and over the last few years have become increasingly significant to the assessment of Islamic societies. After a long period of fixation on textual materials, which reflected the influence of the classical Middle East scholarship, contemporary researchers are investigating real political processes without disregarding the role of religio-cultural traditions and modern ideologies. A number of authors are currently rethinking the significance of fundamentalist Islam in the process of social change as the – provisionally – final stage of this development (see Chapter 4). The question of whether Islamic fundamentalists may play a constructive role in eliminating authoritarianism, however, can be answered only if we keep another theoretical option in mind: the theory of authoritarianism.

It is significantly less homogeneous than the theory of democracy, perhaps because democracy has generally been studied in light of its development within the context of Western modernity, while authoritarian political power is as old as human history, and just as diverse. As a rule, modern-day comparative political science pays significantly more attention to political transformation and democratization than to authoritarianism, which seems to represent 'the old', that which must be overcome (see, for example, Jahn 2006; von Prittwitz 2007). At present, comparative political science directs most of its energy to the issue of change and may thus be overlooking important trends in modern authoritarianism. Yet these may be of greater significance than the modern forces of democratization for a long time to come. As a result, the potential of research to uncover key insights is left untapped. The role that developmental dictatorship has played in Western history and its current importance to the Islamic world remains unclear. This is particularly significant given that the Islamic world is now, more than ever, taking its lead from the model of China. It is also unclear whether traditional rule and modern neo-patrimonialism are really only significant in the Islamic world. Within the Western democracy, ever greater attention is being paid to clientelism and corruption. How, then, are we to describe the precise difference from Islamic countries?

One of the key debates in Western political theory – on the difference between authoritarian and fascist regimes – has yet to be considered in light of a rigorous comparison of Islam and the West. This can probably only be explained in light of the susceptibility of Western research on democracy to academic fashions. This difference is by no means purely academic; it carries a powerful political charge. With respect to the political sphere, the term 'fascism' evokes total antagonism and an end to any 'policy of appeasement' vis-à-vis movements or systems that seem to have parted company with the last scraps of political rationality. If, on the other hand, we posit that the appropriate parallel to Islamic regimes and such contemporary movements as Islamic fundamentalism is, in fact, classical dictatorship, this opens up a whole range of possible ways of dealing with the Islamic world politically, from war and boycotts to de-escalation and policies of détente to cooperation. This chapter focuses on this crucial question, primarily by attempting to contextualize the key term 'Islamofascism' and discussing the question of anti-Semitism in the Islamic world. We also take a brief look at the debate on the authoritarian temptations facing Western democracies in the wake of the attacks of 11 September 2001 and examine a topic that as yet plays a very small role in comparative research, though it touches fundamentally on the problem of a given society's authoritarian character: 'modern slavery', which is prohibited in all political systems but is apparently becoming a component of the legal and social reality in both the Islamic and Western worlds on the tide of modern processes of migration.

'ISLAMOFASCISM': DEAD END OF POLITICAL RATIONALITY?

In various speeches and statements, President George W. Bush referred to Islamic radicalism and terrorism as an 'Islamic fascism' that wishes to destroy the freedom of the Western world.[1] Well-known critics of Islam, such as Daniel Pipes and Norman Podhoretz, have popularized terms such as 'Islamofascism' in the public and intellectual spheres. Since the Iranian Revolution of 1978–9, fundamentalist Islam has often been compared to fascism, as in the debate between Michel Foucault, who saw the Iranian Revolution as a source of revolutionary hope, and French Middle East specialist Maxime Rodinson, who criticised fundamentalist Islam as a form of 'archaic fascism' (see Afary and Anderson 2005, 233; Khalid 1979).

The arguments for equating Islamic fundamentalism with fascism include its anti-Semitism, its anti-Americanism, its evocation of a glorious civilizational past in which the source of liberation from present crisis can be discerned, and the strict internal hierarchy and organization of Islamic fundamentalist movements. In his book *Fascism: Past, Present, Future*, Walter Laqueur identified demagogic populism, the rejection of democracy and a 'fanatic belief in violence' as elements permitting comparisons between Islamic fundamentalism and fascism (Laqueur 1996, 167). In his book *World War IV: The Long Struggle Against Islamofascism*, influential neo-conservative thinker Norman Podhoretz characterizes the struggle against Islamic fundamentalism as a contemporary variant on the historical battle against National Socialism and Soviet totalitarianism (Podhoretz 2007). Probably the best known American critic of Islam, Daniel Pipes, differentiates between Islam and Islamofascism but identifies fundamentalism as a kind of fascism.[2] According to Pipes, Islamic fundamentalists aspire to change fundamentally the basis of the political system, including that of the USA. They form a state within the state, and there is a danger that they might infiltrate Western democracies to fascist ends.

These contributions are worth discussing; since 11 September 2001 an increasing number of commentators have used the term 'Islamofascism' as a political catchword, but their statements are intellectually inaccessible and have no analytical significance. One example is the self-published work of Canadian Craig Read, *Fascism and Paganism. A Brief Comparison of Nazism, Communism and Islam*. Read locates the roots of European fascism in Islamic-Arab paganism (Read 2006). In response to such polemics,

---

[1] President Bush and Secretary of State Rice Discuss the Middle East Crisis, Office of the Press Secretary, 7 August 2006, http://www.whitehouse.gov/news/releases/2006/08/20060807.html (18 February 2008).

[2] Daniel Pipes, Islamism is Fascism, 2001, http://www.danielpipes.org/article/81 (12 February 2008).

German political scientist Claus Leggewie has warned of the dangers of misusing the term Islamofascism: 'Is it really necessary to make this risky historical analogy in order to underline the importance of coming to terms with Jihadism? Can Western democrats be torn from their inertia and navel-gazing only if we, including the most elite circles, reach for the big guns of Hitler comparisons'?[3]

Whether and how 'normal' authoritarian rule can be distinguished from the fascist exercise of power is still subject to dispute. A classical argument is put forward by Hannah Arendt: while authoritarian rule generally means the despotism of an individual or clique, totalitarianism is distinguished by rule in the name of a natural or transcendent law, generally enforced by a single leader backed by the bureaucratic apparatus of a party or movement. The hallmark of this form of rule is that the people are at the mercy not so much of a dictator's or monarch's arbitrary whims but rather the systematic 'cleansing', restructuring and *Gleichschaltung* of much of society. Thus, total government is not superficial tyranny, but a system that raises both inner- and outer-directed terrorism to the status of law (Arendt 1951).

Modern comparative political science still adheres to this fundamental distinction. Volker von Prittwitz, for instance, places fascism, 'terrorist fundamentalism' and totalitarian Stalinism and Maoism on the same level, as all these ideologies and movements have developed fundamentalist-eschatological worldviews; distance themselves from all forms of pluralism and legally constrained government; make use of technological modernity and deploy violence in cynical and brutal ways (von Prittwitz 2007, 63). Von Prittwitz points out that a religion-inspired ideological foundation may also be combined with other elements (such as democracy). But he includes Islamic fundamentalism in the definition of fascism, even if it does not involve the use of terrorism. He nonetheless calls for the precise structures of fundamentalist organizations to be studied on a case-by-case basis with respect to their 'possible transitions to authoritarian models'.

In light of these qualifications, we may understand von Prittwitz as excluding reformist Islamic interpretations from any suspicion of fascism, as they display a form of Islamic political thought that is grounded in religion but is neither anti-pluralist nor oriented towards a single leader or violence. The question remains of the extent to which the various

---

[3] Claus Leggewie, Islam und Moderne: Wider das wachsende Misstrauen, [Islam and modernity: against the growing mistrust], *die tageszeitung*, 30 January 2007.

currents of Islamic fundamentalism wishing to replace the secular state with Sharia – through violence, political means or both – should be regarded as fascist.

We might first expand von Prittwitz's catalogue of the criteria of fascism by including chauvinist-expansionist nationalism, social corporatism and Social Darwinism. It must be conceded, however, that expansionism was and is also characteristic of other autocracies and does not, therefore, represent a genuine distinction, though it is a key feature we cannot do without. Further, Social Darwinism appears in fascism but not in Marxist-Leninist or Maoist totalitarianism, which of course advocate the ideal of the socially just society.

Thus, we may meaningfully discuss a number of features in comparing Islamic fundamentalism and fascism, including:

- Racism and mass killings by the state
- The *Führerprinzip,* or leader principle, and rejection of democracy
- Rejection of legal restraints
- Socioeconomic corporatism
- Social Darwinism
- Expansionism

Racism and mass killings by the state. Classical European fascism had a clear-cut concept of The Enemy towards which it directed its efforts to 'cleanse' society of the 'racially' inferior. In Marxist-Leninist totalitarianism, this distinction was transferred from heredity to social class. Despite the bloody Stalinist class wars, this had the fundamental advantage that people could be assigned to the new ruling class of workers and peasants based on their position within the processes of production. The Nazi concept of race, on the other hand, was biologically closed; whether one was a member of the master race or inferior race, one's fate was sealed at birth.

Islamic fundamentalism makes a basic distinction between believers and non- or unbelievers. But conversion to Islam is open to all and presents no insurmountable obstacles, thus religious affiliation does not constitute a closed category that sets apart friend from enemy. As to the question of whether there is a fundamental animosity between Muslims and non-Muslims which would point to a fundamentalist programme of annihilation, the argument must proceed on a number of levels. The International Crisis Group distinguishes between political, missionary and Jihadist Islamic fundamentalists (for a more in-depth discussion of this, see Chapter 7). Despite their intolerant goals, which they pursue in various ways, it is clear that neither the political nor missionary Islamic groups and organizations are fundamentally preoccupied with waging war against 'unbelievers'. What political Islamic fundamentalists have in mind is the re-establishment of the old institution of dhimmi status, which grants to non-Muslims a right to exist and to autonomy on the basis of Sharia. While this is out of sync with the demands for equality that characterize the modern Western-style democratic constitutional state (secularism), it does not even come close to being a programme of annihilation.

This is fundamentally different in the case of the small minority of 'global Jihadists', who preach an apocalyptic battle against all unbelievers at the End of Days (although they lack anything remotely akin to the firm political programme characteristic of the historical fascists, which makes the modern Jihadists seem more like crypto-fascist sectarians or anarchists). 'Irredentist Jihadists', such as Hamas or Hezbollah, occupy a problematic position. Their real origins lie among nationally oriented political Islamic fundamentalists. In light of the special circumstances of foreign occupation, however, at least some of their members believe it necessary to use violence. These groups in principle share the traditional Muslim tolerance of non-Muslims, such as Jews and Christians, and do not aspire to mass annihilation. But a tense and dangerous relationship exists between the ethnically and nationalistically charged view that Israel is The Enemy and the traditional view of Jews, which was never unprejudiced, so that there is always a danger that the image of Jews will be 'ethnicized'. In some cases, 'the Jew' becomes an enemy supposedly bent on the annihilation of Muslims, against whom Muslims must defend themselves, an idea which sometimes comes very close to the notion of a worldwide Jewish conspiracy. Nevertheless, these groups lack any religiously or politically grounded ideologies of the annihilation of Jews or other non-Muslims (see Chapter 7).

The Führerprinzip, *or leader principle, and rejection of democracy.* Any movement in which only a tiny minority supports the principle of dictatorial leadership would represent a very peculiar form of fascism. The very splintering of Islamic fundamentalists into numerous different groupings points to their lack of any consistent desire to embrace political subordination. Only extremely marginal groups within this spectrum now wish to re-establish the caliphate. It is true, as we have seen, that the major modern Islamic organizations such as the Parti de la Justice et du Developpement (PJD), Egypt's Muslim Brothers and Al-Wasat Party (Centrists), Yemen's Islah (Reform Party), Jordan's

Islamic Action Front, Kuwait's Islamic Constitutional Movement and Bahrain's Al-Wifaq (National Accord) call for the reestablishment of the Sharia, but they are also committed to the democracy-oriented principles of the separation of powers and the party and parliamentary system. In no major Islamic fundamentalist organization does the leadership enjoy anything like the undisputed status held by Hitler and Mussolini within their movements.

However, we should not forget that during the period in which organized fundamentalism emerged under the leadership of the Egyptian Hassan al-Banna in the late 1920s, the rejection of pluralism was one of the movement's basic features. It thus seems entirely possible that elements of authoritarian rule might be revived, though Al-Banna set out no coherent concept of rule. The Sunnite Islamic fundamentalists in Sudan and Afghanistan who came to power through revolution and violence quickly came to embrace the principle of dictatorship, though with changeable leaders, alliances and major internal upheavals: a problem that was particularly well-illustrated by former leader of the Sudanese Islamic fundamentalists and later political prisoner Hassan al-Turabi. In the minority Shiite tradition, some dictatorial clerical leaders enjoy a high degree of legitimation, such as Sheikh Hassan Nasrallah of the Lebanese Hezbollah or Ayatollah Khomeini and his successor Khamenei in Iran. Even so, the outstanding importance of the leading imams is disputed. The internal conflicts over the leadership of the Iraqi Shiites, between Grand Ayatollah Ali al-Sistani and the radical cleric and political leader Muqtada al-Sadr, for example, are good evidence of this. Overall, it is impossible to say with absolute certainty what relationship the large Islamic fundamentalist organizations have to dictatorship and democracy. This may suggest a parallel with European fascism, which also used the existing democracies for its own advancement in its early stages, only to destroy them later on.

Rejection of legal restraints. In his influential book, *Stufen der Machtergreifung* ('Stages of the Seizure of Power'), Karl Dietrich Bracher writes about the relationship of National Socialism to the law and to the legal system: 'The total state reverses [the legal obligations of the democratic constitutional state]; explicitly and consciously according to the wishes and power-related needs of its leadership, it creates its own "law", which is declared a straightforward tool of uncontrollable power: as embodiments of the reason of state, totalitarian goals take precedence over all moral, natural and human rights-based or religiously based legal concepts' (Bracher 1983). In the present context, two things

are noteworthy about this analysis. First, German fascism is presented as
a movement that denied all legal obligations. Second, a religious foundation for law is expressly understood as an alternative and opposite pole
to fascism.

As a rule, Islamic fundamentalists oppose the central position of human-
made positive law, wishing to replace it with 'divine law'. Conflict with
the secular state was thus inevitable. But this stance in no way means that
legal obligations *as such* are denied. Islamic law is a centuries-old, highly
complex legal corpus, an independent system of law that requires legal
interpretation. While the Nazis were able to put an end to the existing
order by means of enabling acts, this is quite impossible in the case of the
Islamic casuistic system, and Islamic law thus entails the capacity to place
limits on Islamic-fundamentalist claims to power. Legal interpretation
can be controlled over the short-term with violence and by the intimida-
tion of the clergy, but it can never be entirely done away with, such that
a latent tension inevitably arises between every dictatorial leader and the
law. In any case, there is no question of legitimacy above the law as in the
case of Hitler. On the contrary, it is Islamic law that provides the Islamic
fundamentalists with political legitimacy in the first place.

The objection can of course be made that modern Islamic fundamentalists reinterpret old legal texts in an eclectic, amateurish and superficial way. But the dualism of laypeople and theologians generates
internal tensions whose effects are felt even in the Iranian revolutionary system: Khomeini's legal constructs, above all the pre-eminence of
the supreme legal scholar (*velayat-e faqih*), were and are contested. In
favourable political circumstances, this independence of Islamic law may
certainly be allied with progressive, democratic forces. For some observers, the Islamic fundamentalists' eclecticism with respect to the Sharia
is also a hopeful sign. Within the modern state, Islamic fundamentalists would undoubtedly emphasize certain features of Islamic law and
ascribe outstanding status to Sharia as a *source of law* or symbolic entity.
But they could scarcely avoid recognizing much of the existing positive law,[4] as it is far more differentiated and appropriate to modern-day
realities, with respect to economic law for example. In any event, there is
a fundamental distinction between the ideological distance from the law
which is characteristic of European fascism and the legal rectitude of the
Islamic fundamentalists, which is raised to the status of a core ideological

---

[4] See the remarks by the Carnegie Endowment on the dearth of legal initiatives put forward
by Islamic organizations: Brown et al. 2006; see also Chapter 3.

programme. Unlike fascism, Islamic fundamentalism is not a form of neo-paganism. As renowned researcher on violence Walter Laqueur puts it, 'Hitler did not engage in Jihad and he did not want to impose anything like the Sharia'.[5]

Socioeconomic corporatism. Islam does not feature any uniform economic doctrine, and it includes both conservative and more liberal views on basic economic issues, with respect to the legitimacy of charging interest, for example (Nienhaus 2000). Large parts of the Iranian economy were nationalized following the Islamic Revolution. In view of incessant economic crises, however, privatization and liberalization have for years formed part of Iranian economic policy. Large fundamentalist opposition groups such as the Egyptian Muslim Brothers are far more economically liberal in outlook than the Iranian leadership. Though there are a number of open questions with respect to the charging of interest, they propagate the idea of the free market economy as a remedy to state corruption and mismanagement, advocate anti-monopolist policies and reject state control of the economy. They thus preach the polar opposite of an economy incorporated into the state and are committed to the idea of a developing middle class.[6] This economically liberal course has been taking shape within the Muslim Brothers for decades. It places them very much within the mainstream of Islamic economic theory, which some radical interpreters endow with a strongly anti-capitalist tenor but which for the 'political Islamists' (as the International Crisis Group defines non-violent, mainstream Islamic fundamentalists) entails no fundamental animosity towards the economic interests of the individual. If implemented, an anti-capitalist approach would shake the foundations of Islamic doctrine, such as the institution of alms-giving (*zakat*), whose goal is social equalization but which amounts to the tacit approval of social inequality. The system of religious endowments (Arabic sing. *waqf*) also implies the autonomous provision of social services within Muslim communities, a provision which, in much the same way as the Christian churches, could not simply be incorporated by the state.

---

[5] Walter Laqueur, *The Origins of Fascism: Islamic Fascism, Islamophobia, Antisemitism*, Oxford University Press, 2006, http://blog.oup.com/2006/10/the_origins_of_2/ (17 February 2008).

[6] Frederik Richter, Wirtschaftspolitik der ägyptischen Muslimbrüder: Korruptionsbekämp fung als Allheilmittel?, [The economic policy of the Egyptian Muslim Brothers: the fight against corruption as a panacea?], http://www.qantara.de/webcom/show_article.php/_c-468/_nr-538/i.html (18 February 2008).

Iranian state Islamic fundamentalism was marked by a tendency to nationalize the economy, particularly in its initial stages. Yet even in this far-reaching model, no extensive form of social corporatism has taken hold that might bear comparison with the National Socialist model, in which every sphere of life, from the economy through the associations to the media was controlled by the political leadership. Despite close ties to the revolutionary system, the Iranian merchants (*bazaris*) represent an independent, traditional middle class economic sector. For much of the history of the Islamic Republic, Iran's media landscape, too, has been subject to far fewer controls than has been assumed by outside observers. Books are censored; yet, monthly magazines were long excluded from censorship, and the large press market also underwent comprehensive liberalization in the era of President Mohammad Khatami (1997–2005) (Amirpur et al. 2000). That this process of opening was later reversed and the policy of reform suppressed certainly underlines the arbitrary nature of Islamic fundamentalist rule in Iran. But it also points to a lively dualism of state and society which did not exist in the fascist systems of Europe. In many fields, Islamic fundamentalist rule in Iran, notably the revolutionary leader and his Guardians of the Revolution, is a kind of parallel system that oversees rather than incorporates enduring political and social institutions, without depriving them of their relative independence. Nor is there any party comparable to the Nazi Party, which occupied a central place in society and into which much of German society was integrated. The classical process of institutionalization around the Shiite clergy places clear limits on the establishment of parallel national organizations.

Social Darwinism. Nazism cultivated a rigid form of Social Darwinism. The preservation of the species (the 'Aryan race') was seen as the state's responsibility, 'racial hygiene' was pursued through forced sterilization and eugenic programmes, and women were forced to bear children for the system while separated from their partners and families. There is no counterpart to these policies in the Islamic fundamentalist scene, unless we wished to suggest a link with the kind of group formation and anti-familial brainwashing common in ultra-radical circles in order to prepare for suicide bombings and terrorist attacks. But this would presumably be a dead end, because the motives here are not attributable to Social Darwinism. Various Islamic fundamentalists cultivate a sometimes pronounced bodily cult centred on the 'purity' of Muslims, but this is bound up with a form of ritualized everyday practice which has nothing to do with eugenics. On the contrary, all political and missionary Muslim fundamentalist organizations do charitable work and try to attract supporters through active efforts to compensate for the lack of social welfare provision within secular systems (see Chapter 2).

Expansionism. Fear of the expansionist tendencies of fundamentalist Islam have been expressed time and again in the West since the Iranian Revolution of 1978–9. In the eyes of many observers, expansionism, world domination and 'holy war' belong together.[7] In 1979, the German magazine *Stern* declared: 'Islam is preparing to conquer the world'.[8] What seemed realistic about this idea at the time was that, in the shape of fundamentalist Islam, a force had appeared whose constant emphasis on the community of Muslims (*umma*) appeared to endanger the authority of the nation state. Over the course of the last three decades, however, it has become clear that, notwithstanding its fraught theoretical relationship to the concept of the nation, *in practice* Islamic fundamentalism pursues realpolitik in much the same way as other systems. Regardless of its at times aggressive anti-American and anti-Western rhetoric, even a state such as Iran has so far waged no expansionist wars. Shireen T. Hunter argues in this connection: 'It would be equally erroneous to view the conduct of all Iranian foreign policy as the fanatical pursuit of a millenarian dream or a quest to establish a so-called Islamic world-order (...). It would be more appropriate to analyze Iran's behavior during the last decade as that of a revolutionary state at different stages of internal consolidation and adaptation to its external setting' (Hunter 1990, 4; see also Karabell 1996, 84). In recent years, it has become clearer than ever that the nationalist principle and the dividing lines between religious groups (Sunnites versus Shiites) now dominate almost entirely the thinking of Islamic fundamentalist states and fundamentalist movements (Roy 2007), with the exception of the cross-border financial aid which states such as Saudi Arabia and Iran constantly make available to kindred movements. Hence, specific Islamic fundamentalist governments may very well act in chauvinistic ways in future – but there is no question of fundamentalist Islam featuring any systematic expansionism that would permit comparison with European fascism. Once again, it is only the small 'global Jihadist' terrorists groups that may be rightly considered to reject national sovereignty.

---

[7] Heinz Nussbaumer, Das Licht aller Gläubigen gegen die Sonne der Arier [The light of all believers against the sun of the Aryans], *Die Welt*, 10 March 1979.

[8] Die Macht des Propheten, [The power of the Prophet], *Stern*, 15 March 1979.

We could continue to pursue the comparison between Islamic fundamentalism and fascism in light of further criteria. But we would increasingly be forced to question whether these should really be considered core aspects of any meaningful definition of totalitarianism and fascism. If Hannah Arendt regarded hatred of the ruling elites as one of the essential traits of German Nazism, we might identify anti-elite iconoclasm as a key feature of fascism in general. In this connection, German historian Götz Aly has gone as far as to compare the student protests of the 1968 generation with National Socialism, as both movements preached struggle and radical action against the ruling elites (Aly 2008). But this demonstrates the weakness of an eclectic comparison that equates two historical phenomena in light of an isolated criterion. Iconoclasm and anti-elitism are undoubtedly parallel features of National Socialism and a fair number of political movements, including the Iranian Revolution, whose key hallmarks included the ousting of the Shah elites and the ending of bourgeois institutional domination (see Chapter 2). German philosopher Peter Sloterdijk has much the same thing in mind when he asserts that Islamic fundamentalism is a case of a totalitarian 'young men's movement' that acts as a focal point for pent-up social rage (Sloterdijk 2006, 344; see also 'Conclusion' in this book). These kinds of remarks are easy to criticize, for they are factually incorrect: modern Islamic fundamentalism is by no means a movement made up solely of men; it is also supported by women, and it is not primarily a youth movement, though the demographic pressure created by young people without prospects has certainly contributed substantially to its rise. But there is a more serious objection, which may be raised against both Aly and Sloterdijk. Is the existence of an iconoclastic youth movement really sufficient evidence for us to justify comparisons with European fascism or totalitarianism? The French Revolution and many other events in world history also embodied such tendencies without being classified as totalitarian or fascist.

In defining what is specific to fascism, we may posit an order of precedence, with racism, policies of racial annihilation and Social Darwinism as its most contemptible features. Corporatism, too, distinguishes fascism from classical authoritarian rule, which involves the despotism of an individual but does not necessarily permeate society in any total way. The *Führerprinzip*, hostility to law and expansionism, meanwhile, are present in one form or another in all types of authoritarian rule. To sum up, the great majority of large Islamic fundamentalist organizations subsumed under the heading of 'political Islamism' by the International Crisis Group fail to fit with the definition of fascism in almost every respect.

They preach neither violent 'cleansing' nor racial fanaticism nor Social Darwinism, and though have a tendency to evoke ethnic-religious bogey-men, they are not apocalyptic movements. They despise secular law but feel bound by Islamic law and, at least in the case of the majority Sunnite version of Islam, have long since given up the idea of a single leader (the caliphate). Only some of them are corporatist and – in practice, at least, over the last thirty years – are no more expansionist in orientation than other forces and political systems. Mainstream Islamic fundamentalism, as studied for example by the Carnegie Endowment for Peace (Brown et al. 2006), is far more reminiscent of radical Protestant movements of earlier centuries than of European fascism. It features strong missionary inclinations and religious zeal, is intolerant and politically motivated, but is not incapable of coming to terms with other parts of society. Unless it is based on the ideology of an extreme minority of 'global Jihadists', Islamic fundamentalism cannot be placed on the same level as European fascism, despite some superficial similarities. It is thus quite wrong to speak here of total power, while the notion of total war is equally incorrect.

Far more, though not all, of the criteria making up the definition of fascism apply to 'global Jihadism', in other words those Islamic groups that preach the active and violent spread of Islam and total holy war, such as the Al Qaeda network of Osama Bin Laden or the GIA in Algeria. In view of the massacres of 'unbelievers' (usually lax Muslims) carried out by the GIA, we may certainly speak of a deliberate programme of annihilation. Analogies with the Khmer Rouge or Nazis suggest themselves. So far, though, none of these groups has managed to take national power, which would allow them to pursue far-reaching corpo-ratist objectives. Structurally, moreover, they are often more anarchistic than hierarchical and leader-oriented. These groups behave like radical anarchists and sectarians. They lack the systematic political and mili-tary character of the Khmer Rouge or European fascists, a result in part of their lack of public support. Despite his fundamental willingness to regard Islamic fundamentalism and fascism as parallel phenomena, even Walter Laqueur ultimately recognized that it might be more analytically productive to replace 'the fascist label' with different classifications of authoritarian rule in the Muslim world (Laqueur 1996, 223).

We find the opposite tendency in the work of certain authors. Frequent comparisons between Hitler and Gamal Abdel Nasser or Hitler and Saddam Hussein suggest that, not just the Islamic fundamentalist state, but also its secular Arab counterpart is fascist. If, as we have seen, reli-gious doctrine and organization may in certain respects be a hindrance

to total power and the destructive inclinations of a given individual and
his clique, is not secular dictatorship the closer parallel? Should we not
speak of 'Arabofascism' rather than 'Islamofascism'? We will leave to
one side the fact that Nasser was embroiled in wars (Yemen, Israel), that
Hussein attacked Iran, and that both modelled themselves on the USSR in
constructing their political systems (state capitalism, one central party).
Despite pronounced concepts of The Enemy, their ideology of power did
not revolve around racist or other forms of mass annihilation based on
enmity towards specific groups. Even Hussein's mass murder of the Kurds
was rooted in his desire to maintain his power in the face of secession-
ist movements. The vast majority of the political murders he carried out
were the manifestation of a quite classical despotism. The development
of Nasser's and Hussein's power perhaps featured elements of the USSR's
totalitarian rule and of the Warsaw Pact, but even this comparison is
valid only to a limited extent: in the field of the economy for example,
the 'Arab socialism' which both dictators espoused never succeeded in
diminishing the key importance of private commerce and agriculture.

Rather than the total transformation of society, Social Darwinist or racist selection and world conquest, it is classical autocracy, in other words
the despotism of an individual, that is the key characteristic of existing
authoritarian power in the Muslim world. There are occasional borrowings from modern Eastern European-style totalitarianism, but these are
not consistently developed. It is thus only in small terrorist groups of
'global Jihadists' that protofascist thought plays a significant role, though
here it is fractured by anarchistic and sectarian tendencies.

ANTI-SEMITISM OR THE RISK OF ETHNICIZATION

It can scarcely be disputed that Jews have been able to live out their lives
with far greater security in the Muslim world than in Christian Europe
over the last two thousand years. While the motif of Jews as 'Christ kill-
ers' long endured in the Christian world, the Koran explicitly recognizes
Judaism as a religion of the book (*ahl al-kitab*). In Europe, religious
motifs became interwoven with social stigmas such as the 'miserly' or
'greedy' Jew, frequently resulting in violence against Jews in Russia,
Poland, Germany and elsewhere. As recently as the Second World War,
German and Polish Jews fled to Muslim countries, particularly Turkey.

The Koran does contain passages that can be interpreted as anti-Jewish,
but their target is Jews as a *Personenverband*, a grouping based on personal ties, rather than as members of a particular religion or as human

beings. While European anti-Semitism denounced Jews as 'subhuman' on account of racial qualities imputed to them, Jews in the Koran are not inferior, but are regarded as both the friends and enemies of God at different points in the text. Thus, the Koran (along with the Hadith, the oral tradition relating the activities of the Prophet Muhammad; Arabic: sing. *Hadith*, pl. *Ahadith*) provides no essentialist definition of Jews but considers Judaism from a religious perspective, as a religion and religious community which is related to Islam and which is to be tolerated. Muhammad concluded the Medina Treaty with the Jews and others, guaranteeing them religious autonomy. The Jews in and around Medina were not expelled and killed because of their faith but because they formed self-contained groups within the Islamic polity of Medina and were even allied with hostile Arab tribes (Paret 2005). But in any case the fundamental tolerance of Judaism as a religion ensured 1400 years of relatively tolerant coexistence between Jews and Muslims under Muslim rule throughout the Middle East (Aziz 2007). The West, with its long history of persecution of the Jews, lacks such a tradition.

However, the ambivalent attitude which Jewish *Personenverbände* inspired in the Prophet Muhammad appeared once again in connection with the foundation of the state of Israel in 1948. The waves of Jewish immigration that changed living conditions in Mandate Palestine in the early twentieth century, slowly at first but with increasing intensity during the 1930s, triggered resistance and animosity on the part of the Arabs. In the course of the various Arab-Israeli wars, most of the Jews living in Arab countries emigrated as tensions with the Muslim Arab population increased. Of the major Jewish communities still living in countries such as Egypt, Morocco and Yemen in the early twentieth century, almost nothing now remains (Krämer 1982). While European-style pogroms and murder are practically unknown in the Middle East, and the anti-Zionist tenor of Arab politics after the Second World War has not eliminated traditional religious tolerance, it has triggered a sharp increase in anti-Jewish feeling in much of the Arab world.

In the words of Bernard Lewis: 'The volume of anti-Semitic books and articles published, the size and number of editions and impressions, the eminence and authority of those who write, publish and sponsor them, their place in school and college curricula, their role in the mass media, would all seem to suggest that classical anti-Semitism is an essential part of Arab intellectual life at the present time – almost as much as happened in Nazi Germany, and considerably more than in late nineteenth and early twentieth century France' (Lewis 1986, 256). We are not dealing here with a race-based anti-Semitism that aspires to liquidate the Jews as in the case of the Nazis. The ethnic and linguistic affinity between Arabs and Hebraic Jews is simply too great for that. This is a nationalistically motivated anti-Judaism, though certain sections of the Arab public in particular no longer distinguish sufficiently between Zionists and Jews. This concept of Jews as The Enemy, charged with ethnic motifs, is a very real contemporary problem.

Distinguishing between European and Muslim Arab anti-Semitism is no easy task, but it is an essential one. The effort is hampered by the fact that, while there have as yet been no attempts at, or calls for, the systematic annihilation of Jews either within Islamic fundamentalism (apart from small terrorist groups) or in any Islamic country, time and again nauseating expressions of support for the deeds of the Nazis are to be heard. During the 1961 trial of Adolf Eichmann, organizer of the Holocaust, Hannah Arendt noted: '(N)ewspapers in Damascus and Beirut, in Cairo and Jordan, did not hide their sympathy for Eichmann or their regret that "he had not finished the job"; a broadcast from Cairo on the day the trial opened even injected a slightly anti-German note into its comments, complaining that there was not "a single incident in which one German plane flew over one Jewish settlement and dropped one bomb on it throughout the last world war"' (Arendt 1963, 10).

What such observations lack, however, is acknowledgement of the fact that Jews continue to be recognized as human beings, believers and citizens by the states of the Islamic world. Egyptian president Gamal Abdel Nasser (1952/54–70), for example, often described as a new 'Hitler' in the West, pursued a quite sophisticated policy with respect to Jews. On the one hand, he slandered them, presenting them as the bogeyman in the struggle against Israel. On the other hand, he assured the tens of thousands of Jews living in the country until 1967 of his fundamental support. In 1963, for example, he attended the ordination of the last Egyptian chief rabbi, Chaim Duweik, in a synagogue in Cairo.[9] Would Hitler have done this? Certainly not. His successor Anwar al-Sadat's visit to Jerusalem in 1977, the Oslo agreement between the PLO and Israel, the numerous meetings and common initiatives characteristic of Arab and Israeli civil societies in the 1990s – these things do not point to any unbridgeable ideological enmity, but rather to the political vulnerability of Muslim- or Arab-Jewish relations. There is a risk that ethnic-religious concepts of The Enemy will develop, take hold and become politically

---

[9] 'All die perversen Helden', [All the perverse heroes], *Der Spiegel*, 28 November 1977.

virulent; such concepts are dangerous, but they are a standard feature of political cultures the world over. Arab Muslim anti-Semitism is not anchored in racism in the way that any equation of Islam, Islamic fundamentalism or secular Arab nationalism with the ideology of the Nazis might imply.

Historian of the Middle East Gerhard Höpp has pointed out that the idea of any correspondence between Arab and Nazi anti-Semitism is untenable in light of the history of the Second World War (Höpp 1994). According to Höpp, one of the arguments that has frequently been put forward highlights the emergence during the war of homemade protofascist movements such as the ultra-nationalists around Antun Saada in Syria. This grouping often deployed a symbolic language similar to National Socialism, but espoused no anti-Jewish ideologies. These protofascist groups also included the Christian Falangists in Lebanon. They were characterized not by anti-Jewish racism, but by small-state nationalism or religious particularism. They did not cooperate with the Nazis.

The fact that the Grand Mufti of Jerusalem, Haj Amin al-Husseini, sympathized with the Nazis during the Second World War is far better known than the fact that this was of minor significance within the Arab world. Fewer than a thousand Arabs fought on the side of the Axis powers while, Höpp tells us, almost half a million fought for the Allies, among them Algerians, Tunisians, Moroccans and Palestinians. The key reason the sympathies of many Arabs lay with fascist Europe was not Hitler's racial ideology, but the fact that 'the Axis' was the enemy of their enemy, the colonial powers of Britain and France. The logic that my enemy's enemy is my friend also applied to Germany's relationship to the Arabs: they were tolerated as allies, but many statements by German diplomats and Nazis of the time, according to Höpp, suggest that they were despised as 'subhuman' just as much as the Jews. In the eyes of German Nazis, Arabs too were racial 'Semites'.

The basic patterns of a strategic but by no means fundamental sympathy with National Socialism still survive in parts of the Muslim world. Often, anything which damages and poses a political challenge to Israel and its Western backers, especially the EU, is welcomed. This applies to the great attention paid to the trials of Roger Garaudy, a French Holocaust denier, in the Arab world. It also applies to similar statements by Iranian President Mahmud Ahmadinejad during the 'cartoon controversy' of 2006. There are good reasons for believing that Ahmadinejad's statements on Israel and the Holocaust should be regarded as a political manoeuvre intended to highlight Western double standards with respect to freedom of speech. But this does *not* mean that Islamic fundamentalist Iran has ever intended, or intends now, to annihilate Jews, though living conditions for Jews have deteriorated there.

Compared with the Jews in the Ottoman empire, Jews in Iran have historically often faced greater difficulties. Within the complicated religious milieu of Iran, home of the dissident Shiite branch of Islam and a large number of minority religions such as the Baha'i, as well as a large Jewish community, the rule of Mohammad Reza Shah Pahlavi (1953–78) is considered the heyday of the Jewish community. Pahlavi's modernism, his Western orientation and, above all, his goal of creating strong bonds with the national minorities and rigidly anti-Islamic policies (such as compulsory removal of the veil) are among the key reasons the Jews were respected and influential minorities during this era (Menashri 1991, 2002). After Khomeini took power in 1979, it initially appeared that, while Iran's secular character under the Shah had protected the Jews, the Islamic Revolution threatened their existence. Khomeini declared the Jews the 'fifth column' of American Imperialism. But he soon moderated this stance and again began to distinguish between Jews and Zionists in public speeches. He emphasized the equality of religions – a position that shows many similarities to the fusion of recognition and populist stigmatization often exhibited by Western politicians with respect to Middle Eastern immigrants. As individuals and affiliates of a religion, Jews in Iran are protected by the state ideology – a crucial and fundamental difference from European fascism. At the same time, they are frequently the targets of populist attacks (Menashri 2002, 400).

Assessing the Palestinian Islamic fundamentalists of Hamas is a more complicated task. Its ideology is violent and oriented towards national liberation. As its violence is at times deliberately aimed at civilians, we may classify Hamas, together with all 'Jihadist' groups that have declared 'holy war' against the West, as 'terrorist', despite fundamental differences from Osama Bin Laden's Al Qaeda (see Chapter 7). But is Hamas also anti-Semitic? A number of authors have answered in the affirmative (Küntzel 2002; Robinson 2004, 131).[10] The diction of Hamas's charter does, in fact, feature unmistakable anti-Semitic traces, above all when Jews are blamed for the problems of the world and

---

[10] See also the review of the book by Alexander Flores at: http://www.isf-freiburg.org/verlag/rezensionen/kuentzel-djihad_rez-flores.html (20 February 2008).

the 'Protocols of the Elders of Zion' are cited as pseudo-scientific evidence. Yet the charter does not call for the elimination of the Jews. Rather, it explicitly expresses the view that Jews and Muslims could live together in peace under Muslim rule(!) (Baumgarten 2006, 58 ff.). Even Hamas, then, sees no religious ideological basis for the destruction of the Jews and Judaism. Rather, after the fashion of conspiracy theories, it attacks not only Israel but Jews as a whole, thus creating an ethno-religious concept of The Enemy. Jews are significant, not as Jews, but as national enemies. Hamas is thus replicating its own view of the story of Muhammad, who preached coexistence with Jews but rejected any Jewish claim to power.

Hence, despite borrowing language and motifs from European fascism, the basic problem of Hamas ideology is not a racist policy of annihilation – as Israeli historian Moshe Zuckermann states, this is a specifically 'Western, Christian phenomenon'[11] – but rather an overdrawn ethno-religious concept of The Enemy within a struggle for national self-assertion. The Jews are constructed as an ethnic group: a form of ideological construction typical to nationalist modernity (as it happens, this has been qualified in the last few years as representatives of Hamas have repeatedly distanced themselves from the anti-Jewish passages in the Hamas charter; Hroub 2006, 31 ff.).

We must keep in mind, though, that such concepts of The Enemy may form part of a policy of mass annihilation. They are dangerous ideological models, as wars in Yugoslavia and elsewhere have shown time and again. But they have nothing to do with the specifically racist and genocidal anti-Semitism that emerged in Germany in the absence, moreover, of any genuine conflict with Jews. As in Iran, the Islamic fundamentalism of Hamas expresses not genocidal fanaticism but claims to power. The idea of dividing the former 'Palestine' into Israeli and Palestinian states, in other words recognizing the existence of an independent Jewish state not under Muslim rule, is something that Hamas has yet to embrace. The desire for re-conquest is supported with by an overdrawn oppositional notion of the enemy that criticizes, not the colonialism of Israeli settlements, but Jews *as such*. But this also means that after any political resolution of the Middle East conflict, this form of anti-Semitism would

---

[11] Die Logik der Okkupation. Eine Diskussion mit dem israelischen Historiker Moshe Zuckermann [The logic of occupation. A discussion with Israeli historian Moshe Zuckermann], in: *Sozialistische Positionen*, http://www.sopos.org/aufsaetze/3cee936fd4a2e/1.phtml (20 February 2008).

in all probability be greatly reduced. How quickly progress can be made was evident in the first few years after the Oslo Accords of 1993, when, among other things, then foreign minister Shimon Peres at a conference in Casablanca, Morocco set out Israel's plans for the economic development of the Arab Middle East. This was by no means a period of total reconciliation, but it did show the cultural flexibility of the Arab Islamic world.

That the anti-Semitism of the Middle East conflict is nationalistic rather than fascist and genocidal is also apparent in the fact that there are parallels on the Israeli side. As a rule, nationalistic concepts of the enemy exist like mirror images on both sides; fascist concepts of the enemy, in contrast, entail a one-sided imperative to destroy. As early as the mid-1980s, in his book *Arabs and Jews*, which won the Pulitzer Prize, David K. Shipler showed that the Israeli Jewish perception of Arabs was also laden with stereotypes and concepts of the enemy (Shipler 1986). In recent times, the minister for strategic planning in the cabinet of Prime Minister Ehud Olmert, Avigdor Lieberman, repeatedly called for ethnic cleansing, large-scale execution of Palestinians, deportations and the unlawful settlement of land, earning him worldwide criticism for inciting hatred against Palestinians.[12] He even called for thousands of political prisoners to be drowned in the Dead Sea, offering to provide the buses to transport them there.[13] In 1994, Israeli citizen Baruch Goldstein carried out a massacre inspired by his hatred of Arabs. In 2004, rabbis justified the killing of civilians.[14] These examples show that many Israelis, including political leaders, have fundamental reservations about Arabs. What is more, through the 'law of return', which guarantees every Jew in the world Israeli citizenship, the Israeli state itself blurs the boundary between Judaism as a *religion* and Zionism as a form of *Jewish nationalism*. Hence, ethnicization from outside (by Arabs or Muslims in general) must at least in part be seen as a reaction to ethnicization from within (by Israelis), though such anti-Arab views are distortions in that, whatever the state of Israel does, many Jews in the world do not feel represented by its policies.

[12] Jonathan Steele, The Rise of the Rightwinger Who Takes His Cue from Putin, *The Guardian*, 2 November 2006.

[13] Entry in Wikipedia, http://en.wikipedia.org/wiki/Avigdor_Lieberman (21 February 2008).

[14] Israeli Rabbis: Don't Spare Civilians, http://osdir.com/ml/ballistichelmet.heads/2004–09/msg00033.html (21 February 2008), original text: Khalid Amayreh, Israeli Rabbis: Don't Spare Civilians, 7 September 2004, www.Aljazeera.net (21 February 2008).

DEMOCRATIC POLYARCHIES AND THE CHANGING FACE
OF AUTHORITARIANISM: DICTATORIAL TEMPTATIONS

Even if we reject the theory of Islamic fascism, variants of authoritarian rule constitute the predominant model of political power in the contemporary Islamic world. The core criteria of any democracy, such as the ability to vote a government in or out of office, free elections and the safeguarding of human rights have been realized in only a few countries (see Chapter 3). It is meaningless to deny how fundamentally the political systems of most Muslim countries differ from those of North America and Europe. However, more meticulous comparison reveals shades of grey that qualify any black-and-white division into Islamic authoritarian and Western democratic systems. In fact, various political systems in Islamic countries have developed into democracies, while many other countries are characterized by liberal transitions and proto-democratic political trends. What is more, Western democracies, particularly since 11 September 2001, have exhibited tendencies towards political developments of dubious democratic legitimacy. Are the democracies of the West and the modernizing autocracies of the Islamic world moving closer together in how they exercise power?

In North Africa, the Middle East and Central, South and Southeast Asia there are significant differences in the character of authoritarian rule, making it difficult to lump their political systems together under the same heading of 'authoritarianism'. Pakistan, despite being ruled by military dictator Pervez Musharraf, held parliamentary elections in February 2008 that marginalized his party – a prelude to his resignation the same year. Similar developments are familiar from Iran, where a dualism of democratic and authoritarian structures has developed, one that also characterized twentieth-century Turkey.

In the Arab world, this kind of dualism is evident only in embryonic form in a small number of countries. With the exception of Lebanon, there are essentially no free elections that might change the formulation of political objectives. Monarchies and elected governments do coexist in Morocco and Jordan, but the freedom of electoral processes is no more guaranteed there than in Egypt. Many Arab countries have, however, seen major progress in the fields of freedom of expression and media freedom, though these revolutions in the public sphere have so far failed to develop sufficient system-changing momentum to trigger democratization. Particularly as a result of cross-border Arab satellite television and the Internet, authoritarianism finds itself confronted by a new form of critical public sphere, one that points to a changing political culture and indicates that the distance between rulers and ruled is growing (K. Hafez 2008a, 2008b). In February 2008, the ministers of public information of many member states of the Arab League resolved to tighten up licensing regulations for the media: a clear sign that the authoritarian state feels challenged by media and in the public sphere. However, because a number of countries, such as Lebanon and Qatar, which are centres of media activity, rejected the resolution, there is little prospect that media policy will in fact be tightened up.

What kind of authoritarianism is it that struggles to cope with the published opinions of the media? How long can it survive? What developmental tendencies can be discerned? British and American researchers have long subdivided authoritarian political systems into 'hard' and 'soft' varieties. Hard authoritarian systems penetrate society, economy and the public sphere. In the contemporary Arab world, this applies primarily to Libya, Tunisia, Syria, Sudan and Saudi Arabia, and has long applied to Iraq. The revolutionary states, in particular, took their lead from the model of the USSR, though their form of totalitarianism, as discussed earlier, never emulated this model in any comprehensive sense – the economy, for example, was never vigorously collectivized. Soft authoritarian systems allow a greater degree of coexistence between state and society. Such systems, which currently include Egypt, Morocco and Jordan in the Arab world, allow considerable freedom of opinion. At times, they even tolerate criticism of the government, which is still against the law, although it is far from unusual for the government to respond with arrests and other sanctions, highlighting a state of profound legal uncertainty. Soft authoritarian systems are attempting to improve the economic output of their ailing state capitalist systems through privatization and a process of international opening, without, however, giving up ultimate control of economic policy. They are also strengthening participative political institutions (such as parliaments), though this is not intended to challenge the ruling elites. In other words, states of this kind show a tendency towards the increased manipulation and clientelist infiltration of superficially democratic institutions. The academic literature shows no firm agreement on which and to what degree these criteria must be developed to justify the labels of hard or soft authoritarianism. While scholars more or less agree that Arab countries can be divided into one or other of these categories, Iran is often considered a special case because it features aspects of both systems, such as relatively free elections and strict religious regulations (Chapter 3).

In a little noticed paper, even Bernard Lewis, one of the hardest critics of political conditions in the Islamic world – a man who greatly influenced the policies of George W. Bush, who was never likely to be accused of playing down political realities – recognizes that Arab, Middle Eastern and Central Asian political systems are becoming increasingly differentiated. He distinguishes between 'traditional autocracies' (mainly the kingdoms and emirates of the Arabian Peninsula), 'modernized autocracies' (Jordan, Egypt, Morocco), 'fascist dictatorships' (Syria and Iraq under Saddam Hussein), 'radical Islamic regimes' (Iran and Sudan) and the 'Central Asian republics', this last category being introduced by Lewis not as means of classifying political systems but in order to underline the regional, cultural and historical independence of Central Asia (Lewis 2003b, 215 f.). Leaving to one side the fact that this system is incomplete (In which category would we place Tunisia and Algeria for example?), that too much weight is placed on ideological differences (Are radical Islamic regimes not essentially revolutionary regimes very similar both to 'fascist dictatorships' and 'modernized autocracies'?) and that, as argued above, fascism as a concept is misleading, Lewis nonetheless acknowledges that some Islamic autocracies are in fact undergoing a process of limited modernization.

This is a good place to recall that many Western democratic systems also experienced long periods of 'enlightened monarchy' (in Prussia for example) and modernist dictatorship (as in Spain) before becoming democratic. This does not mean that we can discern political processes in the contemporary Islamic world that might be described as political 'reforms from above'. In the research on political transformation, this terminology is reserved for a deliberate and substantial pro-democratic shift in the character of a political system (the Gorbachev model). Elites, especially in the Arab world, are not at present promoting any clear-cut reformist dynamic. In the interests of ensuring the survival of the authoritarian system, however, many governments find themselves compelled to pursue a policy of limited liberalization.

As early as 1993, Francis Fukuyama suspected that the concept of soft authoritarianism, also known as 'neo-authoritarianism', would become more popular and might emerge as a competitor to Western democracy as a role model of political development.[15] However, Fukuyama and

---

[15] Jay Branegan, Is Singapore a Model for the West?, Time, 18 January 1993, http://www.time.com/time/magazine/article/0,9171,977490,00.html?iid=chix-sphere (21 February 2008).

others above all had in mind prosperous Southeast Asian states such as Singapore and perhaps China in more recent times, a country whose soft authoritarianism is becoming apparent primarily in the economic sphere, while other aspects of its power remain hard authoritarian (Pei 2000). This form of developmental dictatorship is, in fact, attracting increasing support in other parts of the world. As stated by Joseph S. Nye, professor at Harvard University and one of America's best-known political scientists, China's global resonance as a developmental model is growing – something that Nye calls 'soft power', as intellectual and cultural influences often have a greater impact within international politics than the capacity for military intervention.[16] Can 'soft authoritarianism' become 'soft power'?

This question becomes interesting when we cease to consider it in isolation and place it in the context of the critique of Western democracy, which has been increasingly vehement since 11 September 2001. While the West repeatedly called on the Islamic world to move towards democracy, following the attacks on the World Trade Center and the Pentagon, there were increasing signs that Western democracies were regressing in an authoritarian direction. In his book *The Sorrows of Empire*, renowned Asia expert Chalmers Johnson argues that following these attacks and the Iraq War of 2003, the USA finds itself on the way to becoming an imperialistic and militaristic state (Johnson 2004). As evidence of this, he cites the USA's permanent entanglement in wars across the world, the gradual restriction of constitutionally guaranteed civil rights, the system of propaganda, as exemplified by the campaign of disinformation undertaken by the American government before the war in Iraq ('weapons of mass destruction') and looming economic ruin. In this view, the internal and external crises characteristic of imperialistic policies are closely connected (see Chapter 6), though Johnson does not go into detail here. What exactly does he mean when he refers to the destruction of domestic freedoms? Will the encroachments of the Patriot Act inevitably result in a militaristic state and 'regime change'? Much of Johnson's vision is hypothetical. But it is true that American law is being sidestepped in certain institutions, in the Guantánamo penal facility for example.

Following the attacks of 11 September and the wars in Afghanistan and Iraq, Sheldon S. Wolin of Princeton University suggests that an 'inverted

[16] Joseph S. Nye, The Rise of China's Soft Power, *The Wall Street Journal Asia*, 29 December 2005.

totalitarianism' is gaining momentum in the United States (Wolin 2008). In contrast to classical authoritarianism, the author asserts, in this system of rule democratic institutions are not smashed but hollowed out. Rather than openly destroying democracy, inverted totalitarianism poses as its protector. Wolin characterizes 11 September as comparable to the Reichstag fire – a symbolic event that ushered in the de facto abolition of democracy. The existence of parallel political structures – a state under the rule of law *and* one that engages in torture (Guantánamo, Abu Ghraib), where there is freedom of opinion *and* propagandistic manipulation of the media by governments ('weapons of mass destruction' in Iraq) – is the sign of a democracy managed by small elites. If Wolin is right, then Weimar came to grief as a result of its 'thin' democratic political culture. Classical democracies such as the USA, meanwhile, in which the belief in democracy is deeply rooted, are gradually hollowed out rather than abolished through coups d'état.

The critique of the reliability of democracy is also growing in other parts of the Western hemisphere. In a widely read essay, Australian Daniel Ross develops his vision of the impending emergence of 'violent democracy' (Ross 2004). According to Ross, following the political trans-formation of 1989–90, Western democracy entered an era of 'divinity' in which it assumed that it no longer had any internal or external enemies. New horizons are to be opened up by means of an aggressive global expansion powered by capitalism, armed force and culture (Ross 2004, 25). Just as Nazism believed itself to be taking on the Jews, the West, Ross argues, is now battling against an invisible enemy, Islamic terrorism. Ross makes it clear that the scale of the destruction is not comparable and that Al Qaeda is very real, but asserts that the ethical dimensions of the battle against the enemies of freedom and democracy are becoming increasingly nebulous (Ross 2004, 140).

A growing number of critics are assailing retrogressive domestic poli-cies and restrictions on civil rights. They see a crisis in Western democ-racy, in which social institutions are too weak to defend themselves against the erosion of the liberal constitutional state, as exemplified by state attacks on Arabs and Muslims in the USA, which seem to be usher-ing in a new 'McCarthy era', sometimes by bypassing the justice system (Hagopian 2004). The media, intended as a corrective force, is at the same time increasingly being manipulated by government propaganda, its role called into question by restrictive anti-terrorism laws, up to and including the coercive detention of journalists and dismissals for the wrong kind of reporting (Hess and Kalb 2003; Miller 2004; Schechter

2003; Thussu and Freedman 2003; Tumber and Palmer 2004; Zeliser and Allan 2002). When governments ignore public opinion, we might extend the critics' arguments to suggest that this weakened public sphere is ceasing to function as a 'fourth estate' linking the people with the executive. This applied to the governments of Spain and Italy, which followed the transatlantic hegemon of the USA into war in Iraq despite clear public opposition.

This autocritique of Western democracy is certainly worth considering. It leads on to the question of whether it is really possible to divide up the partially modernized autocracies of the Islamic world on the one hand and the democracies of the Western world on the other into two ideal types. Perhaps we need to come up with a more precise definition of the 'real type' – in Max Weber's sense – of both these political forms. Such ideas were first put forward by the likes of Hannah Arendt, who not only warned of the dangers of authoritarianism and totalitarianism, but also described the authoritarian temptations of democracy (Arendt 1951). In modern political science, Robert A. Dahl's concept of polyarchy has proved a useful approach. In contrast to monarchy and oligarchy, rule by an individual or a small number of people, Dahl describes democracy as rule by the many, while referring to any full development of popular sovereignty as an ideal typical, unattainable state (Dahl 1971, 1989). When, for example, Dahl declares equal access to the public sphere for all and the general availability of alternative political information essential elements of a developed polyarchy, it is clear that this is not fully realizable, as barriers to access to the public sphere vary greatly according to socio-demographic factors such as education. Particularly in the USA, this has given rise to a powerful movement known as 'public journalism' over the last twenty years, one highly critical of the dearth of opportunities to participate in the public sphere open to the average American citizen (Forster 2006; Merritt 1998; Rosen 1999). Many critics have pointed to the lack of legitimacy of professional journalism, whose critical function is impaired by a lack of internal media freedom, the interests of capital and political influences (Donsbach 1982; Herman and Chomsky 1994).

The difference between the still underdeveloped but increasingly participatory public sphere in many Islamic countries (K. Hafez 2001, 2008a, 2008b) and the reality of freedom of opinion within Western journalism is still large, but no longer fundamental. It is highly questionable whether we can still speak of two entirely different media systems. However, the greatest difference lies in other subsystems of society, above all in the political system in the narrow sense of the three classical powers. Despite the justified critique of Western democracy that has emerged in the aftermath of 11 September, it is indisputable that the degree of internal violence in the developed democracies is now at its lowest historical level. Jochen Hippler's assumption that authoritarian states often feature a remarkably low level of political violence while some democratic states – he cites India and Colombia as examples – are marked by a high level of violence (Hippler 2006, 69 f.) is misleading. Neither state is a developed democracy in the Western sense and each only just meets the minimal criteria of political system change: free elections and unhindered changes of governments as well as freedom of opinion. Under the difficult conditions pertaining in developing countries and unstable nation states, the consolidation of the constitutional state is a multi-generational project. It is not the democratic system that produces violence but rather its complex socioeconomic environments. The authoritarian system, even in its most modernized form, produces its own political violence, as evident in so-called 'modern autocracies' (Lewis) such as Egypt, where many thousands of political prisoners are behind bars. An authoritarian system, such as a military dictatorship, may restore order over the short term in a country wracked by civil war – but this is far from making it an alternative system for the reduction of internal violence.

With respect to forms of political rule, the gulf between most countries of the Islamic world and the West is still large. It must be recognized, however, that forward leaps may occur very rapidly indeed and in countries such as Turkey, Indonesia, Bangladesh, and to some extent in Lebanon too, have in fact done so. Under favourable historical circumstances, the modern (soft) autocracy in the Islamic world, challenged by a robust opposition, might meet the basic criteria of democratic system change within a very brief time span. Few observers would have thought countries such as Japan and Korea capable of doing so after the Second World War. But the East Asian example also points to the fact that structural conditions are vital to the further development of democracy in the Islamic world. Without them, stagnation and disappointment would quickly set in. As an ally of the USA, Japan enjoyed its protection, allowing it to develop economically and socially. The Middle East, particularly in light of the conflicts in Israel/Palestine, Afghanistan and Iraq, for which the West bears much responsibility, and the ongoing policy of containment with respect to Iran, lacks preconditions favourable to the development of modern autocracy into genuine democracy.

MODERN SLAVERY: A COMMON CHALLENGE

For some time, the social sciences have been preoccupied by a new concept that lies on the margins of the topic 'political violence' but is nonetheless closely bound up with it: 'modern slavery'. Unlike classical slavery, it no longer refers to a legal status, but to a factual situation in which people are deprived of some of their freedom in terms of labour laws or in a physical sense, as in forced prostitution, the exploitation of illegal immigrants or other fields of systematic unethical treatment. Generally speaking, social factors, such as having a poor family back in the home country, make it subjectively impossible for the individuals concerned to seek legal protection (Follmar-Otto 2007, 64). As slavery is officially prohibited within all the political systems of the Western and Islamic worlds, at first sight the phenomenon of 'modern slavery' seems to have nothing to do with political and legal systems. We are nonetheless dealing here with *political* violence, because some of the causes as well as possible solutions are very closely connected with political systems.

It is estimated, for example, that hundreds of thousands of illegal immigrants work in the French catering trade alone.[17] With falsified documents, they often pay social insurance contributions based on the lowest of wages. If they wish to claim benefits under the health insurance scheme, these are often withheld because of their forged documents. But because such cases are not reported, there is no response from the political sphere and the underground economy continues to thrive. Of the many millions of modern slaves worldwide, more than 10 percent are thought to live in the industrialized countries (McQuade 2007). Other centres of slavery are countries such as India, China, and the Arabian Gulf states with their many foreign workers, many of whom live in disgraceful conditions. Restrictive immigration policies increase the social pressure on the illegal sector and strengthen the basis for exploitative working conditions akin to slavery. Only in recent years has a political awareness of the problems facing this sector gradually begun to emerge in the Western industrialized countries, in South Asia and in the Arabian Gulf states.[18]

From a historical point of view, the British led the way in abolishing classical slavery. But the slavery was made illegal throughout the Ottoman

---

[17] Dorothea Hahn, Pariser Luxusköche verderben den Brei [Top-class Parisian chefs spoil the broth], *die tageszeitung*, 15 February 2008.

[18] Kuwait, for example, announced improved protection for domestic workers in 2008. More than 200 representatives of the job placement sector from Sri Lanka and Kuwait signed a corresponding declaration of intent. IPS Weltblick, 28 April 2008.

empire only shortly after its abolition in the United States in 1889 (Segal 2001, 155). On the Arabian Peninsula, slavery endured far longer in certain places: in Saudi Arabia it was abolished only in the 1960s. But this developmental lag is an exception akin to the late introduction of female suffrage in Switzerland (1971), Liechtenstein (1984) or the canton of Appenzell (1990). Historically, Arab society was marked by a centuries-old cultural rift. On the one hand there existed a brutal slave trade, yet on the other the Koran condemned racism, and it was significantly easier for slaves to advance socially and gain their freedom within the Ottoman empire than in the Christian West. Arab society featured a double standard with respect to its slaves very similar to that regarding animals in modern society in light of factory farming and mass slaughter: people are fond of animals while largely suppressing moral concerns. The British colonial masters in the Middle East displayed similar hypocrisy. While children were still working themselves to death in British mines in the late nineteenth century, missionary pressure to abolish slavery was brought to bear on the Ottoman empire, which did at least contribute to advances in this regard. France prohibited trade in slaves in its colonial possessions from the mid-nineteenth century, but often used those emancipated as a source of cheap labour.

Critics of the concept of 'modern slavery' point out that migrants generally enter a country voluntarily, and the criterion of abduction, as with classical slavery, is therefore lacking (Follmar-Otto 2007, 65). Nonetheless, unethical exploitation is a fact. Furthermore, trade in human beings is still going on, above all in the context of the tremendous disparity in wealth between North and South, and particularly in the case of the abduction of children who are later adopted. We can also refer to the slave trade in cases involving abduction, deceit and coercion (Sölkner and Uhl 2007).

In sum, there are certain parallels between the Islamic world and the West. The classical slave trade involved transactions between the Middle East, Europe and America at the expense of African and Asian peoples, and this trade was abolished at about the same time. Today, both the Islamic world and the West are confronted by the problem of modern slavery. It remains to be seen whether further development of the Western constitutional state and of industrial health and safety regulations will ensure that more is done to combat this phenomenon in future.

6

Imperialism: Autocracy, Democracy and Violence

The events of 11 September 2001 ignited a scholarly debate on the new US imperialism. The war on Iraq only added to the impression that the United States – and Europe in its wake – is practicing a form of imperial rule that lacks sufficient basis in international law through military intervention, wars and occupation regimes. The concept of imperialism, long regarded as an outdated postulate of Marxist theory and had largely disappeared from the academic world, has become respectable again, though there is no final clarity about how to define it. Within the political sphere, however, both left- and right-wing interpreters of world politics essentially agree that there is a Western claim to power that goes beyond the Western nation state, though the goals, legitimacy and necessity of Western intervention are greatly contested. Political violence is by no means entirely banished or proscribed in the West but is justified in contemporary terms.

How does this compare with the expansionist tendencies of Islamic states? The Arab world, Turkey, Iran and Indonesia also have an imperial history – but do they have an imperial present? Certainly in embryonic form, sometimes even in the form of chauvinistic cultural aspirations, but only to a limited degree as a political reality. There is a possibility of border disputes and bilateral wars. Given the political weakness of Islamic states, however, no country is now in a position to make good on any imperial aspirations to rule several countries and regions, as occurred so often throughout the history of the Islamic world. Comparison of the Islamic and Western worlds reveals a marked asymmetry in how political violence is practiced. While the former's primary problem is justifying violence *within* the state, the latter attracts criticism because of its use of force *beyond* its borders. Only in those cases where political violence takes the form of terrorism, rather than being a means of exercising power, do extremist forces within the Islamic world continue to harbour global aspirations. The Islamic world is carrying out 'domestic colonization' in the form of authoritarian violence; the West, on the other hand, is carrying out acts of international violence and waging bloody wars.

In the international context, are the Western democracies ultimately more violent than the Islamic states, which are often regarded as 'fascist' or totalitarian? Scholars are now looking at connections between the nature of the political system of democracy and international violence in quite new ways. Immanuel Kant's postulate of 'eternal peace', according to which the republican nature of the state constitutes a basis for world peace, must be rethought in view of the relations between the Western democratic countries and the authoritarian Islamic states. But even if Kant was wrong, does it mean that Marxists who assumed that the primacy of Western economic interests is the driving force of imperialism were right? Western imperialism must be discussed, not only against the background of its economic drivers, but also in light of the hidden weaknesses in the democratic system, which exhibits its own legitimatory constraints. The West's relations with the Islamic world will largely depend on how it structures the relationship between domestic and international political violence in future.

THE WEST IN THE MIDDLE EAST: A PANOPLY
OF INTERNATIONAL VIOLENCE

The ancestral homelands of Western democracy, the old democracies of the United States and Britain, spent much of their history in a political condition that we would now describe as semi- or pre-democratic, at best. Slavery was abolished in the late nineteenth century, only a little more than one hundred years ago. In countries such as the USA, Britain and Germany, women gained the right to vote only from 1918 on. Until then, subtracting slaves and women, less than half the population actually enjoyed full civil rights, and these countries were advanced in this respect. In France female suffrage was introduced only in 1944 and in Italy, in 1945. These facts are relevant to the topic of imperialism because they show that the classical European colonial powers were still developing countries in democratic terms. Only in this light can we understand how they managed to exist, in some cases for a very long time, in a state of ideological schizophrenia in which the civic-republican freedom of their own populations contrasted with the servitude of the colonized peoples. It is true that in the nineteenth century, civil liberties became more popular in the old democracies and in many European countries gradually prevailed over the old monarchical orders. But the definition of 'citizen' was conceived as narrowly as possible. In any case, women, slaves and colonized peoples were excluded from this category.

Again, only in this light can we understand the brutality of European colonial rule: around thirty million Africans were carried off into slavery, and many millions died in the colonial wars waged by the British, French, Belgians, Spaniards and Germans (LeVine 2005, 50 f.). The human costs were very high, but so were the economic ones, and these still contribute greatly to the disparity in wealth between North and South. The Indian subcontinent was responsible for around 25 percent of worldwide manufacturing production in 1750, while the contemporary figure is less than 5 percent (LeVine 2005, 52); a downward trend that is certainly due in part to internal crises but also to military rule and exploitation by the West. It is not just the classical colonial powers of Spain and Portugal, responsible for the annihilation of entire peoples in South America, that had few scruples about using violence in their colonial territories. The same is true of the modern colonial powers of Britain, France and Germany. Their actions were governed by an economic logic, and this meant showing no consideration for human life in the colonized territories. At best, the colonized countries were left with vague hopes of eventually being civilized by their colonial masters – a vision that was more pronounced in France than in Britain, where such colonialists as Lord Cromer, governor of Egypt, made no secret of their contempt for the local population. In countries, such as Iraq, created after the First World War, British colonial rule was brutal (Simons 1994).

It is thus no surprise that the United States' rise to the status of leading global power after the Second World War awakened great hopes in the former colonial territories (Hafez 2003). By promoting the League of Nations in the First World War and emphasizing the right to national independence, American president Woodrow Wilson set new standards. While colonial states such as Belgium in the Congo or France in Algeria were still fighting for the remnants of their colonial power into the 1960s, the United States distanced itself from colonialism. The USA itself came into being as a result of an anti-colonial tradition. When Britain, facing bankruptcy after the Second World War, returned its mandate over Palestine to the United Nations in 1947, the USA felt compelled to involve itself more deeply in Middle Eastern politics. The founding of the state of Israel and the subsequent Arab-Israeli war of 1948 created a conflictual dynamic that was impossible to evade. In the Cold War, every regional conflict threatened to become a proxy war between the super-powers of the USA and USSR. There was not yet a close alliance between the USA and Israel. On the contrary, the first country to recognize Israel was the USSR, while American efforts were directed towards integrating the Arab states into a system of alliances in order to contain the Soviet Union. Among other things, the Baghdad Pact signed in 1955 incorporated Turkey, Iran and Iraq into the 'Northern Front' intended to contain the USSR. In the Suez Crisis of 1956, Eisenhower sharply condemned the military attack by Britain, France and Israel, describing it as a colonialist action towards a now independent country, Egypt, and no longer in keeping with the times. The USA thus established itself in Middle Eastern eyes as a country continuing the political tradition of Woodrow Wilson, co-founder of the League of Nations, a power without a colonialist past seeking new ways of dealing with the region based cooperation.

The decisive early years of American policy on the Middle East began, a time during which the inconsistency of American foreign policy goals became increasingly clear. On the one hand, Wilson's post-colonial doctrine demanded cooperative ways of dealing with the young states of North Africa, the Middle East and other parts of the Islamic world, such as Indonesia and India (with its large Muslim minority). On the other hand, the West's growing need for oil and its desire for Cold War supremacy required that the Middle East states submit to American interests: a requirement now increasingly met through military and economic pressure as well as secret service activities. In 1953, following Iran's nationalization of its oil resources, the USA toppled the democratic government of Mohammad Mosaddeq with the help of the CIA, installing Mohammad Reza Shah Pahlavi as ruler – an act for which the USA paid dearly twenty-five years later in the form of the pronounced anti-Americanism of the Iranian Revolution. US Secretary of State John Foster Dulles constantly pressured Egyptian president Gamal Abdel Nasser was to join an American military alliance. As one of the leading lights of the non-aligned movement, he refused (Aronson 1986). In response, the USA, not only imposed economic sanctions (Bumbacher 1987), but from the 1960s on, increasingly focussed on its ally Israel. That this option necessarily involved accepting the Israeli occupation of the West Bank and Gaza, in breach of international law, quickly showed that the desire for political hegemony was beginning to gain the upper hand in American foreign policy over the USA's best anti-colonialist intentions. Not by supporting the state of Israel as such but by de facto accepting settler colonialism in the occupied territories, in response to which only half-hearted diplomatic initiatives were proposed and which repeatedly received the US moral support in the UN Security Council, the USA made itself partly responsible for the conquest and settlement of the land and the expulsion and colonialist subjugation of the Palestinians.

The politics of American hegemony in the second half of the twentieth century was hardly a matter of direct military occupation as in traditional colonialism; instead, it was a mix of support for the colonial projects of friendly states, cooperation with authoritarian regimes (in Morocco, post-Nasser Egypt, Jordan, Saudi Arabia and the Gulf states) and violent intervention as in Iran in 1953. This political approach, referred to as 'neo-colonial' by some observers, was increasingly supplemented by a further component: the large-scale provision of weapons to friendly states, which progressively destabilized the Middle East. President Ronald Reagan opted for a policy of 'containment' towards Iran, which had pulled out of the Western alliance after the Islamic Revolution, and attempted to prevent the Revolution from spreading across the region by arming Iraq and encouraging it to attack Iran. This war ultimately cost one million lives, with neither side making significant territorial gains. Without American weapons and satellite reconnaissance that revealed Iranian positions, Iraq would never have been able to wage this war. The fact that the USA, as later emerged in the Iran Contra affair, had also supplied Iran with weapons, laid bare the cynical power politics that pervaded American foreign policy.

This policy followed much the same course in Muslim Southeast Asia. The independent National Security Archive (NSA) of George Washington University in Washington DC published documents in late 2001 which show that in 1975, then President Gerald Ford and his secretary of state Henry Kissinger gave the Indonesian President Suharto their consent to invade East Timor.[1] The transcript of a conversation that took place on the eve of the invasion verifies that Ford expressed understanding for 'the situation' and for the eventuality of 'rapid or drastic action' from Suharto. Kissinger pointed out that it would be necessary to present any action taken by Indonesia as an act of self-defence in order to reassure international public opinion. He also warned of the need for a 'quick military success' and gave assurances that in this case reaction within the USA

---

[1] The National Security Archive, accessible at: http://www.gwu.edu/~nsarchiv/NSAEBB/ NSAEBB62/ (24 February 2009).

could be kept under control. This transcript is part of a series of released documents relating to the US-Indonesian dialogue on East Timor from 1975 and 1976. Approximately 230,000 people died in the invasion.

John K. Cooley has documented an embarrassing history of US support for militant Islamic fundamentalists (Cooley 1999, 5, 89, 109, 219 ff.). In the 1980s, the United States – and Britain and France to some extent – trained Afghan and Arab groups in specialist camps for the anti-Soviet resistance in Afghanistan. During this period, the United States spent around 36 billion dollars waging secret wars in Afghanistan and Central America. At the same time, the USA accepted an enormous boom in the drug trade, which was now flourishing in Afghanistan. Peter Dale Scott has described the combination of drug- and resource-related policies and geopolitics as a key deep structure of American foreign policy (Scott 2004). To this day, regional states such as Iran continue to suffer from the flood of Afghan opium.

The Islamic resistance was of course supported by other states as well. It seems to have been crucial, however, that the USA took part in this 'game' as the most powerful player, on an equal footing with countries such as Iran, Iraq and Sudan, now referred to as 'rogue states'. It can of course be argued that there was no alternative to supporting the Islamic fundamentalist resistance to the Soviet invasion. Nevertheless, the USA was quite willing to see an entire region, all the way to Algeria, destabilized by the so-called 'Afghans' – marauding Arab or other combatants from Afghanistan – following the Soviet withdrawal. The United States' strategic alliance with the Islamic fundamentalists disintegrated in the 1990s when these groups noticed that, following the Gulf War of 1991, the USA was permanently stationed in Saudi Arabia. For militant groups such as those around Osama Bin Laden, the so-called 'holy war' (*jihad*) against the occupiers began in 1998 with the attacks on American embassies in Nairobi, Kenya and Dar es Salaam, Tanzania.

We have now learned that the history of Afghanistan was quite different than was long assumed. In an interview with the *Nouvel Observateur* in 1998, former advisor to President Jimmy Carter, Zbigniew Brzezinski, declared that the USA had actively lured the USSR to Afghanistan by means of secret service activities in the summer of 1979, in other words, before the Soviet invasion.[2] According to Brzezinski, the aim was to inflict

---

[2] The CIA's Intervention in Afghanistan, Interview with Zbigniew Brzezinski, President Jimmy Carter's National Security Adviser, *Le Nouvel Observateur*, Paris, 15–21 January 1998, accessible at: http://www.globalresearch.ca/articles/BRZ110A.html (23 February 2008).

on the Soviet Union a defeat akin to that suffered by America in Vietnam and undermine the Soviet system. The plan worked. The Russian defeat in Afghanistan contributed a good deal to the fall of the USSR, but at the expense of Afghanistan, which descended into decades of civil war. The interview with Brzezinski lays bare the fundamental Machiavellianism of American foreign policy:

Nouvel Observateur: When the Soviets justified their intervention by asserting that they intended to fight against a secret involvement of the United States in Afghanistan, people didn't believe them. However, there was a basis of truth. You don't regret anything today?

Brzezinski: Regret what? That secret operation was an excellent idea. It had the effect of drawing the Russians into the Afghan trap and you want me to regret it? The day that the Soviets officially crossed the border, I wrote to President Carter: we now have the opportunity of giving to the USSR its Vietnam. Indeed, for almost 10 years, Moscow had to carry on a war unsupportable by the government, a conflict that brought about the demoralization and finally the breakup of the Soviet empire.

Nouvel Observateur: And neither do you regret having supported the Islamic fundamentalism, having given arms and advice to future terrorists?

Brzezinksi: What is most important to the history of the world? The Taliban or the collapse of the Soviet empire? Some stirred-up Moslems or the liberation of Central Europe and the end of the cold war?

Nouvel Observateur: Some stirred-up Moslems? But it has been said and repeated: Islamic fundamentalism represents a world menace today.

Brzezinski: Nonsense! It is said that the West had a global policy in regard to Islam. That is stupid. There isn't a global Islam. Look at Islam in a rational manner and without demagoguery or emotion. It is the leading religion of the world with 1.5 billion followers. But what is there in common among Saudi Arabian fundamentalism, moderate Morocco, Pakistan militarism, Egyptian pro-Western or Central Asian secularism? Nothing more than what unites the Christian countries.

The American wars in Afghanistan in 2001 and Iraq in 2003 should in many ways be seen more as a continuation of the imperial US foreign policy than as aberrations in American history. It is true that the predominant theory of hegemony that was characteristic of American foreign policy, as espoused by such leading lights as Kissinger and Brzezinksi (Brzezinski 1997), implied the primacy of protecting US interests through diplomacy and multilateral alliances. The deployment of military force to secure American interests was, however, never ruled out as *ultima ratio*. The neo-conservative policies of President George W. Bush following the attacks of 11 September were also more of a strategic variant than a political revolution. Under Bush, the USA clearly shifted to an old form of imperial policy: direct military intervention and long-term occupation. The 'asymmetrical' nature of wars against terrorists, which were regarded as a form of privatized violence, served as the main justification. With large contingents of troops, military bases and parallel political structures, without which national governments can make no decisions, the USA and European countries now have a presence in the Middle East and Central Asia on a scale not seen since the colonial era. Herfried Münkler rightly refers to the 'return of the empire' (Münkler 2005a, 224).

After the loss of many millions of lives during the colonial period, political violence perpetrated by Western democracies has again become par for the course. An estimated 100,000 people died in the second Gulf War on Iraq in 1991, mainly as a result of Anglo-American air strikes. Data on civilian casualties of the war in Iraq of 2003 differ widely. The most conservative estimate, the Iraq Body Count, assumes a figure of around 90,000 deaths by 2008;[3] estimates by the specialist London-based international medical journal *The Lancet* are far larger (Riehm 2006). Regardless of possible justifications, there can be no doubt that the foreign policy of Western democracies involves large-scale political violence.

WESTERN DEMOCRACY AND INTERNATIONAL VIOLENCE: FROM 'ETERNAL PEACE' TO 'HUMANITARIAN IMPERIALISM'

There is no agreement in the scholarly literature as to what exactly the terms 'empire' and 'imperialism' mean. Clearly, the question of whether a given act of military incursion into sovereign territory has been sanctioned by international law, in other words by a UN resolution, is of fundamental importance. We might, for example, point to the difference between the American wars in Afghanistan in 2001 and Iraq in 2003. While the UN justified the war in Afghanistan as a kind of 'war of pacification' (Münkler 2005b) triggered by an attack on the USA, the Iraq War received no legitimacy in international law. It was waged solely in the interests of the United States and its allies. It remains a matter of dispute whether the key factor was security or an economic interest in Iraqi oil. Iraq had not attacked the USA, and there was no evidence of any link with terrorism. What was clearly evident was that Iraq possesses the second-largest oil reserves in the world, so that any lengthy occupation, based on the so-called 'Korea model', for example, would have a

---

[3] Iraq Body Count, http://www.iraqbodycount.org/ (22 February 2008).

lasting impact on China and America's other emerging Asian competitors. In controlling Iraq, and already exercising a decisive influence on Saudi Arabia, America would control the markets and economic powers of the future.

Alongside legality, the way in which power is exercised is important to defining the concept of empire. Empire requires that one country comprehensively control another (Porter 2004), though whether *direct* rule is required is subject to controversy (Jaberg and Schlotter 2005). Does an empire exist only in cases where one country is entirely occupied, governed and dominated by another, or is it enough when a given country indirectly exercises a decisive influence on local political forces by means of an overwhelming military presence or threat? Some authors would make a distinction between imperial and hegemonic rule. But this is ultimately a conceptual dispute. Modern imperialism, also known as 'neo-imperialism', may intervene rapidly and on a massive scale even in remote regions, conditional upon the possession of highly developed modern military technology. It exercises power through a skilfully arranged system of military bases and through a diplomatic 'advisory system'. In Iraq, for example, the USA has formally returned power to the Iraqi government. In Baghdad, though, one of the world's largest American embassies, with a staff of thousands and backed up by the massive US military presence, de facto exercises a decisive influence on day-to-day politics.

Hence, if 'imperialism' means a state exercising unlawful and decisive power over another, the next question is: Is this even possible in the case of a Western democracy? Can a Western democracy act in an imperialistic way? Many theorists have sought to describe the connection between the internal structure of a political system and its conduct in the wider world. One of the most famous is undoubtedly Immanuel Kant with his 1795 treatise *Eternal Peace* (Kant 2005). In it, Kant sets out reasons for the hopeful idea that a republican state in which the citizens themselves must decide the question of war and peace might form the basis for world peace.

In recent years, and particularly after 11 September and the ensuing Middle East wars, Kant's thesis has again been subject to contentious debate among political scientists. Kant's views are borne out empirically in the sense that democratic states do, in fact, wage fewer wars *against* one another. The fact that vital questions of war and peace are no longer subject to the despotic rule of an autocrat, together with the checks and balances of democracy, have clearly had a pacifying effect. On closer inspection, however, we find reason to doubt that democracy has a *generally* pacifying effect (Habermas 1996, 192–236). The same mechanisms that prevent wars between democratic states seem not to work with respect to wars against non-democratic states. As noted, Western democracies have waged many wars beyond their own territory, causing death on a massive scale: in the Vietnam War alone, the USA killed around one million Vietnamese. The list of US military interventions and wars is so long that it would take several pages to list them all.[4]

How, then, are we to explain this peculiar rift between the internal peaceableness of democracy – with respect to its own population and other democratic states – and its aggressive readiness for external wars? This state of affairs may perhaps be expressed most simply by a psychological formula produced by Jean-Christophe Rufin, who refers to the 'dictatorship of liberalism': the idea that democracies' high degree of domestic pluralism engenders an urgent complementary need for an international bogeyman in order to secure social cohesion (Rufin 1994). In this view, the process of demarcating democracy from the external world, sometimes through war, is the real identity-forming factor in the post-modern constitution of Western democracies.

But this thesis is highly speculative and rooted in a questionable view of mass psychology. It is not democracy as such that represents a danger to the world around it. Rather, the large, economically strong military powers of the West are securing their political and economic sinecures through military action. This would mean that it is only smaller and weaker democracies, those, moreover, not incorporated into military alliances with larger states, which are 'good' democracies in the Kantian sense. Madagascar, then, but not Britain. On the other hand, this would also mean that if all the states in the world were democracies, a battle of the stronger against the weaker might ensue. It is not democracy as such that seems to reduce the risk of war, but democratic reason coupled with an understanding of one's own weakness.

Despite the fact that in democracies the people determine their own fates and those of their children, certain arguments do in fact suggest that the political system of democracy is prone to errors. Christopher Daase has summarized the weaknesses of democracy in both psychological and power-political terms (Daase 2004, 56 ff.):

---

[4] See Zoltan Grossmann's list in 'A Century of US Military Interventions from Wounded Knee to Afghanistan', http://www.zmag.org/crisesCurEvts/Interventions.htm (15 February 2008).

- Democratic elections may encourage patriotic sentiments – a state of affairs known in communication science as the Rally Round the Flag phenomenon (Mueller 1973).
- Successful wars against other states may divert attention away from internal problems.
- As a system featuring a high degree of self-legitimation, democracy de-legitimizes every other political system; authoritarian rule, however 'modern' it may be, is regarded as 'unjust rule'. From an ideological point of view, it then becomes legitimate to attack any authoritarian state in order to liberate its people.
- Particularly during times of crisis, democratic pluralism is curbed by emergency institutions in favour of small 'rapid-reaction' groups of decision-makers (kitchen cabinets, security committees, crisis management bodies, emergency laws); this increases the efficiency and speed of war-related decision making and also diminishes the republican supervision so highly regarded by Kant.
- The democratic compulsion to achieve consensus, or at least to get large majorities on board, leads to the extension of war aims in order to rally together as many political factions as possible. For example, naked economic interests appeal mainly to conservatives, humanitarian goals to the political left, while security concerns tend to resonate across the political spectrum.

All these arguments suggest that Western democracies have an intrinsic, systemic susceptibility to waging war on autocracies. This clearly qualifies Kant's notion that democracies are peace loving compared with non-democratic political regimes. Kant's vision of 'eternal peace' still applies only internally, not externally. We might identify extenuating circumstances for the period before the First World War and even up to the Second World War for at the time, as the obvious example of many countries' late introduction of female suffrage shows, democracy was not yet fully developed along modern lines. But if only a part of the population was able to participate in democracy, only this part – namely, all non-slaves and non-women – was in a position to prevent wars.

But what has happened since the Second World War? It is striking that a number of post-war Western theorists have discussed the relationship between political systems, foreign policies and international politics but have come to quite different conclusions than Kant. On closer inspection, these conclusions bear out Daase's list of democratic flaws. Even a cursory survey shows that there is at present no consensus on a 'democratic world peace', not even a minimum consensus of the kind developed by democracies, in the wake of modernity, to limit internal power and subject it to legal regulation – a consensus which now forms the basis of a well-founded critique of autocracy throughout much of the Islamic world (see Chapter 1).

While all Western theorists condemn authoritarian rule within the state, many of them justify imperial, in other words authoritarian, rule beyond it. The distinction between internal and external spheres – internal peace and external chaos – has even become fundamental to theory building. Robert Cooper, the leading foreign policy advisor to former British Prime Minister Tony Blair during the Iraq War of 2003 called quite openly for a 'new imperialism' (R. Cooper 2003). The 'pre-modern' state, by which he means most countries outside of Europe and North America, represents a danger to the West as a base for terrorists, and only 'defensive' imperialism offers any prospect of getting the chaos under control. Cooper's distinction between spheres of civilisation and chaos is strongly reminiscent of the older thought patterns of colonialism. According to Cooper, democratic civilization and authoritarian or terrorist barbarism are two opposing entities, which means that Western democracy must protect itself. An inescapable analogy suggests itself: just as the Catholic Church repeatedly disregarded its own principles throughout history in order to ensure its survival (which it justified as guaranteeing that these principles would be respected in future), democracy, too, must resort to the barbaric instrument of war to ensure the survival of civilization. The significant thing about this argument is that democracy is in principle regarded as peace loving and less expansionary than autocracy – which, as we have seen, is empirically correct only to a very limited extent, namely, with respect to other democracies.

The neo-conservative circles around President George W. Bush have also made repeated use of these motifs, often with a fair degree of contempt for the arguments of the realist school (Kissinger and Brzezinski), which simply – and brutally but openly – cited national power interests as central to decisions on war and peace (Henning 2006; Keller 2008). But the neo-conservatives also put forward another argument, to which Cooper pays little attention, which Bush and Blair put into play as they attempted to justify the 2003 Iraq War, in order to, as Daase would put it, broaden the political coalition. Having initially focussed on Saddam Hussein's alleged weapons of mass destruction and supposed links to terrorist organizations, in other words, highlighting *external* threats to Western democracy, they increasingly began to argue that regime change in Baghdad was important in order to safeguard human rights and initiate a democratic process. The imperial approach of American neo-conservatives is not only 'defensive' in Cooper's sense but also justifies itself as 'humanitarian'.

There are a number of things worth noting about such ideas. *First*, a look at history reveals that humanitarian justifications were already part of the ideological arsenal of the colonial era (Gong 1984; Salter 2002, 35–7). This brings out the precarious legitimacy of an interventionist logic: violent occupation and domination, the large-scale destruction of human life and exploitation of countries (oil treaties, control of China, see above) can scarcely be classed as humanitarian actions. The humanitarian argument was justifiable in the Second World War in view of genocide; it was hardly credible in the oil-rich former colonial territories of the Middle East. *Second*, after some initial hesitation, many members of the Democratic Party in the United States fell into line with the neo-conservatives around George W. Bush and supported the Iraq War. It is clear that the introduction of the humanitarian argument did in fact open up the prospect of creating a broad pro-war coalition. Even former liberal intellectuals such as Harvard professor and now leader of the Canadian Liberal Party Michael Ignatieff suddenly came out in favour of a shift to 'humanitarian imperialism'. In view of the breakdown of the Wilsonian idea of national independence, Ignatieff concedes, the world must again embrace the imperial idea, only this time, as it were, with altruistic motives (Ignatieff 2003, 122). It was not just conservative forces that proved susceptible to the imperialist idea. Even seasoned European liberals such as Jürgen Habermas began to waver. Struck by the fall of a statue of Saddam Hussein in Baghdad in April 2003, he asked whether, despite the violation of international law and the high-tech military attack, the American war in Iraq might not be legitimate after all (Habermas 2004, 32).

The thrust of Herfried Münkler's contribution is quite different. He underlines the difference between intervention imposed from outside and an imperialism desired by the local people because, in view of their wretched predicament, they would rather place themselves under foreign rule than continue to endure it (Münkler 2005a). In the Middle East context, this throws up the question of whether some Iraqis welcomed the American war of 2003 despite American violation of human rights. This idea is highly speculative. There was no spontaneous welcome for the USA as liberators in Iraq – the toppling of the statue, as we soon learned, was staged by US troops. Moreover, particularly under the generally authoritarian conditions of intervention, the amount of support within a population cannot be objectively gauged and is open to manipulation by small political cliques. The Iraq War of 2003 was a classic example of cooperation between an imperial power and a local elite, which was favoured and supported by the US government, got allowed to be involved in its plans and used as a means of legitimation. The most famous example was the Iraqi opposition in exile under the leadership of Ahmed Chalabi, a grouping whose criminality became apparent after the US invasion. In most world historical situations, Münkler's imperialism 'by invitation' is a variant on the old power-political principle of 'divide and rule', a technique mastered by the European colonial powers, which always involved forging alliances with indigenous cliques. There can be no legitimate 'invitation' to take on the role of empire.

Nonetheless, after 11 September and in light of the totalitarian-fascist danger they believed they could discern in the Islamic world, even self-confessed opponents of an imperial approach and long-time believers in multilateralism began to support, or at least hesitantly sympathize with, the neo-imperial policies of the United States. Yet these new converts overlooked the fact that if we compare Islam and the West over the last century, Western forces have been the aggressors far more often than Islamic ones. In other words, the self-defence theory is wide of the mark. And they ignored the enormous humanitarian costs, the huge number of victims of 'humanitarian' wars, along with the motives of power and enrichment – ultimately nothing new – behind which humanitarian arguments are concealed; these are motives that no policy of invitation by local power cliques can relativize. In light of the great successes of democracy all over the world, Wilson's ideas of national self-determination have by no means been proved wrong. But countries that were once colonial territories often continue to struggle with the consequences of artificial borders and forms of rule that were installed and stabilized from outside. Regardless of these criticisms, however, after 11 September it became apparent that imperialism and imperial violence were still present within Western culture and, following a brief phase of post-colonial thought, proved all too easy to reactivate.

This was true not only in the United States. It is interesting to note that in the USA there is much overlap in the way left-wing critics of globalization such as Naomi Klein and right-wing journalists such as Robert Kagan assess Europe's role in world politics. Both accuse Europe of following the USA's lead. They suggest that Europe is, on the one hand, essentially pursuing the same power-political goals as the USA, and on the other, laying claim to a morally superior position through criticism of American imperialism (Kagan 2003).[5] And the West as a whole does in fact continue to accept neo-imperialism. In France, for example, despite its opposition under President Jacques Chirac to America's war in Iraq, a debate on the re-evaluation of French colonial history began soon after the events of 11 September. Article 4 of a law passed on 23 February 2005 states: 'Les programmes scolaires reconnaissent en particulier le rôle positif de la présence française outre-mer, notamment en Afrique du Nord'.[6]

France's temporary confrontation with the United States over the Iraq War of 2003 cannot disguise the fact that French policy on Africa strongly resembles American foreign policy. Paris pays no heed to the multilateralism of the United Nations, emphasizes the civilizing, missionary character of its policies, and pursues a nuclear-weapons policy that violates international agreements (Speckmann 2007; see also Brüne 2005). A country like Germany pursues its interests primarily through transatlantic relations and support American action of the kind seen in Afghanistan, including militarily support, though this was sanctioned by the United Nations and cannot be described as 'imperialistic' in a narrow sense. Yet Berlin's efforts to distance itself from the breach of international law in the American prison camp in Guantánamo are weak and far from credible. Are the European countries satellites of the American Empire?

There are many Western critics of the prevailing policy of neo-imperialism. Michael Hardt and Antonio Negri criticize the strong-arm mentality of globalism since the attacks of 11 September and underline that global politics should be played out within a globally integrated democracy rather than a new empire (Hardt and Negri 2004). John Pilger's reports provide an inside view of modern imperialism (Pilger 2002). In Europe, in order to stake out an agenda distinct from imperialism, the democratic left – post-communists in France and Italy and the Greens – is attempting to formulate a new policy that facilitates cross-border intervention in the cause of peace and at the same time respects the fundamentals of international law, installing the United Nations as the key actor. The European people's parties, however, whether of the conservative or social

---

[5] See the interview with Naomi Klein in LeVine 2005, p. 235.
[6] 'The educational programmes acknowledge in particular the positive role of the French presence abroad, notably in North Africa'. French historians protested against this law, seeing it as legislative interference in the writing of history: L'appel des 19 historiens: Liberté pour l'histoire!, http://www.ldh-toulon.net/spip.php?article1086 (25 February 2008).

democratic camps, above all the Labour Party of Tony Blair and Gordon Brown, have long since embraced neo-imperialism.

It would be wrong to claim that contemporary neo-imperialism is simply reverting to the worldview of the colonial era. Imperialism justifies itself afresh in each historical era. While the 'imperial peace' of earlier times put little faith in the colonial subjects' capacity to achieve civilization and saw the protection of human rights as the responsibility of the colonial powers, contemporary ideas are quite different. George W. Bush and other champions of humanitarian imperialism constantly emphasized that their chief concern is to give the peoples of the world the chance to achieve freedom. In this sense, neo-imperialism does not in any way take its lead from Samuel Huntington's culturalist view of a world of unchangeable cultural antagonisms. The contemporary neo-imperialist approach is not only the source of straightforward power-savvy cynicism, but also a humanistic sense of mission and the notion that those often despised as 'barbarians' in the old colonialism are capable of learning. We are left, however, with a new kind of Orientalist worldview. Because of its military strength, the Islamic world has historically been regarded in the West more as an alternative civilization than as the site of savage barbarism. In this sense Bush and other neo-imperialists, in fact, believed the Islamic world to be capable of learning the Western lifestyle and Western democracy (see also Tibi 1984). However, they also never questioned the superiority of the democratic system and imposed it by force. The resources of the world – oil, above all – are seen, as it were, as a just reward for this costly act of educating Islamic civilizing. The new imperialism has an enlightened view of human beings, but remains repressive and violent.

The Western neo-imperialism of the twenty-first century is no simple case of regression extending from Kant, theorist of a republican peace among nations, to Carl Schmitt, German scholar of constitutional law during the interwar period who assumed that political action is impossible in the absence of us-and-them distinctions between peoples (Schmitt 2002). Rather, contemporary neo-imperialism embodies the attempt to complete Kant through Schmitt: war for human rights and democracy based on a concept – however coherent it may or may not be – of totalitarianism and fascism as the enemy. This notion is transferred to Islam with the aim of enforcing human rights and democracy. There are no barbarians now, but 'the barbaric' is still with us, and the notion of civilization and counter-civilization, of an Orient and Occident engaged in violent struggle, is alive and well.

ISLAMIC IMPERIALISM: A CULTURAL REMNANT

Historically, one state's imperial endeavours have often been justified with reference to another's ambitions, transforming political and economic motives into a defensive mission. This idea of self-defence is also present within the modern imperial mindset of the West, but it is not focussed solely on the danger of asymmetrical wars against terrorists. The imperial efforts of Middle Eastern states, above all Iran, are also frequently cited as an argument for military intervention, particularly in conservative political circles.[7] Can we justly view imperialism as a key characteristic of contemporary Iran, along with the Arab countries and other Islamic states? If so, how does this proclivity manifest itself?

Fundamentally, the Islamic states are not currently in a phase of active imperialism, though the imperial past continues to make itself felt in many respects. Jochen Hippler rightly points out that while around one quarter of the world's population consists of Muslims, they were responsible for 'only' five of around 150 million victims of genocide in the twentieth century, as this mass annihilation was concentrated in Germany, Europe, the USSR and China (Hippler 2006, 20). There is not to claim that Islamic civilization is culturally superior. Historically, it is just as well acquainted with the phenomenon of imperialism as is the West. Subsequent to the political and military decline of its erstwhile empires and for 'lack of opportunity', any imperial tendencies in the Islamic world have been much subdued. Like the United States, with its annihilation of native Americans, or the European colonial empires, the Turkish state's massacre of Armenians in the early twentieth century and its ongoing conflict with the Kurds show that the effects of Islamic countries' historical imperialism are still being felt in the present. Much the same goes for the conduct of Islamic states in North Africa. Yet these are generally the after-effects of an older Islamic imperialism rather than features of Islamic countries' contemporary policies.

The classical imperial age of the Islamic world lasted until the fifteenth century. Constantinople was captured in 1453. Interestingly, as Ephraim Karsh points out, even during this period Islam was not the predominant element in expansion. Alliances with non-Muslims were the order of the day. Subject peoples were not forced to convert, and the 'Islamic state'

---

[7] See for example Scott Sullivan, China Must Stop Ahmadinejad, http://www.theconservativevoice.com/article/24002.html (25 February 2008).

had long since become basically absolutist (Karsh 2007, 33, 46, 66 f.). The Islamic state practiced classical Oriental despotism. Because the state was strong, this despotism also made itself felt in imperial policies. Many a Byzantine ruler preferred Islamic rule to the religious fanaticism of the Crusaders, which, moreover, concealed a range of economic motives (Karsh 2007, 74 ff.).

What must be discussed, however, is Karsh's supposition that Islamic expansionist tendencies are evident throughout history, even into the present (Karsh 2007, 5). Is there a line of continuity innate to Islamic or Middle Eastern imperial endeavours that extends from the classical period to Gamal Abdel Nasser, Ayatollah Khomeini and beyond? One of Karsh's key ideas is that the pan-Arabism and pan-Islamism of the twentieth century were essentially imperial projects (Karsh 2007, 7). But he overlooks the fact that neither of these endeavours was concerned with territorial expansion, but rather with uniting the Islamic countries in order that they might confront neo-colonialism or neo-imperialism with renewed vigour. With the exception of marginal extremist groups, which continue to propagate an expansive 'holy war', this was the main thrust of the pan-Arab and pan-Islamic movements. Gamal Abd El Nasser, who ruled the United Arab Republic of Egypt and Syria from 1958 to 1961, was more of an Arab Bismarck than an Arab Napoleon. He was at least as popular in the rest of the Arab world as he was in Egypt itself.

It is no doubt true that these sympathies were based in part on Nasser's unequivocal opposition to the state of Israel, an opposition that was in breach of international law and which Israeli historians rightly view as neo-imperialist. Yet Israel was a special problem because the settler colonialism of the Zionist movement provoked an Arab claim to power. It is nothing less than paradoxical to interpret Nasser's anti-imperialism, which he formulated in collaboration with the unaligned movement and its leading exponents, such as Nehru, Castro and Tito and which he put into practice in the Suez War, as itself 'imperialist'.

Many other developments, in North Africa for example, may also be considered the after-effects of an imperial policy pursued by Islamic states in the past and not its continuation in the present, with two striking exceptions relating to the Sahara nations. Morocco annexed first parts then the whole of Western Sahara following Spain's departure in 1976. Libya has involved itself in a number of wars over the last few decades, both in Chad and Sudan (Darfur), though only for brief periods. Egypt's current role in Sudan exhibits little of its former influence there. The Darfur crisis in Sudan can hardly be considered an indication of contemporary Arab imperial aspirations, as the Arab central government in Khartoum is basically fighting to thwart the secessionism of a distinct Arab-Islamic section of its population. This may be seen as intra-national civil war or even genocide (Prunier 2005), which brings out once again the undemocratic character of Arab regimes, but is not a case of expansive imperialism.

The last political leader in the Middle East to pursue imperial aspirations through war was Saddam Hussein: in 1980 when he attacked Iran (with American support), and in 1991 by invading Kuwait. Here again, though, we are dealing with centuries-old border disputes within the Islamic world, which the Western colonial powers partly brought about when they divided territories into states after the First World War. The Kashmir conflict is another remnant of the division of colonial India into separate states. It is not genuine evidence of imperial schemes hatched by Pakistan. What the example of Pakistan shows, however, is that rather than military *intervention*, the contemporary Islamic state often opts for more subtle means of *intercession*: the training and funding of political and paramilitary organizations which, for example, operate in Afghanistan from bases in Pakistan.

Thus, what we can discern in the Islamic world are the remnants of imperialist policies. As a whole, however, the Islamic states are part of what we might call, borrowing from Herfried Münkler, a post-imperial space (Münkler 2005a, 213 ff.), which is now serving the United States and its allies in Europe as a zone of imperial expansion. It is not the Islamic world that is advancing on the West, but vice versa. All in all, if we compare Islam and the West, we must inevitably conclude that the use of imperial force is part of the Islamic past and of the Western present. The Islamic world is quite right to complain that it is currently the victim of Western neo-imperialism.

This does not mean that the Islamic states have fully resolved the problems of their own imperial past. Today, while imperialism in the Islamic world is not a power-political option, it often continues to exist as a cultural ideal. In much the same way as the former world power of Great Britain struggled to make the mental switch to its diminished status in twentieth century, the Arab states in particular have yet to come to terms fully with their loss of political significance on the world stage. There has been very little reappraisal of Middle Eastern colonialism, though this is scarcely possible under the authoritarian conditions that pertain in most countries, as any attempt to come to terms with history in this way comes up against the limits of *raison d'état*. These countries lament the return of Western imperialism, while failing to acknowledge their own historical legacies of expansionism, just as the West often overlooks its own remnants of political repression – from 'modern slavery' to Guantánamo to an imperial foreign policy.

7

Terrorism and Non-violent Resistance: Extremism and Pacifism Across Cultures

Since the events of 11 September 2001, terrorism has been one of the key topics of the contemporary era. But how great is the threat of terrorism in reality? Before the attacks on the World Trade Center and the Pentagon, a number of conflict analyses had deemed the security risks posed by terrorism to be negligible; far less significant, in any case, than the threat to life and limb posed by state authoritarianism and wars between regular armies both within and between states (Scheffler 2000). But it is also beyond doubt that terrorism as a form of privatized violence that targets civilians has increased, as is evident, for example, in the attacks on New York and Washington, DC[1] (2001), Bali (2002), Madrid (2004), Jakarta (2004/2009) and London (2005). In the future, terrorism involving biological, chemical or nuclear weapons could increase the human costs dramatically. Nonetheless, in its survey of threats to global security, the United Nations identified terrorism as just one of numerous dangers. It attached just as much importance to wars between nations, civil wars, and the production of and trade in weapons. The report also expressed the view that terrorism is a threat to some, but by no means all, countries of the world.[2]

While the true extent of the threat posed by terrorism remains a matter of controversy, the psychological impact of this form of violence, which

---

[1] It would be more precise to say that the attacks took place in New York and *near* Washington, DC, because the Pentagon building that was attacked is in Arlington, Virginia.

[2] A more Secure World: Our Shared Responsibility (2004), Report of the Secretary-General's High-level Panel on Threats, Challenges and Change, New York: UN Department of Public Information.

is practiced by underground groups, is tremendous. So far, the fear of terrorism exceeds its destructive power many times over. Western publics tend to link terrorism with Islam. This is understandable: While there are other forms of terrorism in the world, it is Islamic terrorism (Jihadism) that most aggressively targets people and institutions in the Western industrial states. Whereas Tamil terrorism, for example, has remained limited to a particular region, Islamic terrorism has taken on a global dimension, warranting a bespoke typology. At the same time, we must bear in mind that, in terms of the numbers of both victims and attacks, the Islamic world itself is worse affected by Islamic fundamentalist terrorism than the West. It is a case of Muslims fighting Muslims. Terrorism is, therefore, just as much a threat to the Islamic world as to the West. When we analyze the causes of the phenomenon, however, we find sometimes profound differences between the Islamic and Western worlds.

While there is an excessive awareness of Islamic fundamentalist terrorism in the West, non-violent resistance and peaceful protest against Western policies, both far from unusual in the Islamic world, largely escape the West's attention. The mass media, Western and non-Western, almost entirely ignores the fact that the Islamic world has a long and ongoing tradition of non-violent resistance, which is practiced daily. It is wrong to consider pacifism a Western invention that might, at most, be inspired by East Asian religions and philosophies but not by Islam. There is an urgent need for comparative research on pacifist traditions in Islam and the West.

A TYPOLOGY OF ISLAMIC TERRORISM: IS TERRORISM TYPICALLY ISLAMIC?

In defining terrorism, it seems useful to make a distinction between forms of violence and motives for violence. Motives matter in that each terrorist act is initially justified by a political or ideological objective. In the absence of a political motive, unlawful violence is merely criminal, not terrorist. Terrorism targets a political system or harbours various political-ideological motives of a nationalist, ethnic or religious tenor. States, too, may practice terrorism – so-called state terrorism – if they violate their own or international laws, which they also do for political reasons (by engaging in torture or illegal killings, for example).

Any meaningful definition of the term 'terrorism' must focus on violence against civilians. Illegal military wars waged by regular armies or guerrilla struggles carried out by armed paramilitary units against armies or going on between guerrilla armies are sometimes described as 'terrorist'. However, this definition is contested because it defames armed struggle which is in conformity with international law, for example armed resistance against illegal occupying forces. But the victims of paramilitary violence now include civilians, and this makes it terrorism. At the same time, we can discern a change in civilian targets in the last few years. Modern terrorism is no longer primarily concerned with assassinating political decision-makers. Rather, it attempts to disseminate its political messages indirectly by threatening and killing, indeed sacrificing, entirely innocent civilians.[3] In the 1970s, the German Red Army Faction (RAF) was still abducting politicians; Egyptian President Anwar al-Sadat was murdered by Islamic fundamentalist terrorists – in the twenty-first century, terrorists blow up skyscrapers, occupy schools and theatres or detonate bombs in public places.

The International Crisis Group subdivides contemporary Islamic fundamentalism (which they label, 'Islamism') into three major groups: Islamic political movements, Islamic mission and Islamic armed struggle (Jihadists), this last being further divided into three subgroups: internal, irredentist and global Jihadists.[4] According to this organization, Islamic fundamentalist movements, such as the Egyptian Muslim Brothers, or other groups whose compatibility with democracy was studied by the Carnegie Endowment for International Peace (Brown et al. 2006) profess their acceptance of the nation state, forego violence and aim to achieve evolutionary political change. This may well be problematic in terms of democratic theory (see Chapter 3), but it is neither revolutionary nor violent. At most, such groups merely claim the right to resist foreign occupiers but not the national government, even if they harshly criticize or even reject the current political system. 'Missionary Islam', groups such as Al-Tabligh wa al-Dawa or Al-Takfir wa al-Hijra, do not have political goals and are not violent despite their religious radicalism (Rashwan 2007). They, in fact, represent a return to the early days of Islam, promoting a generally ascetic lifestyle as a means of creating identity and as a source of strength amid the crises of Muslim modernity. While the origins of the Salafiyya movement, which inspired the modern reformist political Islam of the twentieth century, can be traced to the

---

[3] I owe the distinction between victims and target groups to a remark by Ms. Hanan Badr, currently completing a PhD on the reception of terrorism in the West and the Arab world at the University of Erfurt.

[4] Understanding Islamism, loc. cit.

guiding intellectual forces of Jamal al-Din al-Afghani and Muhammad Abduh (see Chapter 1), 'neo-Salafiyya' emerged more or less as a by-product. With such authors as the Egyptian Sayyid Qutb, who was executed in 1966, it provided the key thinkers that inspired modern Islamic fundamentalist terrorism.

Groupings which are prepared to deploy violence and terrorism – in other words, violence against civilians – are generally referred to as 'Jihadists' and have historically often been renegades who rejected the political or 'missionary Islamism' that they originally embraced. The vast majority of missionary Islamists renounced violence and professed their commitment to peaceful means, but small groups became increasingly radicalized and developed into what we now know as Islamic Jihadist or Islamic fundamentalist terrorist groups. Of the three Jihadist subgroups the Crisis Group identified – internal, irredentist and global Jihadists – irredentist Jihadists, such as the Palestinian Hamas, present the greatest analytical problem. Because they not only fight against foreign occupation but also practice violence against civilians, they have – with respect to *forms of violence* – clearly ceased to engage in legitimate resistance as it is understood in international law. However, as far as their *motives for violence* – regaining territory – are concerned, they remain within the framework of international law, at least to the extent that they merely demand the return of the territories to which a given people are entitled. In the case of the Palestinian Hamas, the struggle to take back the areas of the West Bank and Gaza Strip occupied by Israel in 1967 conforms to international law, particularly given that there is still no state of Palestine that could sign a peace treaty. What is illegal, however, is the more far-reaching demand for the return of 'all of Palestine', which includes the modern state of Israel. Were Hamas to embrace a two-state solution, we could definitively regard it as a hybrid of illegal forms of violence and legal motives for violence. We look again at this in-between position when we analyze the difference in the assessment of Hamas in the West and in the Islamic world.

This complex assessment of 'irredentist Islamism' does not apply to the 'global Jihadists', whose motives are very difficult to grasp because they pursue no political programme[5] but are apocalyptic in nature, revolving around a final confrontation with Jews, Christians and all non-Muslims, a category that includes 'lapsed Muslims'.[6] While it is true that

[5] Ibid, p. 17.
[6] Ibid, p. 16.

the global Jihadists use the same forms of violence as the irredentists, that is, suicide attacks, hijackings, etc., the reasons for their struggle vary so greatly that the relations between different factions tend to be antagonistic. While irredentists wish to regain lost territories for the people and to this end are capable of many doctrinal compromises, up to and including integrating forces that are clearly secular, the global Jihadists systematically target Muslim populations that oppose their aims. In contrast to the irredentists, the global Jihadists do not regard the death of Muslims as unavoidable 'collateral damage' but rather, as in the case of the GIA underground army in Algeria in the 1990s, as an act of religious purification and the enforcement of claims to power against 'unbelievers' in their own ranks, an approach that can only be described as proto-fascist (though systematic violence against Muslims is controversial even among the global Jihadists). Whereas the irredentists are often popular among their own populations, who view them as the last resort in the struggle against occupation, this is rarely true of the global Jihadists. They are considered alien elements, as are the Arab fighters under Osama Bin Laden in Afghanistan.

While the widespread rejection of global Jihadism following 11 September was also evident in the Arab-Islamic world, it is no exaggeration to state that the Islamic world and the West view irredentist Jihadism – in other words Hamas or Hezbollah – utterly differently. The West overwhelmingly rejects these groups, above all because of their attacks on civilians, but they enjoy broad support within the Islamic world because of their opposition to Israel, particularly in light of the fact that Israel claims a far larger number of Palestinian civilian victims by blowing up buildings, arbitrarily killing civilians, imposing collective punishment and engaging in torture. How differently irredentists are judged is apparent, not only when we compare Arab and Western media, but also when we consider public opinion in general.

How do these differences of opinion come about? Can they be explained merely by differing political interests, with terrorism or state terrorism being an accepted and approved means of realizing territorial claims? Or does Islamic terrorism have cultural and religious roots – an idea that has been repeatedly put forward in the wake of Samuel Huntington's thesis of the 'clash of civilizations'? (Marshall 2006, 30 f.). This idea seems backed up by the fact that non-state terrorism has in recent decades frequently been perpetrated by Islamic fundamentalist groups. A number of facts, however, cast doubt on the supposition that Islam has a special cultural proclivity for terrorism:

1. The phenomenon of terrorism is not restricted to the Islamic world.
2. Terrorism existed in the Islamic world before the rise of Islamic fundamentalist movements.
3. Excepting situations of occupation, Jihadism is the preserve of a minority within Islamic fundamentalist movements, namely ultraradical groupings.

Comparison of world regions shows that terrorism occurs across the globe. Between 1980 and 2001, the Tamil Tigers carried out 75 of the 186 acts of terrorism for which we have evidence (Hippler 2006, 84 ff.). More recent acts of terrorism have been carried out by groups such as Japanese Aum Shinrikyo, which carried out gas attacks on the Tokyo underground, or the Peruvian Shining Path, whose hostage taking and massacres have cost thousands of civilian lives. Though Islamic fundamentalist terrorists have been highly active in the first decade of the twenty-first century, the problem of terrorism is not specific to any world region, culture or religion.

In today's Islamic world, Jihadists often use radical interpretations of Islam to justify terrorism. Yet the religion of Islam, its theology, cannot be the real cause of terrorism; this is apparent in the simple fact that Middle Eastern terrorism is older than Islamic Jihadism. It is true that there have been fundamentalist Islamic groups since the foundation of the Muslim Brothers in 1928. But these groups have carried out terrorist attacks only since the 1980s, for example, the attack by Islamic Jihad on President Anwar al-Sadat of Egypt in 1980. Secular nationalists such as the Palestinian Liberation Organization (PLO) carried out acts of terrorism in the early 1970s, such as the hijacking of airliners or the massacre of Israeli athletes during the 1972 Olympic Games in Munich. To this day, some of the 'Islamic suicide attacks' in such countries as Iraq are carried out by secular groups (Hippler 2006, 84 ff.). This clearly shows that extremist groups did not need to wait for the rise of Islamic fundamentalism, its arguments couched in religious terms, in order to find an ideological breeding ground for terrorism. Modern nationalist ideas and even certain forms of Middle Eastern communist thought, inspired by Western thought and politics, performed the same function (for example, the Popular Front for the Liberation of Palestine [PFLP]). There is no genetic link between Islam, religion and terrorism, though Islamic theology, law and tradition are certainly amenable to instrumentalization.

We must qualify the connection between Islam and terrorism in a third sense. Only within a minority strain of Islamic thought is the relationship between religion and political violence interpreted so as to constitute a basis for terrorist acts. Three main currents of a theory of violence can be discerned within the Islamic tradition (Bennett 2005, 198 ff.): the most important is the theory of just war, which states that violence is permitted only as a defensive measure and in cases of attack from outside the Islamic world. In addition there are the smaller schools of Islamic thought: Jihadism, a theory of offensive and total war, and Islamic pacifism, which we look at later in this chapter.

According to the moderate reading backed by most contemporary scholars (Abu-Nimer 2003, 26 ff., 35; Bennett 2005, 219 ff.), in Islam, war is permitted only if the intention and consideration of the appropriateness of the means allows no other approach – the cause of liberating Muslims from aggressors, for example. Even in war, violence should be deployed proportionally, and civilians must not be targeted. The essence of this doctrine is that the so-called 'House of Islam' (*Dar al-Islam*), in other words, territory with a majority-Muslim population, may be defended but not expanded by force. Wars must not be fought for the sake of mission and conversion.

It is primarily the thinkers Sayyid Qutb and Sayyid Abul Ala Maududi, popular among extremist Islamic fundamentalists, who have pushed for an offensive 'holy war' (Bennett 2005, 198 ff.). In this view, the Dar al-Islam is in a permanent state of war with the Dar al-Kufr, the territory of the 'unbelievers'. Peace will be granted only in the beyond. Extremists sometimes make a historical connection between themselves and the caliphs, the successors to Muhammad who actively expanded Arab territory and ushered in the Islamic imperial period. Today, this interpretation is the preserve of a small terrorist minority which, as we have seen, is referred to as Jihadist, though the irredentist Jihadists (Hamas among others) essentially represent the intersection of moderate and radical views.

The presence of both a moderate, defensive theological justification and a radical, offensive for political violence finds correspondence in the Christian tradition, though these approaches rose to prominence at different times in the Islamic and Christian worlds. Vilho Harle has written: 'Islam has been often perceived as a military doctrine due to the concept of jihad, which is normally rendered in English as "holy war." This is incorrect: According to classical Islam, no human activity is holy or sacred, and especially no war can be so. It is another matter that

Islam – just like Zoroastrianism, Judaism and Christianity – has motivated peoples to make war on behalf of the religion and their God, for good against evil. (…) (The) doctrine as such does not imply any more violence than Christianity does' (Harle 2000, 75, 77).

The image of the Christian martyr has cropped up repeatedly throughout history (Davis III 2004). For the Christian warrior, however, it was not Jesus Christ who served as role model as Jesus had broken with the traditional Judeo-Christian figure of the belligerent Messiah who purifies the world and reveals the true faith. After the death of Christ, however, the Christian martyr figure increasingly evolved from the suffering pacifist into the Christian warrior-martyr, as exemplified by the legendary figure of St. George of Lydda/Palestine, which arose in the fourth century. Richard the Lionheart later chose George as the patron of his crusade. Over the centuries, Muslims and Christians have developed near-identical notions of the "just war". In Christianity, the key elements included the teachings of St. Augustine or the early medieval theology of the French monastery Cluny, whose abbot Odo (926–44) argued that wars can be waged for good reasons, making them 'holy wars' (Davis III 2004, 251). This idea was interpreted in an offensive and radical way during the Crusades and in a defensive and moderate fashion during attacks by Islamic states on European powers, and it lives on in the discourse of evangelists such as Billy Graham, whose utterances feature unmistakable traces of the doctrine of holy war. Faith, so Graham tells us, is permanent war against sinners and sin (Davis III 244). In the West, the metaphor of offensive purification is very popular with certain Christian-inspired sects such as Scientology, as became apparent in January 2008, when American actor Tom Cruise, a famous adherent, called for the purification of the world in an internal video that was later made public.

Over the last century, Protestantism has produced a large number of legitimatory models that justify the deployment of violence as morally acceptable and make just wars seem possible. Prominent American theologian Reinhold Niebuhr laid the moral philosophical ground for America's entry into the Second World War with his doctrine of ethical perfectionism in relation to violence (Childless 1974). The human being, according to Niebuhr, is essentially sinful and violence is immanent to life. The important thing is to keep the use of violence within reasonable bounds, but not, as with the pacifist denial of all violence, to refuse to take social responsibility. For Niebuhr, 'necessity' and 'responsibility' were the key criteria with which the use of violence should be aligned.

In the Protestant church, doctrinal progress was made after the Second World War when, influenced by the development of nuclear weapons and other instruments of mass destruction, an increasing number of interpreters considered just war to have become infeasible and called for a shift towards pacifism (Honecker 1995, 416 ff.). That this interpretation has not taken hold throughout the Christian churches, and that it is still quite possible for churches to push for 'just wars', was evident on 17 February 2008, when the former Serbian province declared independence and the Orthodox Church in Belgrade called on the government to mobilize the army and occupy Kosovo.

This one example lays bare the ultimate impossibility of assuming that neither Christianity nor Islam has definitively closed the door on offensive and radical interpretations of 'just violence'. In the contemporary Islamic world, at any rate, an extremist interpretation is par for the course among Jihadists. The various schools of Islamic thought use the Prophet Muhammad to their own ends. He is a role model for both pacifists and terrorists, each group referencing different deeds and periods of his life to support their ideas.

It is also difficult to assign certain strands of Islamic fundamentalism to the various Islamic interpretations of violence. Whereas global Jihadists such as Osama Bin Laden have clearly taken their lead from the extremist teachings of Sayyid Qutb, irredentist groups such as Palestinian Hamas are hybrids of defensive mainstream and offensive Jihadist thought. As previously noted, they claim national defence as their justification and limit themselves to the recuperation of national territory, without aspiring to expand their struggle beyond it. This is a legitimate stance within the framework of classical Islamic law and is open to attack only to the extent that Hamas demands more than a two-state solution. At the same time, Hamas rejects the Islamic protection of civilians, a component of classical teachings on just war, and has clearly taken an extremist turn with its suicide attacks. Here, the organization is *not* firmly anchored in traditional ideology, and the sympathy it is shown by some Islamic scholars is a sad example of a break with tradition in the Arab world that has ushered in a violent modernity. The systematic killing of civilians underlines the development of a special form of extremist violence that pursues no anarchist goals but attempts to achieve its at least partially legitimate aims by means of illegitimate violence (against civilians) – violence of a kind that conflicts with both international law and classical Islamic teachings.

Numerous authors have begun to redefine their view of groupings such as Hamas and Hezbollah in recent years. Glenn E. Robinson calls for a distinction to be made between Islamic fundamentalist groups that occasionally use terrorism, such as Hamas with its record of agreeing lengthy cease-fires, and those which always use terrorism, such as the global Jihadists; otherwise, we risk overlooking the core character of Islamic fundamentalist organizations as part of a political movement (Robinson 2004, 112). Helga Baumgarten makes a similar argument, pointing out that Hamas has been democratically legitimized through elections, even as it aspires to reconquer *all* of Palestine (Baumgarten 2006). The Israeli state, too, has yet to embrace an unambiguous two-state policy. It continues, in essence, to occupy the West Bank and allows its settlement in breach of international law. But Hamas' use of violence against civilians must be rejected as extremist as a matter of principle (Baumgarten 2006, 117). Baumgarten makes the interesting point that it would be possible to sign a treaty with Hamas, such as the one between Lebanese Hezbollah and Israel in 1996, which would essentially bring an end to attacks on civilians. Unfortunately, Baumgarten states, Israel is unwilling to countenance such a treaty (Baumgarten 2006, 189).

For now, then, the scholarly literature is far less critical of Hezbollah than of Hamas. Augustus Richard Norton, one of the best-known American Middle East specialists and expert on Arab civil society, describes Hezbollah as an organization that almost exclusively engages in legitimate military resistance to the Israeli occupation (Norton 2007). Hezbollah carries out suicide attacks only against military installations (see also Harik 2005, 2). Israel, according to Norton, has killed far more civilians in its struggle against Hezbollah. Some Hezbollah activities, such as the abduction of soldiers, must however, be described as terrorist. To a certain extent, in light of its impressive record of providing social services, Hezbollah even commands the respect of Lebanon's secular government (Metzger 2000, 175 ff.). Hezbollah is in a sense highly conservative; yet, it is breaking away from the traditional view of the non-working woman, and women form a taken-for-granted part of the movement. Many authors now put forward the hypothesis that Hezbollah's progressive inclusion in politics and society would help open up the organization further, irrespective of its financial support from Iran (Harik 2005, 3).

Whatever our final assessment of Hamas and Hezbollah, it is clear that Islam's relationship to terrorist violence is complex. Terrorism across the world is far from being an exclusively Islamic phenomenon, and not all forms of terrorist violence in the Islamic world can be put down to

Islamic fundamentalists. When religious justifications play a role, the similarities in how Christianity and Islam attempt to come to terms with violence are generally more striking than the differences. Both religions have produced moderate and radical interpretations. A small subset of currently active Islamic fundamentalists has clearly departed from traditional Islamic teachings by adopting an extremist interpretation of the religion.

CAUSES OF TERRORISM: HOLY WAR AS A BLEND OF MADNESS AND RATIONALITY

If the causes of Islamic fundamentalist terrorism cannot be found in the religion of Islam, where do they lie? A great many authors cite two key reasons that fundamentalist terrorism has emerged in the last thirty years: *authoritarian violence*, as practiced by Islamic regimes, whether secular or religious, and *imperialist violence,* in the form of repression and exploitation by external governments. Terrorism, then, is a form of reactive violence. Paradoxically, the self-image of many terrorists, especially the global Jihadists, goes far beyond this kind of defensive perspective. We must inevitably ask whether those who resist attempts to suggest a genetic link between terrorism and Islam sanction this rationalizing interpretive about-face. Is terrorism really the weapon of the 'little guy' against authoritarianism and imperialism? Is terrorism really the 'instrumentally rational political tool of a structurally inferior party to conflict'? (Hippler 2006, 89). Plainly, the real dividing lines in interpreting terrorism run not between religions or cultures, but between modes of interpretation within cultures, some of which place the emphasis on its political rationality, others underlining its psychological-individualist characteristics.

Islamic fundamentalist terrorism is interpreted structurally by some scholars in the United States (M. Hafez 2003, 2004; Wiktorowicz 2004b). Here, the systematic repression of an opposition fighting for increased political participation and social improvements in, for example, such countries as Algeria, Egypt, Tunisia, Jordan and Pakistan, is identified as underpinning the development of terrorism (M. Hafez 2003, 27–70). Even 'modern authoritarianism', with its consequence-free and controlled electoral and democratic rituals, would, according to this view, be unsuited to prevent a strengthening opposition to dictatorships from committing extremist acts. Yet the experiences of these countries have often been quite different. In Tunisia, despite lasting political repression, no terrorist

Islamic fundamentalism has developed. In Jordan and Pakistan, on the other hand, there has been sometimes marked political violence despite relatively extensive opportunities for political participation. It is important to realize that terrorism is more likely to arise when the organizational existence of Islamic fundamentalist political movements is threatened, alongside general political repression (M. Hafez 2003, 71–108).

If these authors were right, then terrorism would be a rational reaction to state repression and organizational persecution. To reverse the argument, terrorism could be avoided by tolerating the non-violent political activities of Islamic fundamentalist movements. Is it possible, then, that terrorism could be eliminated through genuine political integration, at least in those places where the imperialist use of violence plays a subordinate role, in other words, in countries that are not directly occupied? Certain international experiences, with the Red Army Faction (RAF) in Germany, for example, raise doubts about this thesis. There was no ban on political participation in West Germany in the 1960s and 1970s, nor was the survival of radical political groups threatened unless they incited violence; yet, this did not prevent the rise of RAF terrorism.

Another intellectual approach that can be ascribed to the structuralist school is the supposition, widespread in the anti-globalization movement, that terrorism is chiefly the consequence of external violence (Pintak 2003; Sardar and Davies 2002).[7] In this view, imperialism and terrorism are mutually dependent and stabilize one another. The simple answer to the famous question, 'Why do they hate us?', originally posed by the *Christian Science Monitor* following the attacks of 11 September, is: because they have every reason to! The idea here is that present-day neo-imperialism is ignored in the West and triggers a terrorist counter-reaction in the Islamic world.

While it is undoubtedly true that authoritarian repression and imperial power politics continue to exist, it is highly doubtful that they sufficiently explain terrorism for the following reasons:

- It is by no means the case that state repression *inevitably* provokes a violent reaction, let alone terrorist acts against civilians. Not all opposition to repression is violent. This raises the question of whether repression is really a sufficient explanation for terrorism.

---

[7] See, for example, Lev Grinberg's text 'Symbolischer Völkermord' [Symbolic genocide] on the website of Attac-Deutschland, http://attac-gk.net-hh.de/index.php?id=372 (3 March 2008).

- Even if we assume that terrorism is a consequence of repression, it is also *cause* of repressive structures. In the Middle East, it made the police state even worse, further reduced participatory spaces and helped bring about the renaissance of imperialism.
- Certain phenomena relating to repression, like social injustice, play scarcely any role in extremist ideologies, such as that of the global Jihadists. The Al Qaeda organization headed by Osama Bin Laden has never prioritized the social question (Guelke 2006, 252), though it does have much to say about imperialism.

Undoubtedly, social and political violence *may* be among the factors motivating terrorism, but we must go beyond this line of argument. Ultra-radical groups that spilt from the Muslim Brothers, such as Al-Jihad al-Islami, arose when Egypt was still under authoritarian rule, but the survival of the Muslim Brothers *as such* was no longer threatened. Since the time of the Anwar al-Sadat government in the 1970s, the Muslim Brothers have existed in a state of tolerated semi-legality. Despite being officially banned, the group takes part in elections on other parties' lists. Inevitably, then, repression was eased, and we must interpret terrorism not only in structural but also in psychological terms. Terrorism has been shaped by certain key figures, such as the Egyptian Aiman al-Zawahiri. Individuals such as the former leader of Hamas, Sheik Yassin, have also played a role in their groupings' embrace of armed struggle or acts of terrorism against civilians (Baumgarten 2006, 48 f.).

Terrorism is not caused solely by the realities on the ground; it is also influenced by the way certain individuals perceive these realities. It is these individuals who decide whether evolution or revolution is the most effective way to change a given political situation. The concept of 'rational choice', which has taken hold in political science via perception theory and decision theory, does not assume that people behave rationally; instead they engage in rational reflection based on their values and personal cost-benefit calculations of possible actions (Allingham 2002). Identical social conditions may therefore lead individuals to reach different conclusions. These may appear rational to the individual extremist but are generally condemned by society as a whole because they are not motivated by any generally accepted goals, and/or the means of achieving these goals are considered unethical and largely ineffective by most people.

A psychological alternative to the structuralist analysis of terrorism is provided by Olivier Roy and others who claim that the 'global Jihadists' have long since broken loose from the local causes of structural violence and that they 'no longer have any connection with the "real" Muslim world that they supposedly represent' (Roy 2006, 295, 285 ff.). In tune with Roy's interpretation one could argue that the global Jihadists, organized in their brotherhoods, no longer subject their actions to any kind of rational reflection, systematically cordoning themselves off from the corrective of reality while using various techniques to brainwash their members. It is unclear, however, whether such interpretations are culturalist or psychological. Can terrorism be explained as a psychological defect in which religion merely serves as an ideological prop?

Having contested a purely culturalist interpretation of terrorism before, we must acknowledge that perhaps the most common view of terrorism posits an interplay of religion and madness. The colloquialism 'religious fanaticism' contains both phenomena: religion and psychopathology. Drawing on the work of Eric Voegelin, Barry Cooper refers to terrorism as a kind of a spiritual-philosophical disease, which he also calls 'pneumopathology' (B. Cooper 2006). There is a risk here of drifting into culturalist arguments, which currently suggest that only Islam has the potential to produce political fanaticism, while Christianity, in particular, claims to have lost this potential (Weinstein 2006, 99). But this is not an inevitable corollary of the thesis of terrorism being a spiritual-philosophical disease. In modern system theoretical interpretations of terrorism, religion – any religion – becomes an ideological environmental factor. Like 'poverty', 'religion' is a milieu within which terrorist actors and their counterparts interact, perceive and misperceive – no more and no less. Religion can be the stone pit for 'madness' – it is not the madness itself.

Muslims living in the West, the Muslim diaspora, provide an example of how structuralist approaches may be fruitfully combined with interpretations anchored in the psychology of religion or in ethnopsychology. To understand the spread of Islamic terrorism in the twenty-first century, we require multi-perspectival approaches rather than simple answers. Ultimately, we would have to decide which theory is the most plausible on a case-by-case basis. The second and third generation of immigrants has escaped the political repression found in their countries of origin, but conflicts still have an indirect impact because of their identification with the Islamic countries. That this may sometimes lead to terrorism is shown by the British bombers of 7 July 2005, who had grown up in the United Kingdom. A structuralist interpretation of such events may be valid because, despite living in the United Kingdom, those involved may make an anti-imperialist identification with their country of origin, which is not necessarily pathological. The argument often put forward against the structuralist interpretation of terrorism, that the key actors were middle class and suffered no political persecution in the United Kingdom, ignores the possibility that these individuals might incorporate distant problems into their own life stories through the process of identity transfer (Guelke 2006, 251). Those who dispute this would struggle to explain why Moses, the privileged son of a king, set off with the Jews for the Promised Land. Furthermore, the descendents of Muslim immigrants in the West may grow up in a milieu marked by subtle discrimination, the victims of overt or covert racism.

If we take our lead from these structural reflections, we must inevitably conclude that the USA and European countries with high levels of immigration are ill-advised to pursue a neo-imperialist agenda, as even seemingly well-integrated individuals may find rational reasons for acts of terror through identificatory transfer. If the older form of colonialism was directed against distant subjects, contemporary neo-imperialism targets citizens of an immigrant background, not in constitutional terms, but certainly in a wider political sense.

We must bear this structural interpretation in mind when considering the psychological variant often favoured by Western media. Scholars like David Cook and Olivia Allison also state that it is 'perceived victimization' rather than real discrimination that is crucial to terrorism (Cook and Allison 2007, 128). We might well describe the terrorist acts of young British Muslims in London as the madness of the brainwashed, which exists only because people manoeuvre themselves, from a great distance, into a collective pattern of thought that leads to extremist activities. In reality, it is clear that terrorism has never had any real prospect of achieving liberation from internal or external repression – on the contrary, it has at times helped bring about this repression in the first place, as is evident, for example, in the Afghanistan war, which was the consequence of the attacks of 11 September. Comparative political science has repeatedly shown that violence is not a particularly successful strategy of social transformation (Zimmermann 2006; see also Chapter 4). Hence, regardless of the legitimate and rational *motives* which *may* apply to a particular terrorist, the *means of violence* which he deploys must be regarded as the result of a 'pathological' misperception.

Thus, while the critique of authoritarianism and imperialism is largely justified, the notion that terrorism is unavoidable is wrong and raises it to the status of political act of liberation from structural repression.

At the same time, it is difficult to deny that terrorism may be rationally motivated. The extremist psychology of the perpetrators, blinded by religious and ethnic motives, does not entirely rule out legitimate structuralist interpretations. A meaningful profile of the individual terrorist would be imperative here. We may assume, particularly in the early stages of terrorist recruitment, that arguments centred on political resistance hold great appeal for a large number of sympathisers, though many terrorists are characterized by a degree of psychopathology, which is frequently reinforced by techniques of psychological manipulation.

The public and the media in both Western and Islamic countries approach the phenomenon of terrorism in very different ways. While violence against civilians is universally condemned, as was evident in the initial reactions to the attacks of 11 September 2001 in both the West and the Islamic world (K. Hafez 2002a, 232 f.), significant differences have crept into evaluations of terrorism over the last decade. It is thus no longer possible to speak of a consistent global dialogue on terrorism. In the Islamic media, terrorism is blamed chiefly on the West's militaristic foreign policies and Israeli state terrorism (Glück 2008). From the late 1990s, opinion polls have shown that a majority of Palestinians, including those who previously welcomed the peace process endorsed by Yasser Arafat, now approve of terrorist attacks on Israeli citizens.[8] Similarly, most Israelis now support the use of extreme force against the Palestinians. Authoritarianism as a motivating factor is suppressed in the partially censored media landscapes of the Islamic world, and Muslims are often portrayed as global victims of discrimination. Western media, on the other hand, focus on the cultural-religious background to terrorism (K. Hafez 2002a, 228 ff.) and assert that the problem of terrorism, which is viewed as wholly pathological in nature, can be solved only by political and military means (Glück 2008, 153 f.).

The West and the Islamic world share a tendency to reduce the complexity of terrorism in line with their own ideological models. While the West tends to interpret terrorism in terms of psychology, culture and criminality, the arguments put forward within the Islamic world tend to be structuralist in nature. The irredentist Jihadism of Hamas in particular is understood as rational political action in much of the Islamic public sphere. Certain prominent Islamic scholars are partly to

---

[8] See the relevant remarks in the country reports on the autonomous Palestinian territories in the 'Middle East Yearbook' from 1996 on (edited by Thomas Koszinowski and Hanspeter Mattes of the Deutsches Orient-Institut).

blame for this when they ignore the fact that the end does not always justify the means, something which is recognized in traditional Islamic teachings. A debate on the link between imperialism and terrorism is avoided in the West. Islamic countries, meanwhile, sidestep the fact that this debate also highlights their own repressive politics by blaming the West for everything.

In sum: the terrorists' communicative intention, namely, to achieve more through their sensational atrocities than merely attracting attention on a massive scale, is succeeding to the extent that the West is stoking a fear of psychopathic Islamic fundamentalists – or even Muslims in general. The panic this produces is an important aspect of the threat posed by terrorism. As American policy towards the Middle East shows, it can lead to political overreactions. But the idea that terrorism *also* has structural political causes, at least in the eyes of many sympathisers, requires urgent discussion in the media if we wish to seize the opportunity to understand how political advances can help to end the upsurge in Islamic fundamentalist terrorism. Authors such as Terry Eagleton (2005, 118) and Adrian Guelke are therefore right to criticize the self-censoring characteristic of the discourse on terrorism. As Guelke notes: 'The fervour with which the radical right denies that injustice and inequality have any bearing on the question of terrorism may be self-serving in so far as it indicates an unwillingness to address questions of global equity. (...) (It) does remain the case that the connections between these at a global level are far more tenuous than they are within particular societies. However, the explanation of Al-Qaeda's emergence in terms of the spread of an evil ideology is scarcely more illuminating' (Guelke 2006, 254 f.).

NON-VIOLENT RESISTANCE IN ISLAM AND HOW THE WEST IGNORES IT

Pacifism is a common ideology in Europe and North America, a belief system in which a number of humanist and Christian rationales lead to a fundamental rejection of war and violence. In the USA, the prime example is the quietism-pacifism of the Quakers and the Amish. But the Enlightenment also exercised a significant influence on pacifism, in the form, for example, of Kant's 'eternal peace' and the developing philosophy of human rights. In Western countries, numerous modern peace movements have taken off in the post-war period, notably against the wars in Vietnam, the Gulf wars and the arms build-up during the Cold War. Pacifism and peace movements are not, however, the same thing.

Peace movements are often fairly short-term social movements that unite people with differing motives, very few of whom are consistent pacifists. The collapse of the American anti-war movement prior to America's entry into the Second World War is paradigmatic of the internal differences so often found in peace movements. Many pacifists switched to the pro-war camp because they felt that the exceptional brutality of the Hitler regime ruled out radical pacifism and made the ethical use of violence indispensible (DeBenedetti 1980; Wittner 1984).

Non-violent resistance is related to pacifism. In both Europe and North America, movements have developed that espouse the view that social peace cannot be established solely through the absence of wars; it requires a variety of social and political reforms. Since the aim must be to achieve structural changes, a refusal to go to war is not enough, and this school of thought therefore advocates a philosophy of civil disobedience or non-violent resistance. In Europe, intellectuals such as German scholar Theodor Ebert, influenced by the student protests of the 1960s and 1970s, even supported an approach based on 'non-violent rebellion' in which a crucial distinction was made between illegitimate violence against people and legitimate violence against things (Ebert 1978). In the USA, the most famous proponent of this approach was Martin Luther King with his philosophy of non-violent resistance to racial discrimination. In recent years, the environmental and anti-globalization movements have combined various forms of non-violent resistance. Here, non-violent symbolic actions, in particular, are intended to capture the moral high ground (LeVine 2005, 246 ff.).

Despite these significant traditions, it would be wrong to assume that pacifism and/or non-violent resistance are accepted by majorities in Western cultures. In 1983, conservative member of the German Bundestag Heiner Geißler even went so far as to blame pacifism for Auschwitz. In exaggerated form, this shows clearly that any fundamental rejection of violence and war is seen as a lack of social responsibility by a majority in Western countries; a stance entirely in keeping with the doctrine of just war advocated by Reinhold Niebuhr and other theologians. Civilized violence, but not a total rejection of violence, typifies the contemporary Western attitude. This is evident in the system of collective military security that is characteristic of both the armed forces and NATO, and in the defence of national sovereignty within the context of the United Nations and international law. This prevailing doctrine is frequently criticized by pacifists for sustaining the vicious circle of war and violence. Yet the notion of ethical, defensible, appropriate and just violence remains the

primary culture of the West, and pacifism the secondary culture, advocated at best by a minority of people.

Mark LeVine was one of the first to point out that Islamic pacifist and
non-violent schools of thought and strategies are essentially ignored in the
West. It is no exaggeration to state that the Western world is marked by
a highly selective perception that largely reduces Islam to terrorism and
every conceivable form of violence. Conversely, Buddhism and Hinduism
are perceived as 'peaceful religions'. This, too, is a selective perception,
as a simple example shows. The Dalai Lama, the highest authority in
Tibetan Buddhism (often referred to as Lamaism), is indeed representative of a peaceful religious interpretation of resistance to China, but
Lamaism was largely responsible for centuries of feudal exploitation in
Tibet, something which is only rarely taken into consideration.

Because Islam is typecast as violent, any attempt to reconcile Islam and
pacifism is for many critics like trying to square the circle. Theologically,
we appear to be faced with insurmountable problems because the Koran
legitimizes violence and war, albeit under specific conditions, and above
all, because the Prophet Muhammad himself waged wars. While Christian
justifications for war are always very elaborate, as war seems to contradict the pacifist message of Jesus Christ, we might conclude that war
and violence correspond consistently and fully with the basic character
of Islam. Nonetheless, an Islamic pacifism has managed to develop, and
Christianity and Islam have developed mirror-image methods of exegesis.
Over the centuries, and to some extent to this day, practical Christian
theology has qualified Jesus Christ's radical message of peace, expressed
in the Sermon on the Mount, by producing justifications for war.
Meanwhile, the doctrine of just war is in fact the Koran's main message
on the subject; pacifist teachings exist only on the margins (Abu-Nimer
2003, 33). Islamic pacifists, however, refer mainly to the early period of
the Prophet Muhammad's activities when, despite persecution, he repeatedly forbade his followers to use violence, even for self-defence. The denial
of the pacifist Scriptures (the Bible) by the Christian doctrine of war thus
corresponds to the converse relativization of the Koranic doctrine of just
war by Muslim pacifists drawing on the traditional Islamic writings of
the Hadith. With this epistemological sleight of hand, it becomes quite
possible to establish a connection between pacifism and Islamic tradition.
In some cases, the Koran itself is even being reinterpreted from a pacifist
perspective.

The image of the suffering and persecuted Prophet Muhammad has
taken hold in Sufism and in the Ahmadiyya movement. Both represent

strong popular Islamic currents that preach inner asceticism and purification through the development of the capacity for suffering, and both have moved away from the concept of jihad as a metaphor for the physical waging of war (Abu-Nimer 2003, 45). Modern reformist Islam has taken up these impulses and contributed to the development of an intellectual pacifism. Maulana Wahiduddin Khan explains the superiority of non-violent resistance with reference to the first few years of the Prophet Muhammad's activities in Mecca, when he preached non-violence and peaceful mission (*dawa*).[9] Zeki Saritoprak, drawing on the work of Turkish reformist thinkers Said Nursi and Fetullah Gülen, also cites the example of Muhammad (Saritoprak 2005).

An unusual but elegant argument is found in the work of Chaiwat Satha-Anand, who refers not only to the practice of the Prophet but also to the Koran. Satha-Anand concedes that the Koran permits the use of violence under certain conditions. Yet these conditions no longer pertain in the era of high-tech warfare. Satha-Anand takes the view that the distinction between the guilty and the innocent (civilians) anchored in mainstream Islam no longer makes sense in the age of weapons of mass destruction because it is no longer possible to restrict killing specifically to soldiers. In practice, this means that the Koran must be interpreted as urging abstention from war under contemporary conditions (Satha-Anand 1993, 15). This suggests a line of reasoning that runs perfectly parallel to the pacifist debate within Protestant Christianity after the Second World War. Both Islamic pacifism and Christian pacifism reject the idea, preached by Niebuhr and others, that violence can be deployed in an ethical fashion, emphasizing the destructive power of modern weapons of mass destruction.

The greeting 'Salam' means 'peace' in Arabic, whereas the word for pacifism, *musalama* has connotations of passivity and inactivity in the Arab Islamic world and is therefore rather uncommon. Many modern thinkers, very much in the spirit of Mahatma Gandhi, prefer to speak of non-violent action or non-violent resistance.[10] Recent Islamic history contains numerous examples of non-violent resistance, but these are largely ignored in the West. Islamic fundamentalist organizations also deploy

---

[9] Maulana Wahiduddin Khan, Non-Violence and Islam, http://www.alrisala.org/Articles/papers/nonviolence.htm (15 September 2007).
[10] See Muhammad Iqbal Ahnaf, Towards an Islamic Active Non-Violence Approach, http://islam21.net/main/index.php?option=com_content&task=view&id=114&Itemid=40 (28 February 2008).

non-violent methods. The most famous examples of such resistance include:[11]

- *Egyptian Revolution 1919:* months of non-violent resistance against the British occupation
- *Pashtun resistance 1930:* taking his lead from Muhammad's early pacifism, Abdul Ghaffar Khan, known as Badshah Khan, a close associate of Gandhi, rallied together many thousands of people in what is now northern Pakistan to create his 'army of God' (Khudai Khidmatgar) in order to engage in non-violent resistance against the colonial power of Britain (Easwaran 1999; Johansen 1997; Milton-Edwards 2006, 187 ff.).
- *Iranian Revolution 1977-:* Despite massacres perpetrated by the government, from 1977 on Iranians opposed Mohammad Reza Shah Pahlavi through strikes and boycotts. This non-violent strategy was abandoned only after Ayatollah Khomeini assumed power.
- *Fall of the Sudanese government 1985:* Dictator Jaafar Numeiri was overthrown after several weeks of non-violent demonstrations and strikes.
- *Palestinian resistance 1987-:* since the first Intifada began in the West Bank and Gaza Strip in 1987, the nature of Palestinian resistance has changed; there has been a shift away from the armed struggle of the PLO towards civil disobedience and non-violent resistance.

In addition to these major non-violent movements, non-violent resistance is an everyday element of political life in the Islamic world; from demonstrations by Algerian journalists (late 1980s) and hunger strikes at Palestinian universities (LeVine 2005, 253) to 10,000-strong demonstrations organized by Ayatollah Sistani in Iraq (Berger 2004). We are dealing here with a large number of activities of the most varied kinds.

Palestinian resistance in the first Intifada, which began in 1987 and lasted to 1994, shows very clearly both the potential and the limits of non-violent resistance in the Islamic world. We must bear in mind, however, that conditions in Palestine do not apply elsewhere and that the chances of success for a given effort are closely bound up with the character of a specific trouble spot. Nonetheless, the Intifada illustrates why, despite various attempts, a movement comparable to Mahatma Gandhi's liberation struggle has not so far emerged in the Islamic world.

---

[11] For an overview, see Wiktorowicz 2004b, Zunes 1999.

The first Intifada deployed largely non-violent means (Dajani 1999; Lockman and Beinin 1989; Zunes 1999).[12] Mostly manifestations of upsurge and violence were witnessed by a worldwide audience, especially youths throwing stones at the Israeli army. Far less attention was paid to strike action, boycotts, the withholding of taxes, sit-ins, blockades and other acts of civil disobedience. It is reasonable to assume that the Palestinians' popular uprising influenced world opinion in such a way that the Oslo peace process was able to begin in 1993 via the indirect route of the Madrid negotiations. The peace process ground to a halt only in the late 1990s, when Hamas and other groups increasingly abandoned the strategy of non-violence in favour of terrorism (Zunes 1999, 48).

Muhammad Abu-Nimer points out that the Palestinians' non-violent resistance began four years before the Intifada. He rejects the notion, common in the West, that the uprising was spontaneous (Abu-Nimer 2003, 130 ff.). If he is correct, the Intifada was a feat of organization long in the making, without which it would quickly have collapsed, rather than lasting for years. The central command of the Intifada, the Unified National Leadership of the Uprising (UNLU), planned and organized civil resistance based on the following elements: economic boycotts (such as the closing of businesses), social boycotts (such as general strikes), protest marches, political non-cooperation (such as the non-recognition of Israel), symbolic actions (such as wearing the Palestinian national colours) and the development of alternative structures (such as people's committees) (Abu-Nimer 2003, 151 ff.). Hamas was not part of the UNLU, but it cooperated with many of these measures, and mosques often became centres of resistance (Abu-Nimer 2003, 166). Hamas' main task at the time was to provide a corrective to the occupation economy by setting up charitable and social institutions: the absence of the Israeli labour market, in particular, impoverished the Palestinian population. Christian and secular groups were also involved in the Intifada; Islam was not centre stage (Abu-Nimer 2003, 175).

The rest of the story is well known. Hopes were raised in 1993–95 that the Oslo peace process would facilitate the signing of a peace treaty within five years which would culminate in the implementation of the two-state solution, but the murder of Israeli prime minister Yitzhak Rabin by an Israeli extremist in 1995 transformed the situation. Implementation of the interim agreements was delayed, treaty proposals became half-hearted

---

[12] Stephen Zunes, Nonviolent Resistance in the Islamic World, in: Nonviolent Activist, http://www.warresisters.org/nva0102–1.htm (13 September 2007).

and the Israelis continued to build illegal settlements while Hamas stepped up its terrorist activities: the peace process ground to a halt. The second Intifada, from 2000 onwards, was no longer unambiguously non-violent. Non-violent action has also been deployed in the Palestinian territories in the first decade of the twenty-first century, but only sporadically and without much effect.

A prominent example is the Palestinian village of Bilin in the West Bank. The villagers protested peacefully for two and a half years against the Israeli separation wall, which was preventing farmers from getting to their fields. As a result, Israel's supreme court ruled in 2007 that the wall had to be moved.[13] The group Popular Committee Against the Wall had strictly adhered to non-violent strategies over the years: activists chained themselves to olive trees, demonstrated or built makeshift prison cells, repeatedly enduring arrest and tear-gas and stun-grenade attacks. The group argued that the resistance struggle in general could be lost because some Palestinians were too quick to take up arms, thus forfeiting the moral authority of Palestinian resistance.

Hamas, which has been chiefly responsible for acts of terrorism in recent years, has also frequently deployed non-violent means. In February 2008, for example, Hamas organized a human chain through the Gaza Strip to demand the opening of the borders. However, neither Hamas nor the PLO, which dominates in the West Bank, has adopted a comprehensive strategy of non-violent resistance. Such an approach has repeatedly been thwarted by terrorist acts, and there is no coordinated national policy as there was during the 1987 Intifada, when the PLO recognized the momentum of internal resistance and adapted itself to it.

Why have the Palestinians failed where Gandhi and Badshah Khan succeeded, namely, in achieving non-violent national liberation? It is not because there is no tradition of non-violent resistance in Islam. On the contrary, non-violent action is a daily practice in many Islamic countries. But as the Palestinian example shows, it only rarely leads to a coordinated and focussed national movement. Feuds between Hamas and the PLO are among the key reasons for this in Palestine. While violence is easy to effect, non-violent resistance requires an internal consensus among political factions. Ideological differences must take a back seat

---

[13] Susanne Knaul, Gewaltfreier Protest bringt Erfolg [Non-violent protest brings success] in: *die tageszeitung*, 6 September 2007; Martin Forberg, 'Wissen sie etwas Besseres als den Boykott?' [Can you think of anything better then a boycott?], *die tageszeitung*, 9–10 February 2008.

to a common goal. This succeeded in the case of Gandhi's movement. Differences and problems, up to and including armed conflicts, for example between Pakistan and India, sprang up only *after* independence had been achieved. In contrast, even during the initial stages of the Oslo process, the Palestinians never managed to unite the different camps. Yasser Arafat's strategy of always keeping a number of ministerial posts in his autonomous administration available for Hamas, in case it eventually opted to support the peace process, did not obscure the PLO's aspiration to dominance.

Spontaneous uprisings, as the failed rebellion of Burmese monks in 2007 showed, are no panacea. Non-violent resistance requires a coherent synthesis of political coordination and a grass-roots willingness to implement agreed measures: another reason for the Palestinians' failure lies in the relative absence of lasting and large-scale mass protests in the twenty-first century. Even the best organization will come to grief if it fails to fire the popular imagination. However, the popular response to any non-violent campaign is in part due to the experienced or anticipated suffering caused by a given regime or army of occupation. Abu-Nimer rightly points to the fact that there are significant differences between the realities of occupation in Palestine and India. While the movement of Gandhi and Badshah Khan developed within the context of highly superficial British colonial rule, which could never fully control the enormous Indian sub-continent, in the occupied Palestinian territories about four million Palestinians confront an equally large occupying power in the shape of Israel, which is actively pursuing a policy of colonialist settlement, enjoys enormous military superiority within a very small geographical arena and nips every attempt at resistance in the bud (Abu-Nimer 2003, 143). The first Intifada certainly showed Israel's vulnerability, but its armed forces are now better able to take the necessary defensive action as a result. The rubber bullets, stun grenades, arrests and the blowing up of buildings that are a fact of everyday life in the occupied territory make it harder to mobilize the Palestinian people.

As this example demonstrates, culturalist theories that deny that the Islamic world has any capacity for non-violent resistance or even pacifism, working on the assumption of an inherent propensity for violence, have failed to study carefully the realities on the ground in the roughly sixty Islamic countries. This applies even to those authors who fully acknowledge the basic potential for non-violent resistance in the Middle East. When Mark LeVine alludes to the example of the Zapatista resistance movement in Mexico with respect to the Middle East and North African region, he overlooks the specific conditions underlying this case. It is true that Mexico is an authoritarian state to some extent, but certainly not to the same degree as some Middle Eastern states. Civil resistance in the Iraq of Saddam Hussein was very hard to imagine. But the Zapatistas had and still have another invaluable advantage which Middle Eastern resistance groups have hitherto largely lacked: they enjoy the undivided support of an anti-globalization movement operating on a worldwide scale, without which they would not have been successful (Cleaver 1998). While the Palestinian resistance struggle receives great international attention, it is scarcely conceivable that other political struggles in the Islamic world would meet with a similar response. The internal unity of those resisting, their ability to develop non-violent structures and the nature of the state violence perpetrated against their movements will therefore remain the key criteria for the success of non-violent resistance in the Islamic world.

The academic discussion of the opportunities for, and limits to, the Islamic world's non-violent resistance to occupation and authoritarian rule is still in its infancy. It sometimes seems as though Western publics would fail to recognize non-violent resistance in Islamic countries even if it happens on a large scale. While every terror attack ends up in the evening news, even the most large-scale non-violent events receive at best marginal attention in our media. Abu-Nimer: 'Many analysts, scholarly and popular, fail to recognize non-violent resistance when it does anything but sit, stand, or march right in front of them. Violence is so much easier to recognize, categorize, and analyze; weapons, physical attacks, injuries, and death compel attention' (Abu-Nimer 2003, 139). This not only reflects specific reservations about Islam. Non-violent resistance in other parts of the world receives equally little attention – as in the regions neighbouring Chiapas province in Mexico, which have similar problems that are also largely ignored. Conflict has tremendous news value. Western journalism views violence as key to overcoming news thresholds, laying the foundations for a fatal symbiosis of terrorism and journalism (K. Hafez 1999b, 2002b, 59 ff., 90 ff., 125 ff., 134 ff.). A society in which a visual medium like television sets the tone is particularly likely to develop conservative characteristics. War, violence and security practices lend themselves to visual representation. The politics of peace, on the other hand, based primarily on negotiations, is far less attractive (Scheuer 1999) in this venue.

Systematic comparison of Islam and the West would be of tremendous value in this respect. The Muslim world has a rich tradition of peaceful and civil dispute resolution, but attempts to pursue a strategy of modern pacifism and non-violent resistance have met with limited success. It is true that such approaches have as a rule been no more than peripheral phenomena in Western societies as well, but the experiences of the labour movement, various peace movements and the American civil rights movement show that the traditional societal institutions for settling conflicts are inadequate to the task of defending people against the repression of the modern state, irrespective of whether this state is the authoritarian one in which they are living or a foreign occupier. Particularly in the Middle East, a certain section of the youth has turned to violence because the old social means of ensuring peace have been monopolized by the modern state. Saddam Hussein cooperated with the tribal authorities of Iraq (Jabar 2003) and Gamal Abdel Nasser controlled the traditional Islamic clergy. The current political and social problems in the Islamic world, however, require modern emancipatory movements that would have to overcome the patriarchal gulf between men and women as well as social and ethnic boundaries in order to help the values of pacifism and non-violent resistance gain acceptance (Abu-Nimer 2003, 110 ff.).

Conclusion

From 'Holy War' to Democracy? The Current State of Islamic and Western Modernity

Western discourse, particularly in the mass media and popular culture, but also much of academia and the high-brow cultural scene, imputes boundless radicalism, fanaticism and violence to the Islamic world. Its capacity for social and political change, meanwhile, is frequently denied. Even among the most progressive of Western thinkers, there is a long tradition of support for colonialism when it comes to Islam and the Middle East. Karl Marx himself believed that only the penetration of the religious-feudal stagnation of the Middle East by the forces of Western capitalism could lay the key foundation stones for the emergence of modernity in the region (Turner 1978). For Max Weber, Islam was the antithesis of the Protestant ethic of modernity (Salvatore 1997). We should, however, acknowledge the extenuating circumstances: while these key intellectual figures displayed an 'Orientalist' tendency to deny the Islamic world a capacity for development in light of its contemporary weakness, they were in the good company of the leading experts on Islam and the Middle East of the time.

This has now changed fundamentally. Since the great debate on Western scholarship on the Middle East initiated by Edward Said in 1978, the relevant academic disciplines have undergone a process of profound reform. Anyone now claiming that the Islamic world is fundamentally incapable of making cultural, social or political progress will surely be refuted by most scholars in the field. And anyone now referring to a permanent cultural struggle between Islam and the West – Samuel Huntington and

Bernard Lewis being recent examples – need look no further than modern scholarship on the Middle East for an initiation into the complexity of developments in the contemporary Islamic world, a world marked by processes of democratization, hard and soft autocracies, regional differences and social and cultural transformation. The research on Islam and the Middle East carried out at Western universities and printed by Western publishers has notched up considerable achievements. But it remains a specialist and marginal academic field. It is the Huntingtons and Lewises and the major media and publishing houses that dominate public discourse and the major academic debates rather than this marginal discipline. Much of the time, it is in fact the Oriana Fallacis and Michel Houellebeqs of the world who turn up in the high-street bookstores with their crude Islamophobia, while the real specialists at best make it into the media during periods of extreme crisis. The tendency of Western societies to depict Islam as another world incompatible with modernity, democracy and civilization, ensuring the survival of the old opposition between East and West, even in the 'information society', has prompted UN secretary generals, German presidents and many others to issue public warnings of a new 'clash of civilizations' (see, for example, Herzog 1999).

One contemporary revenant of the Western Orientalist mentality is German philosopher Peter Sloterdijk, who is sometimes described as the most influential living German thinker, a figure known beyond academia in the media and wider public sphere. In his book *Zorn und Zeit* (*Rage and Time*), Sloterdijk rightly states that modern Islamic fundamentalism is a mobilizing force whose recent popularity is anchored in the social problems of the Islamic world. Yet he characterizes Islamic fundamentalism, and in fact often Islam as a whole, as a totally anti-systemic and violence-oriented force vis-à-vis the Western world and modernity and as completely incompatible with them:

By the mid-21st century, if birth rates remain at their current high levels, the new mobilizations [of Islamic fundamentalism] – whether or not they are legitimate in terms of Koranic theology – could, in the Arabian Peninsula alone, influence a reservoir of several hundred million young men for whom the only existentially attractive horizon of meaning is likely to involve embracing projects of self-destruction with a political and religious patina. In thousands of Koranic schools, which have sprung up all over the world as if by magic in recent times, filled with seething surpluses of young men, the restless masses are drilled in the concepts of Holy War. (...) Even experts on this state of affairs have not the slightest idea how the Muslim youth bulge so dramatically underway, the largest wave of surplus young men bent on genocide in the history of the world, might be contained by peaceful means. (...) Thus, however true it may be that the Islamic theocracy rests upon the formally and materially totalitarian aspiration to regulate all human activity in a virtually Islamicized world society in accordance with Koranic law, such a regime would be utterly incapable of responding to the economic, political, technological and artistic realities of the contemporary era. (...) That political Islamism is out of synch with the modern world and is marked by a fundamentally anti-modern attitude is plain for all to see (Sloterdijk 2006, 346–8).

To put it in a nutshell: this book claims the exact opposite. Where Sloterdijk sees only hatred and menace in the Islamic world, the present author cherishes the hope that despite genuine risks from dictatorships, wars, terror and anti-Semitism, *even* and perhaps *especially* political Islam, in all its forms up to and including fundamentalism, might prepare the ground for the political inclusion of the Islamic world in a largely consensual project of modernity. Alongside the spectrum of secular political and social phenomena already in evidence, the Islamic countries might develop a second pillar of a religious-conservative hue, generating the normal dualism of political factions and ideologies characteristic of almost all Western political cultures. To this end, however, secular and religious forces must overcome their still typically authoritarian proclivities. This is a process of internal reform quite familiar to the West: we need only think of the turbulent history of Western political ideologies and forces, which in the case of Europe, broke with dictatorship only a few decades ago.

Perhaps the roots of the widespread notion that politics in the Islamic world is anti-Western and deeply irrational really do lie in the complex relationship between proximity and distance that often exists between political processes in the Islamic and Western worlds. The development of political ideologies, cultures and systems in the Islamic world by no means entirely defies analysis through tried-and-tested Western theories. On the contrary, on closer inspection there is much that must strike us as astonishingly familiar: a clamouring for reforms alongside necessary breaks with tradition, fundamentalist ideological skirmishes alongside social protest, reform logjams and change, and the instability of democratic conditions. Developments often occur in much the same way, though frequently at different points in time. The Islamic world has produced its own variants of modern developments. But does this justify talk of a *separate* modernity or even counter-modernity?

The 'out-of-synch-ness' to which even Sloterdijk refers is in fact partial rather than absolute, and it does not mean total dissimilarity. What is our basis for comparison? Post-war history in its entirety? If so, we soon discover that religion has played a major role in the politics of the Middle East by no means from the very beginning of its modern history, but only since the Iranian revolution of 1978–9. And there were certainly reasons for this return of religious and reformationist politics to the centre of political life, reasons rooted in the specific circumstances of the Islamic world. Unlike the Western countries at the time of the Enlightenment, Middle Eastern states lie within the sphere of influence of Western imperialism, against which Islam has been deployed as an ideology of independence. In contrast to the Western world, secularism in the Middle East did not come about in the nineteenth and twentieth centuries solely in the shape of the idea of liberation from religious constraints: it was administered by authoritarian regimes, cliques and putschists, who deployed it as a bulwark of their otherwise questionable legitimacy, particularly vis-à-vis their Western backers. What could be more logical than to threaten such dictatorships with the mobilizing force of religion?

At the same time, it is by no means the case that secularism is totally disapproved of in contemporary Islamic societies. There are certainly more 'cultural' than strict Muslims in the Islamic world. For them, religion is now no more than a tradition which they often scarcely practice, and there are more atheists than one might think. At a time of neo-conservative re-Islamization, however, it is hard for such people to state their beliefs openly for fear of the social consequences. The tolerance of Islam with respect to itself and to other religions is currently beset by severe problems, but it is still alive. Mass phenomena such as the Arabic news station *Al-Jazeera*, which features daily clashes between individuals of the widest range of ideological backgrounds, show that a secular and pluralist mentality has long since been enjoying its own renaissance. Many people, however, value political Islam, and even anti-secular Islamic fundamentalism, as a political ideology opposed to the prevailing political systems or, at least, the ruling elites. What the West must grasp is that in view of the repressive realities of many secular dictatorships, religion tends to take on emancipatory overtones. Such religion is often reactionary and marked by 'Catholic' intolerance. But this also makes it radical: it rejects the gestures of subservience characteristic of the traditional Islamic scholars and through its break with tradition (which it of course camouflages as the *preservation* of tradition) provokes a general mood within society that a new era is about to dawn in which unjust orders will be swept away.

It is paradoxical but quite true: lifestyles are becoming increasingly individualized and religion is one of the key drivers of this process. The seemingly collectivizing bond of Islam has done nothing to prevent the almost post-modern departures of Islam on the Internet. The systematics of the religious-political schools of thought are becoming ever more complex. Comparison with the West reveals that the Islamic world too features a remarkable juxtaposition of old and new ideologies, of 'radical protestant' views and socially revolutionary projects, through middle class reform projects of a 'neo-Lutheran' hue and revivalist movements to liberal religious reformers. The Islamic world does not, therefore, stand outside of global modernity. Rather, like every other region of the world, it is producing its own blend of highly modern forms of expression. The Islamic world is catching up on processes of reformation, but at the same time, in intellectual-history terms (partly because of the West's influence), is already further advanced than was the Christian Reformation, and it is integrating this syncretism into the political and social conflicts of the industrial-age, and post-colonial societies.

It is by no means only the Islamic fundamentalists who offend against the minimum political consensus of Western modernity that developed following the Second World War – secularism, the constitutional state and the core elements of any democracy, namely electoral freedom, freedom of assembly and freedom of opinion. Sections of both the Islamic-fundamentalist and secular spectrum are out of step with this consensus in various ways. At the same time, however, even most contemporary fundamentalists are no longer committed to authoritarianism, even if they continue to oppose the secular state. 'Christian democratization' is not a privilege of the West, but a reproducible model that has long since taken off in the Islamic world.

Christian democratization in the West, however, developed only on the basis of a functioning social contract and stable democracies – conditions which, with the exception of a small number of countries, do not yet apply in the Islamic world. It is thus no surprise that the political factions correspond to deep social structures, which reveal the true extent of contemporary social shifts. The Islamic fundamentalists are particularly vocal in their aspiration to remove the political and economic elites who are so lacking in social depth. But their claim to speak for society does not go uncontested. Despite their active provision of social services, their visions of a just society have often remained vague. Most fundamentalists are not socialists, but economic liberals with a religious patina. Their domain is the 'small-scale capitalism' of social networks – but could they run entire national economies? The Iranian experience, where state Islam produced nouveau riche classes, suggests not, while the case of Turkey points to an affirmative answer. But what matters at this point in time is the understanding that Islamic fundamentalism does not solely involve religious reflexes but also the 'cultural accommodation of social change', as expressed in the title of what is probably Bassam Tibi's best book. It is not Islam as such that produced fundamentalism, but the function of religion in social transformation.

From the point of view of democratization, the choice between liberalism and radicalism is essentially a question of strategy. The major Islamic fundamentalist organizations today are not of a revolutionary persuasion. With the exception of irredentist organizations, such as Hamas, they renounce violence, but it is chiefly in their rejection of the secular state that they cling to a radical protestant stance that in principle threatens democracy. It is no surprise that authoritarian systems do not produce flawless democrats. The remarkable thing is that the majority of Muslims today want democracy in the first place, a state of affairs which for the most part they have never experienced themselves. The fundamentalists want to remove the existing dictatorships. The friction with fundamental religious claims alone generates a political radicalism that unquestionably makes them the strongest opposition to the existing authoritarian regimes. The European experience shows that because it strengthens the opposition's capacity to oppose, political radicalism may stimulate processes of democratization. Democracies negotiated between radical forces are among Europe's most successful models of democratization (Spain, Portugal, perhaps Northern Ireland in the near future). Moreover, fundamental claims by groups, parties and movements are far from unusual in developed democracies, the old *Fundis* of the German green movement being a prime example.

Radicalism thus generates opportunities for democratization as well as risks. Comparative research on political transformation has yet to consistently apply the insights of the functionalist theory of democracy to the Islamic world. The opposition in Islamic countries is expected to be firmly established within civil society and of a 'Christian democratic' tenor – otherwise it receives no support. The highly positive examples of 'democracy without democrats' – with the exception of the Weimar Republic – are forgotten. Yet the genius of Islamic fundamentalism consists in a quite unique capacity for political combat: as the derivative of an old religious tradition, it is at the very least sure to survive even during periods of authoritarianism; it offers apparent ideological clarity through radical slogans, enjoys a high degree of legitimacy among the general population, can be deployed within the international context as an anti-imperialist ideology and facilitates the creation of a broad social alliance which, despite being concentrated in the lower-middle classes, excludes no social stratum or class.

But fundamentalism is not a wholly positive phenomenon, for it entails the risk of lapsing into authoritarian patterns. Ideological 'grey zones' exist for good reason. If their terms are clear, pacts and alliances with secular forces could therefore expedite integration. While equating Islamic fundamentalism with 'Islamofascism' has become a widespread form of political abuse, comparative studies reveal how unproductive the term is. Fundamentalists do not propagate the violent cleansing of society, racial fanaticism or Social Darwinism. Though they have a tendency to evoke ethno-religious bogeymen, they do not constitute apocalyptic religious movements. They despise secular law, but feel bound by Islamic law and, at least in the case of the majority Sunnite school of Islam, have long since parted company with the idea of a single leader (a caliphate). They are corporatist only to a limited extent and – at least in terms of the practice of the last thirty years – are no more expansionist in orientation than other forces and political systems. With ideas reminiscent of earlier ideologies of 'national liberation', only small terrorist groups enter into fascist territory.

By seeking to safeguard democratization and greater political openness, the West could exercise a significant influence on integrative developments within mainstream Islamic fundamentalism – were it finally to opt for a policy on Islam modelled on approaches such as former German chancellor Willy Brandt's *Ostpolitik* rather than its current support for the authoritarian status quo. Though the Islamic world does not represent a cohesive block like that of the Warsaw Pact, in the post-George W. Bush era the West must attempt to formulate policies on the Middle East and Islam that strike a new balance between making demands and providing encouragement. The West, however, is far from adept at critiquing its own imperialist violence. Western democracies are not experiencing the kind of 'eternal peace' that Kant had in mind. They are in essence defective democracies, a description that Western scholarship normally reserves for developing countries. The predominance of a doctrine that posits a world of pacified democracies versus illegitimate and dangerous non-democracies is the result of the West's tendency to succumb to self-interest and populism. It gives rise to a self-righteous worldview that regards Western violence abroad as a collateral malfunction of the Western political system rather than the norm.

Reflexive modernity? At present, political violence occurs in both the Islamic and Western worlds, though in different forms depending on historical timing and circumstance – as authoritarianism in the first case and imperialism in the second. This generates asymmetries that impede Western examination of its own violence and of its intrinsically violent relationship with Islam. In contrast to the peaceableness of Western civilization and the pacifist message of Christianity, the instrumentalization of Islam to justify acts of terrorism is considered evidence of Islam's cultural propensity for violence. Such stereotypical views fail to grasp the true lesson of any comparative analysis: that both religions have produced very similar theological doctrines of 'just war'. In comparison to this ethically qualified concept of violence, both terrorists and pacifists have remained outsiders in *both* religions and civilizations. In the context of dangers real or imagined, many in the Western industrialized states currently tend to justify even neo-imperialist violence. Their counterparts in the Islamic world, meanwhile, sympathize not with terrorism as such, but with the idea that terrorism is the weapon of the weaker against the Western hegemon. These are widespread misperceptions in urgent need of revision *on both sides*. Military action neither eliminates the causes of terrorism nor is terrorist violence an ethical – or even particularly promising – strategy for tackling political and social problems.

But the West must also recognize that non-violent resistance is a widespread and everyday practice in Islamic countries. Acts of violence are often paid far too much attention, propagating the notion of the young genocidal Middle Eastern male. Clearly, the project of comparative political research and of elucidating the shared features of Islamic and Western modernity is still in its infancy.

Bibliography

Abootalebi, Ali Reza (2000). *Islam and Democracy. State-Society Relations in Developing Countries, 1980–1994.* New York/London: Garland.

Abu Zayd, Nasr Hamid (2006). *Reformation of Islamic Thought: A Critical Historical Analysis.* Amsterdam: Amsterdam University Press.

Abu Zayd, Nasr and Esther Nelson (2004). *Voices of an Exile: Reflections on Islam.* Westport: Praeger.

Abu-Nimer, Mohammed (2003). *Nonviolence and Peace Building in Islam. Theory and Practice.* Gainesville, FL, et al.: University of Florida Press.

Afary, Janet and Kevin B. Anderson (2005). *Foucault and the Iranian Revolution. Gender and the Seductions of Islamism.* Chicago/London: University of Chicago Press.

Agai, Bekim (2006). Fethullah Gülen: Die größte türkisch-islamische Bildungsbewegung [Fethullah Gülen: the largest Turkish-Islamic educational movement], in: Katajun Amirpur and Ludwig Amman (eds.). *Der Islam am Wendepunkt. Liberale und konservative Reformer einer Weltreligion [Islam at a crossroads. Liberal and conservative reformers of a world religion].* Freiburg et al.: Herder, 55–63.

Allafi, Mohammed H. and Sabine Allafi (2003). *Iran an der Schwelle zur Demokratie? Die erste islamische Republik in den Konturen der neuen Weltordnung [Iran on the threshold of democracy? How the first Islamic Republic fits into the new world order].* Frankfurt: Glaré Verlag.

Allingham, Michael (2002). *Choice Theory: A Very Short Introduction.* Oxford: Oxford University Press.

Alterman, John B. (2007). *The Death of Political Islam?* in: *Middle East Notes and Comment,* December, 1 f.

Aly, Götz (2008). *Unser Kampf 1968. Ein irritierender Blick zurück [Our struggle of 1968. An irritating look backwards].* Frankfurt: S. Fischer.

Amin, Samir (1978). *The Arab Nation. Nationalism and Class Struggles.* London: Zed Books.

Amirpur, Katajun, Henner Fürtig and Javad Kooroshy (2000). The Euro-Iranian Dialogue and the West in Iranian Media: Official, Loyalist, and Alternative Views in the Nineties, in: Kai Hafez (ed.). *Islam and the West in the Mass Media. Fragmented Images in a Globalizing World*. Cresskill. NJ: Hampton, 121–40.

Amman, Ludwig (2006). Tariq Ramadan: Die konservative Reform [Tariq Ramadan: the conservative approach to reform], in: Katajun Amirpur and Ludwig Amman (eds.). *Der Islam am Wendepunkt. Liberale und konservative Reformer einer Weltreligion [Islam at a crossroads. Liberal and conservative reformers of a world religion]*. Freiburg, Germany, et al.: Herder, 23–33.

Anderson, Lisa (1990). Policy-Making and Theory Building: American Political Science and the Islamic Middle East, in: Hisham Sharabi (ed.). *Theory, Politics and the Arab World. Critical Responses*. New York/London: Routledge, 52–80.

An-Na'im, Abdullahi Ahmed (1996). *Toward an Islamic Reformation. Civil Liberties, Human Rights, and International Law*. Syracuse, NY: Syracuse University Press.

Antar, Noha (2007). Die Muslimbruderschaft in Ägypten: Zwiespältige Reformer [The Muslim Brothers in Egypt: ambivalent reformers], in: Muriel Asseburg (ed.). *Moderate Islamisten als Reformakteure. Rahmenbedingungen und programmatischer Wandel [Moderate Islamists as agents of reform. Parameters and programmatic change]*. Berlin: Stiftung Wissenschaft und Politik, 63–73.

Arab Human Development Report 2002: *Creating Opportunities for Future Generations (2003)*. New York: United Nations Development Program.

Arendt, Hannah (1951). *The Origins of Totalitarianism*. New York: Harcourt, Brace Jovanovich.

  (1963). *Eichmann in Jerusalem. A Report on the Banality of Evil*. New York: Viking.

Aronson, Geoffrey (1986). *From Sideshow to Center Stage: U.S. Policy toward Egypt 1946–1956*. Boulder, CO: Lynne Rienner.

Ash, Timothy Garton (2004). *Free World. Why a Crisis of the West Reveals the Opportunity of Our Time*. London/New York: Penguin.

Ayubi, Nazih (1991). *Political Islam. Religion and Politics in the Arab World*. London/New York: Routledge.

Aziz, Haris (2007). *Anti-Semitism amongst Muslims, in: Tahir Abbas (ed.). Islamic Political Radicalism. A European Perspective*, Edinburgh: Edinburgh University Press, 71–82.

A More Secure World: Our Shared Responsibility (2004). *Report of the Secretary-General's High-level Panel on Threats. Challenges and Change*. New York: UN Department of Public Information.

Bacevich, Andrew J. (2002). *American Empire. The Realities and Consequences of U.S. Diplomacy*. Cambridge/London: Harvard University Press.

Baer, Gabriel (1962). *A History of Landownership in Modern Egypt, 1800–1950*. London: Oxford University Press.

  (1969). *Studies in the Social History of Modern Egypt, 1800–1950*. Chicago: Chicago University Press.

Baker, Raymond William (2003). *Islam Without Fear. Egypt and the New Islamists*. Cambridge, MA/London: Harvard University Press.

Barber, Benjamin R. (1993). *Jihad vs. Mc World. Terrorism's Challenge to Democracy*. New York: Random House.

Batatu, Hanna (1986). Shi'i Organizations in Iraq: al-Da'wah al-Islamiyah and al-Mujahidin, in: Juan R. I. Cole and Nikkie R. Keddie (eds.). *Shi'ism and Social Protest*. New Haven/London: Yale University Press, 179–200.

Baumgarten, Helga (2006). *Hamas. Der politische Islam in Palästina [Hamas. Political Islam in Palestine]*, Munich: Diederichs.

Bayat, Asef (2007). *Making Islam Democratic. Social Movements and the Post-Islamist Turn*. Palo Alto, CA: Stanford University Press.

Beck, Ulrich, Anthony Giddens and Scott Lash (1994). *Reflexive Modernization. Reflexive Modernization: Politics, Tradition and Aesthetics in the Modern Social Order*. London: Blackwell.

Benard, Cheryl and Zalmay Khalilzad (1984). 'The Government of God': Iran's *Islamic Republic*. New York: Columbia University Press.

Benhabib, Seyla (2002). *The Claims of Culture. Equality and Diversity in the Global Era*. Princeton/Oxford: Princeton University Press.

Bennett, Clinton (2005). *Muslims and Modernity. An Introduction to the Issues and Debates*. London/New York: Continuum.

Berger, Johannes (2006). Die Einheit der Moderne [The unity of modernity], in: Schwinn, Thomas (ed.). *Die Vielfalt und die Einheit der Moderne. Kultur- und strukturvergleichende Analysen [The diversity and unity of modernity. Comparative analyses of culture and structure]*. Wiesbaden: VS Verlag für Sozialwissenschaften, 201–25.

Berger, Rose Marie (2004). *The Hungry Spirit. Nonviolence in Najaf? Will We Recognize an Islamic Peace Movement when We See It?* in: *Sojourners Magazine*. November.

Betz, Joachim and Volker Matthies (1990). Dritte Welt im Abseits? Folgen der Ost-West-Entspannung [Third World out in the cold? The consequences of East-West détente], in: Joachim Betz and Volker Matthies (eds.). *Jahrbuch Dritte Welt 1991. Daten, Übersichten, Analysen [Third World yearbook 1991. Dates, surveys, analyses]*, Munich: C.H. Beck, 35–47.

Binder, Leonard (1964). *The Ideological Revolution in the Middle East*. New York: John Wiley.

Boldt, Hans (1970). Deutscher Konstitutionalismus und Bismarckreich [German constitutionalism and the Bismarckian empire], in: Michael Stürmer (ed.). *Das kaiserliche Deutschland [Imperial Germany]*. Düsseldorf: Droste, p.119–42.

   (1975). *Deutsche Staatslehre im Vormärz [German political science in the Vormärz]*. Düsseldorf: Droste.

Bracher, Karl Dietrich (1983). *Stufen der Machtergreifung [Stages of the seizure of power]*. Frankfurt: Ullstein (orig. 1962).

Bromley, Simon (1997). Middle East Exceptionalism – Myth or Reality?, in: Potter, David, David Goldblatt, Margaret Kiloh and Paul Lewis (eds.). *Democratization*. Cambridge: Polity, 321–44.

Brown, Nathan J., Amr Hamzawy and Marina Ottaway (2006). *Islamist Movements and the Democratic Process in the Arab World: Exploring the*

Grey Zones, Carnegie Papers no. 67. Washington, DC: Carnegie Endowment for International Peace.

Brownlee, Jason (2007). *Authoritarianism in an Age of Democratization.* Cambridge: Cambridge University Press.

Brüne, Stefan (2005). *Europas Außenbeziehungen und die Zukunft der Entwicklungspolitik [Europe's foreign relations and the future of development policy].* Wiesbaden: VS Verlag für Sozialwissenschaften.

Brumberg, Daniel (2003). Islamists and the Politics of Consensus, in: Larry Diamond, Marc F. Plattner and Daniel Brumberg (eds.). *Islam and Democracy in the Middle East.* Baltimore/London: The Johns Hopkins University Press, 268–75.

Brumberg, Daniel and Larry Diamond (2003). Introduction, in: Larry Diamond, Marc F. Plattner and Daniel Brumberg (eds.). *Islam and Democracy in the Middle East.* Baltimore/London: The Johns Hopkins University Press, IX-XXVI.

Brzezinski, Zbigniew (1997). *The Grand Chessboard. American Primacy and its Geostrategic Imperatives.* New York: Basic.

Bumbacher, Beat (1987). *Die USA und Nasser. Amerikanische Ägypten-Politik der Kennedy- und Johnson-Administration 1961–1967 [The USA and Nasser. American policy on Egypt under Kennedy and Johnson, 1961–1967].* Stuttgart: Steiner.

Burgat, Francois (2003). *Face to Face with Political Islam.* London: I.B. Tauris.

Burke, Edmund, III (1988). Islam and Social Movements: Methodological Reflections, in: Edmund Burke and Ira Lapidus (eds.). *Islam, Politics, and Social Movements.* Berkeley: University of California Press, 17–35.

Childless, James F. (1974). Reinhold Niebuhr's Critique of Pacifism, in: *The Review of Politics* 4, 467–91.

Cleaver, Harry M. (1998). The Zapatista Effect: The Internet and the Rise of an Alternative Political Fabric, in: *Journal of International Affairs* 2, 621–40.

Cook, David and Olivia Allison (2007). *Understanding and Addressing Suicide Attacks. The Faith and Politics of Martyrdom Operations.* Westport/London: Praeger.

Cooley, John K. (1999). *Unholy Wars: Afghanistan, America and International Terrorism.* London et al.: Pluto.

Cooper, Barry (2006). Understanding Jihadist Terrorism after 9/11, in: Bradley C. S. Watson (ed.). *The West at War.* Lanham. MD, et al.: Lexington, 41–51.

Cooper, Robert (2003). *The Breaking of Nations. Order and Chaos in the Twenty-First Century.* New York: Grove.

Crecelius, Daniel (1980). The Course of Secularization in Modern Egypt, in: John L. Esposito (ed.). *Islam and Development. Religion and Sociopolitical Change.* Syracuse: Syracuse University Press, 49–70.

Croissant, Aurel, Hans-Joachim Lauth and Wolfgang Merkel (2000). Zivilgesellschaft und Transformation: ein internationaler Vergleich [Civil society and political transformation], in: Wolfgang Merkel (ed.). *Systemwechsel 5. Zivilgesellschaft und Transformation [System change 5. Civil society and political transformation].* Opladen: Leske und Budrich, 9–49.

Daase, Christopher (2004). Demokratischer Frieden – Demokratischer Krieg: Drei Gründe für die Unfriedlichkeit von Demokratien [Democratic peace, democratic war: three reasons for the non-peaceful nature of democracies], in: Christine Schweitzer, Björn Aust. Peter Schlotter (eds.). *Demokratien im Krieg [Democracies at war].* Baden-Baden: Nomos, 53–71.

Dahl, Robert A. (1971). *Polyarchy: Participation and Opposition.* New Haven, CT: Yale University Press.

 (1989). *Democracy and its Critics.* New Haven, CT: Yale University Press.

Dajani, Souad (1999). Nonviolent Resistance in the Occupied Territories: A Critical Reevaluation, in: Stephen Zunes, Lester R. Kurtz and Sarah Beth Asher (eds.). *Nonviolent Social Movements. A Geographical Perspective.* Malden/Oxford: Blackwell, 52–74.

Dallmayr, Fred (2002). *Dialogue Among Civilizations. Some Exemplary Voices.* New York: Palgrave Macmillan.

 (2004). Beyond Monologue: For a Comparative Political Theory, in: *Perspectives on Politics* 2, 249–57.

Davis III, Charles T. (2004). The Qur'an, Muhammad, and the Jihad in Context, in: J. Harold Ellens (ed.). *The Destructive Power of Religion. Violence in Judaism. Christianity, and Islam.* Westport/London: Praeger, 233–254.

DeBenedetti, Charles (1980). *The Peace Reform in American History.* Bloomington: Indiana University Press.

Dieterich, Renate (1998). *Transformation oder Stagnation? Die jordanische Demokratiepolitik seit 1989 [Political transformation or stagnation? Jordanian policy on democracy since 1989].* Hamburg: Deutsches Orient-Institut.

Donsbach, Wolfgang (1982). *Legitimationsprobleme des Journalismus [Problems of legitimacy for journalism].* Freiburg/Munich: Alber.

Duncker, Arne (2003). *Gleichheit und Ungleichheit in der Ehe. Persönliche Stellung von Frau und Mann im Recht der ehelichen Lebensgemeinschaft 1700–1914 [Equality and inequality in marriage. The status of women and men in marital law, 1700–1914].* Cologne et al.: Böhlau.

Eagleton, Terry (2005). *Holy Terror.* Oxford: Oxford University Press.

Easwaran, Eknath (1999). *Nonviolent Soldier of Islam. Badshah Khan: A Man to Match His Mountains.* Tomales: Nilgiri.

Ebadi, Shirin (2006). *Iran Awakening. A Memoir of Revolution and Hope.* New York: Random House.

Ebert, Theodor (1978). *Gewaltfreier Aufstand. Alternative zum Bürgerkrieg [Non-violent rebellion. An alternative to civil war].* Frankfurt: Waldkircher.

Eisenstadt, Shmuel N. (2002). *Multiple Modernities.* New Brunswick: Transaction.

el-Affendi, Abdelwahab (2006). *The Islamist Responsibility in the Arab Democratic Transition, Discussion Paper Presented at the workshop: 'Electing Islamism: Prospects for Democratization in the Arab World'.* University of Westminster. London. November 3–5, 2006.

Engelmann, Bernt (1977). *Einig gegen Recht und Freiheit [United against law and freedom], Deutsches Anti-Geschichtsbuch [German anti-history book],* vol. II. Frankfurt: Fischer Taschenbuch Verlag.

Esposito, John L. and Dalia Mogahed (2007). *Who Speaks for Islam? What a Billion Muslims Really Think. Based on Gallup's World Poll – the Largest Study of its Kind.* New York: Gallup.

Esposito, John L. (1995). *The Islamic Threat: Myth or Reality?* New York/ Oxford: Oxford University Press.

Esposito, John L. and John O. Voll (1996). *Islam and Democracy.* New York/ Oxford: Oxford University Press.

Etzioni, Amitai (2004). *From Empire to Community. A New Approach to International Relations.* New York: Palgrave/Macmillan.

Euben, Roxanne (1999). *Enemy in the Mirror: Islamic Fundamentalism and the Limits of Modern Rationalism. A Work of Comparative Political Theory.* Princeton, NJ: Princeton University Press.

Faath, Sigrid (1999). Systemtransformation als Forschungsgegenstand. Allgemeine Aspekte und das Fallbeispiel Arabische Welt [System transformation as an object of research. *General aspects and the case study of the Arab world]*, in: *Wuquf* 12, 189–252.

Farschid, Olaf (1989). Hizbiya: Die Neuorientierung der Muslimbruderschaft Ägyptens in den Jahren 1984 und 1989 [Hizbiya: The reorientation of Egypt's Muslim Brothers between 1984 and 1989], in: *Orient* 1, 53–73.

Fix, Stefan (2006). Farid Esack: Eine islamische Theologie der Befreiung [An Islamic theology of liberation], in: Katajun Amirpur and Ludwig Amman (eds.). Der Islam am Wendepunkt. *Liberale und konservative Reformer einer Weltreligion [Islam at a crossroads. Liberal and conservative reformers of a world religion].* Freiburg et al.: Herder, 146–54.

Follmar-Otto, Petra (2007). Menschenrechtliche Instrumente gegen Menschenhandel [Tackling the slave trade with the instruments of human rights], in: Jahrbuch Menschenrechte *[Yearbook of human rights]* 2008, ed. by Deutsches Institut für Menschenrechte. Frankfurt: Suhrkamp, 63–76.

Forster, Klaus (2006). *Journalismus im Spannungsfeld zwischen Freiheit und Verantwortung. Das Konzept des 'Public Journalism' und seine empirische Relevanz [Journalism and the fraught balance between freedom and responsibility. The concept of 'public journalism' and its empirical relevance].* Cologne: Herbert von Halem.

Foucault, Michel (1981). *Archäologie des Wissens [Archaeology of knowledge].* Frankfurt: Suhrkamp (Fr. orig. 1969).

Fukuyama, Francis (2006). *America at the Crossroads. Democracy, Power, and the Neoconservative Legacy.* New Haven/London: Yale University Press.

Fürtig, Henner (2000). Iraq as a Golem. Identity Crises of a Western Creation, in: Kai Hafez (ed.). *The Islamic World and the West. An Introduction to Political Cultures and International Relations.* Leiden et al.: Brill, 204–16.

Gall, Lothar and Rainer Koch (eds.) (1981). *Der europäische Liberalismus im 19. Jahrhundert. Texte zu seiner Entwicklung [European liberalism in the 19th century. Writings on its development]*, 4 vols. Frankfurt: Ullstein.

Galtung, Johan (1972). Eine strukturelle Theorie des Imperialismus [A structural theory of imperialism], in: Dieter Senghaas (ed.). *Imperialismus und strukturelle Gewalt. Analysen über abhängige Reproduktion [Imperialism and structural violence. Analyses of dependent reproduction].* Frankfurt: Suhrkamp, 29–104.

Gerges, Fawaz A. (1999). *America and Political Islam. Clash of Cultures or Clash of Interests?* Cambridge/New York: Cambridge University Press.

Gerlach, Julia (2006). *Zwischen Pop und Dschihad. Muslimische Jugendliche in Deutschland [Between pop and Jihad. Muslim youth in Germany]*. Berlin: Ch. Links Verlag.

Ghadbian, Najib (1997). *Democratization and the Islamist Challenge in the Arab World*. Boulder, CO: Westview.

Giddens, Anthony (1994). Living in a post-traditional society, in: Ulrich Beck, Anthony Giddens and Scott Lash (1994). *Reflexive Modernization: Politics, Tradition and Aesthetics in the Modern Social Order*. London: Blackwell, 56–109.

Glück, Antje (2008). *Terror im Kopf. Terrorismusberichterstattung in der deutschen und arabischen Presse [Terror on the brain. Coverage of terrorism in the German and Arab press]*. Berlin: Frank und Timme.

Gong, Gerrit W. (1984). *The Standard of 'Civilization' in International Society*. Oxford: Oxford University Press.

Gräf, Bettina (2006). Yusuf al-Qaradawi: Das Erlaubte und das Verbotene im Islam [Yusuf al-Qaradawi: Islamic notions of the permitted and forbidden], in: Katajun Amirpur and Ludwig Amman (eds.). *Der Islam am Wendepunkt. Liberale und konservative Reformer einer Weltreligion [Islam at a crossroads. Liberal and conservative reformers of a world religion]*. Freiburg et al.: Herder, 109–17.

Grimm, Jordis (2006). *Ergebnisse der Glücksforschung als Leitfaden für politisches Handeln? [The findings of research on happiness as a guide to political action?]*, Discussion Paper no. 14. Flensburg: Universität Flensburg, Internationales Institut für Management.

Gronau, Dietrich (2006). *Luther: Revolutionär des Glaubens [Luther: religious revolutionary]*. Munich: Heinrich Hugendubel.

Guelke, Adrian (2006). *Terrorism and Global Disorder. Political Violence in the Contemporary World*. London/New York: I.B. Tauris.

Haarmann, Ulrich (ed.) (1994). *Geschichte der arabischen Welt [A history of the Arab world]* (3rd expanded edition). Munich: C.H. Beck.

Habermas, Jürgen (1996). *Die Einbeziehung des Anderen. Studien zur politischen Theorie [Inclusion of the other. Studies in political theory]*. Frankfurt: Suhrkamp.

(2001). *Glauben und Wissen. Friedenspreis des Deutschen Buchhandels 2001. Laudatio: Jan Philipp Reemtsma [Faith and knowledge. Speech on receiving the Peace Prize of the German book trade, with a tribute by Jan Philipp Reemtsma]*. Frankfurt: Suhrkamp.

(2004). *Der gespaltene Westen. Kleine politische Schriften X [The divided West]*. Frankfurt: Suhrkamp.

Hafez, Kai (1998). *Review of: Fred Halliday, Islam and the Myth of Confrontation. Religion and Politics in the Middle East*. London/New York: I.B. Tauris, in: asien, afrika, lateinamerika [asia, africa, latin america] 5, 590–93.

(1999a). *Islamic World Information Sources Conference*. Oct. 31 – Nov. 3, 1999, in Riyadh, Saudi Arabia, in: *Orient* 4, 573–76.

(1999b). Medien und Demokratisierung im Nahen Osten. Regionale und globale Einflußfaktoren [Media and democratization in the Middle East. Regional and global influences], in: Nahost Jahrbuch 1998. *Politik, Wirtschaft und Gesellschaft in Nordafrika und dem Nahen und Mittleren Osten [Middle East yearbook 1998. Politics, economy and society in North Africa and the Middle East]*, eds. Deutsches Orient-Institut, Thomas Koszinowski and Hanspeter Mattes. Opladen: Leske and Budrich, 203–8.

(2000). *Islam and the West in the Mass Media. Fragmented Images in a Globalizing World.* Cresskill. NJ: Hampton.

(ed.) (2001). *Mass Media. Politics and Society in the Middle East.* Cresskill, NJ: Hampton.

(2002a). Die irrationale Fehlwahrnehmung des 'anderen': Deutsche und arabische Öffentlichkeitsreaktionen auf den 11. September [Irrational misperceptions of the 'other': the reaction of German and Arab publics to the 11th September 2001], in: Georg Stein and Volkhard Windfuhr (eds.). *Ein Tag im September. 11.9.2001 [A day in September. 11th September 2001].* Heidelberg: Palmyra, 221–46.

(2002b). Journalism Ethics Revisited: A Comparison of Ethics Codes in Europe, North Africa, the Middle East and Muslim Asia, in: *Political Communication* 2, 225–50.

(2003). Ein neuer Kolonialismus. US-amerikanische und europäische Nahostpolitik [A new colonialism. US and European policy on the Middle East], in: Kai Hafez and Birgit Schäbler (eds.). *Der Irak – Land zwischen Krieg und Frieden, Mit einem Vorwort von Hans Küng [Iraq – between war and peace. With a foreword by Hans Küng].* Heidelberg: Palmyra, 40–74.

(2006). Arab Satellite Broadcasting: Democracy without Political Parties, in: *Transnational Broadcasting Studies* 2, 275–97.

(ed.) (2008a). *Arab Media: Power and Weakness.* London: Continuum.

(2008b). The Role of Media in the Arab World's Transformation Process, in: Christian-Peter Hanelt and Almut Möller (eds.). *Bound to Cooperate: Europe and the Middle East II.* Gütersloh: Bertelsmann, 321–39.

Hafez, Kai and Udo Steinbach (eds.) (1999). *Juden und Muslime in Deutschland. Minderheitendialog als Zukunftsaufgabe [Jews and Muslims in Germany. Dialogue between minorities as a task for the future].* Hamburg: Deutsches Orient-Institut.

Hafez, Mohammed (2003). *Why Muslims Rebel. Repression and Resistance in the Islamic World.* Boulder/London: Lynne Rienner.

(2004). From Marginalization to Massacres: A Political Process Explanation of GIA Violence in Algeria, in: Quintan Wiktorowicz (ed.). *Islamic Activism. A Social Movement Theory Approach.* Bloomington/Indianapolis: Indiana University Press, 37–60.

Hagopian, Elaine C. (ed.) (2004). *Civil Rights in Peril. The Targeting of Arabs and Muslims.* Chicago: Haymarket and London: Pluto.

Hall, Stuart (1980). Encoding/Decoding, in: Stuart Hall, Dorothy Hobson, Andrew Lowe and Paul Willis (eds.). *Culture, Media. Language. Working Papers in Cultural Studies, 1972–1979.* London: Hutchinson.

Halliday, Fred (1996). *Islam and the Myth of Confrontation. Religion and Politics in the Middle East*. London/New York: I.B. Tauris.

Hamdy, Iman A. (ed.) (2004). *Elections in the Middle East. What Do they Mean?*. Cairo: American University in Cairo Press.

Hamzawy, Amr (2005). *Political Change in the Arab World: the Challenge of Democratic Islamists*, in: *Dialogue with the Islamic World, Federal Foreign Office*. Berlin: Edition Diplomatie, 10–21.

Harders, Cilja (1998). Die Furcht der Reichen und die Hoffnungen der Armen – Ägyptens schwieriger Weg zur Demokratie [Fears of the rich and hopes of the poor – Egypt's difficult path to democracy], in: Gunter Schubert and Rainer Tetzlaff (eds.). *Blockierte Demokratien in der Dritten Welt [Obstructed democracies in the Third World]*. Opladen: Leske und Budrich, 267–96.

Hardt, Michael and Antonio Negri (2004). *Multitude*. New York: Penguin.

Harik, Judith Palmer (2005). *Hezbollah. The Changing Face of Terrorism*. London/New York: I.B. Tauris.

Harle, Vilho (2000). *The Enemy with a Thousand Faces. The Tradition of the Other in Western Political Thought and History*. Westport/London: Praeger.

Hartmann, Jürgen (1995). *Vergleichende Politikwissenschaft. Ein Lehrbuch [A textbook of comparative political science]*. Frankfurt/New York: Campus.

Hefner, Robert W. (2000). *Civil Islam. Muslims and Democratization in Indonesia*. Princeton/Oxford: Princeton University Press.

(2005). Introduction: Modernity and the Remaking of Muslim Politics, in: Hefner (ed.). *Remaking Muslim Politics. Pluralism, Contestation, Democratization*. Princeton/Oxford: Princeton University Press, 1–36.

Heft, James L. (ed.) (2004). *Beyond Violence. Religious Sources of Social Transformation in Judaism, Christianity, and Islam*. New York: Fordham University Press.

Hegasy, Sonja (2000). They Dare to Speak Out: Changes in the Political Culture of Egypt, Morocco and the Arab World, in: Kai Hafez (ed.). *The Islamic World and the West. An Introduction to Political Cultures and International Relations*. Leiden et al.: Brill, 146–60.

Heikal, Mohamed (1984). *Autumn of Fury. The Assassination of Sadat*. London: Corgi.

Henning, Klaus (2006). *Aufstieg der 'Neokons'. Politische Intellektuelle in den USA und der 'Neue Imperialismus' [The rise of the 'neocons'. Political intellectuals in the USA and the 'new imperialism']*. Cologne: ISP Wissenschaft und Forschung.

Herbert, David (ed.) (2001). *Religion and Social Transformations*. Aldershot et al.: Ashgate/The Open University.

Herman, Edward S. and Noam Chomsky (1994). *Manufacturing Consent. The Political Economy of the Mass Media*. London: Vintage (orig. 1988).

Herzog, Roman (1999). *Preventing the Clash of Civilizations. A Peace Strategy for the Twenty-First Century*. New York: St. Martin's.

Hess, Stephen and Marvin Kalb (eds.) (2003). *The Media and the War on Terrorism*. Washington, DC: Brookings Institution.

Hippler, Jochen (2006). Krieg, Repression, Terrorismus. Politische Gewalt und Zivilisation in westlichen und muslimischen Gesellschaften, mit Kommentaren von Nasr Hamid Abu Zaid und Amr Hamzawy *[War, repression, terrorism. Political violence and civilization in Western and Muslim societies, with commentaries by Nasr Hamid Abu Zaid and Amr Hamzawy]*. Stuttgart: Institut für Auslandsbeziehungen.

Hofman, Steven Ryan (2004). Islam and Democracy, in: *Comparative Political Studies* 6, 652–76.

Honecker, Martin (1995). *Grundriss der Sozialethik [An outline of social ethics]*. Berlin: de Gruyter.

Höpp, Gerhard (1994). Araber im Zweiten Weltkrieg: Kollaboration oder Patriotismus? [Arabs in the Second World War: collaboration or patriotism?], in: Wolfgang Schwanitz (ed.). *Jenseits der Legenden: Araber, Juden, Deutsche [Beyond legends: Arabs, Jews and Germans]*. Berlin: Dietz, 86–92.

Hottinger, Arnold (2000). *Gottesstaaten und Machtpyramiden. Demokratie in der islamischen Welt [Theocracies and power pyramids. Democracy in the Islamic world]*. Paderborn et al.: Schöningh.

Hourani, Albert (1983). *Arabic Thought in the Liberal Age 1798–1939*. Cambridge et al.: Cambridge University Press (orig. 1962).

Hroub, Khaled (2006). *Hamas. A Beginner's Guide*. London/Ann Arbor: Pluto.

Hubel, Helmut (2005). Wie viel Religion ist in den Konflikten des Vorderen Orients? [How much religion is there in Middle East conflicts?], in: Mathias Hildebrandt and Manfred Brocker (eds.). *Unfriedliche Religionen? Das politische Gewalt- und Konfliktpotenzial von Religionen [Unpeaceful religions? Religions' potential for political violence and conflict]*. Wiesbaden: VS Verlag für Sozialwissenschaften, 179–91.

Hudson, Michael C. (1995). Arab Regimes and the Democratization: responses to the Challenge of Political Islam, in: Laura Guazzone (ed.). *The Islamist Dilemma*, Reading, UK: Ithaca, 217–45.

Hunter, Shireen T. (1990). *Iran and the World. Continuity in a Revolutionary Decade*. Bloomington/Indianapolis: Bloomington University Press.

Huntington, Samuel P. (1984). Will More Countries Become Democratic? in: *Political Science Quarterly* 2, 193–218.

Huntington, Samuel (1991). *The Third Wave: Democratization in the Late Twentieth Century*. Norman: University of Oklahoma Press.

Huntington, Samuel P. (1993). The Clash of Civilizations? in: *Foreign Affairs* 3, 22–49.

(1996). *The Clash of Civilizations and the Remaking of World Order*. New York: Simon and Schuster.

Hurd, Elizabeth Shakman (2008). *The Politics of Secularism in International Relations*. Princeton/Oxford: Princeton University Press.

Ibrahim, Saad Eddin (1982). *The New Arab Social Order*. Boulder: Westview.

Ignatieff, Michael (2003). *Empire Lite. Nation-Building in Bosnia, Kosovo and Afghanistan*. London: Vintage.

Ismail, Salwa (2003). *Rethinking Islamist Policies*. London: I.B. Tauris.

Jabar, Faleh A. (2003). Der Stamm im Staat. Zur Wiederbelebung der Stammeskultur im Irak [The tribe within the state. On the revival of tribal culture in Iraq], in: Kai Hafez and Birgit Schäbler (eds.). *Der Irak – Land zwischen Krieg und Frieden, Mit einem Vorwort von Hans Küng [Iraq – between war and peace. With a foreword by Hans Küng].* Heidelberg: Palmyra, 187–207.

Jaberg, Sabine and Peter Schlotter (2005). Imperium, Frieden, Gerechtigkeit: Zur Einführung [Empire, peace, justice: an introduction], in: Sabine Jaberg and Peter Schlotter, Imperiale Weltordnung – Trend des 21. *Jahrhunderts? [Imperial world order – the trend of the 21st century?].* Baden-Baden: Nomos, 7–27.

Jacobs, Andreas (2006). *Reformislam. Akteure, Methoden und Themen progressiven Denkens im zeitgenössischen Islam [Reformist Islam. Actors, methods and themes of progressive thought in contemporary Islam], Arbeitspapier der Konrad-Adenauer-Stiftung* [Working papers of the Konrad Adenauer Foundation], no. 155. Berlin/Sankt-Augustin.

Jahn, Detlef (2006). *Einführung in die vergleichende Politikwissenschaft [An introduction to comparative political science].* Wiesbaden: VS Verlag für Sozialwissenschaften.

Johansen, Robert C. (1997). Radical Islam and Nonviolence: A Case Study of Religious Empowerment and Constraint among Pashtuns, in: *Journal of Peace Research* 1, 53–71.

Johnson, Chalmers (2004). *The Sorrows of Empire. Militarism. Secrecy, and the End of the Republic.* London/New York: Verso (Orig. 2003).

Jünemann, Annette (2000). Support for Democracy or Fear of Islamism? Europe and Algeria, in: Kai Hafez (ed.). *The Islamic World and the West. An Introduction to Political Cultures and International Relations.* Leiden et al.: Brill, 103–26.

Jung, Hwa Yol (ed.) (2002). *Comparative Political Culture in the Age of Globalization. An Introductory Anthology.* Lanham, MD, et al.: Lexington.

Kagan, Robert (2003). *Of Paradise and Power. America and Europe in the New World Order.* New York: Alfred A. Knopf.

Kamrava, Mehran (2000). *Politics and Society in the Developing World.* London/New York: Routledge.

Kamrava, Mehran (ed.) (2006). *The New Voices of Islam: Reforming Politics and Modernity. A Reader.* London/New York: I.B. Tauris.

Kant, Immanuel (2005). *Zum ewigen Frieden. Ein philosophischer Entwurf [On eternal peace. A philosophical outline].* Stuttgart: Reclam (orig. 1795).

Karabell, Zachary (1996). Fundamental Misconceptions: Islamic Foreign Policy, in: *Foreign Policy* 105, 77–90.

Karl, Terry L. and Philippe C. Schmitter (1991). Modes of Transition in Latin America, Southern and Eastern Europe, in: *International Social Science Journal* 128, 269–85.

Karsh, Efraim (2007). *Islamic Imperialism. A History.* New Haven/London: Yale University Press.

Keddie, Nikkie (1988). Ideology, Society, and the State in Post-Colonial Muslim Societies, in: Fred Halliday and Hamza Alavi (eds.). *State and Ideology in the Middle East and Pakistan.* New York: Monthly Review, 9–30.

Keller, Patrick (2008). *Neokonservatismus und amerikanische Außenpolitik. Ideen, Krieg und Strategie von Ronald Reagan bis George W. Bush [Neoconservatism and American foreign policy. Ideas, war and strategy from Ronald Reagan to George W. Bush].* Paderborn: Schöningh.

Kellermann, Klaus (1984). *Pluralistischer Kommunismus? Wandlungstendenzen eurokommunistischer Parteien in Westeuropa [Pluralist communism? Trends of change among Eurocommunist parties in Western Europe].* Stuttgart: Klett-Cotta.

Kepel, Gilles (2000). *Jihad. Expansion et décline de l'islamisme [Jihad. The expansion and decline of Islamism].* Paris: Gallimard.

Khalid, Detlev (1979). Die totalitäre Tendenz im Islam [The tendency towards totalitarianism in Islam], in: *Orient* 3, 27–35.

Khalid, Duran (1982). *Reislamisierung und Entwicklungspolitik [Re-Islamization and development policy].* Cologne: Weltforum Verlag.

Koszinowski, Thomas (1999). Die Ohnmacht der ägyptischen Parteienopposition: strukturbedingt oder hausgemacht? [Is the impotence of opposition parties in Egypt determined by structure or homemade?], in: *Wuquf* 12, 99–123.

Kraidy, Marwan (2008). From Activity to Interactivity: The Arab Audience, in: Kai Hafez (ed.). *Arab Media: Power and Weakness.* New York/London: Continuum, 77–86.

Krämer, Gudrun (1982). *Minderheit, Millet, Nation? Die Juden in Ägypten 1914–1952 [Minority, millet or nation? The Jews in Egypt, 1914–1952].* Wiesbaden: Harrassowitz.

(1987–8). The Change of Paradigm. Political Pluralism in Contemporary Egypt, in: *Peuples Méditerranéens* 41–2, 283–302.

Kühnhardt, Ludger (1991). *Die Universalität der Menschenrechte [The universality of human rights].* Bonn: Bundeszentrale für politische Bildung.

Küntzel, Matthias (2002). *Djihad und Judenhass. Über den neuen antisemitischen Krieg [Jihad and anti-Semitism. On the new anti-Semitic war].* Freiburg, Germany: ça ira.

Kylvas, Stathis N. (2000). Commitment Problems in Emerging Democracies: The Case of Religious Parties, in: *Comparative Politics* 4, 379–98.

Laqueur, Walter (1996). *Fascism. Past, Present, Future.* Oxford/New York: Oxford University Press.

Lawrence, Bruce B. (1987). Muslim Fundamentalist Movements: Reflections toward a New Approach, in: Barbara Stowasser (ed.). *The Islamic Impulse.* Washington, DC: Center for Contemporary Arab Studies. Georgetown University, 15–36.

(1989). *Defenders of God: The Fundamentalist Revolt against the Modern Age.* San Francisco: Harper and Row.

Lerner, Daniel (1958). *The Passing of Traditional Society. Modernizing the Middle East.* Glencoe, IL: The Free Press.

LeVine, Mark (2005). *Why They Don't Hate Us. Lifting the Veil on the Axis of Evil.* Oxford: Oneworld.

Lewis, Bernard (1986). *Semites and Antisemites.* New York/London: Norton.

(2003a). *The Crisis of Islam. Holy War and Unholy Terror.* New York: Random.

(2003b). A Historical Overview, in: Larry Diamond, Marc F. Plattner and Daniel Brumberg (eds.). *Islam and Democracy in the Middle East.* Baltimore/London: The Johns Hopkins University Press, 208–19.

Lipset, Seymour Martin (1960). *Political Man.* London: Heinemann.

Lockman, Zachary (2004). *Contending Visions of the Middle East. The History and Politics of Orientalism.* Cambridge: Cambridge University Press.

Lockman, Zachary and Joel Beinin (eds.) (1989). *Intifada. The Palestinian Uprising against Israeli Occupation.* Boston: South End.

Löwenthal, Richard (1986): Staatsfunktionen und Staatsform in den Entwicklungsländern [The functions and form of the state in developing countries], in: Franz Nuscheler (ed.). *Politikwissenschaftliche Entwicklungsländerforschung [Political science research on developing countries]*, Darmstadt: Wissenschaftliche Buchgesellschaft, 241–75 (orig. 1962).

Marshall, Paul (2006). Understanding Radical Islam, in: Bradley C.S. Watson (ed.). *The West at War.* Lanham, MD et al.: Lexington, 29–40.

Marx, Karl (1904). *A Contribution to the Critique of Political Economy.* Chicago: Charles Kerr (orig. 1859).

Matthies, Volker (2005). Eine Welt voller neuer Kriege? [A world brimming over with new wars?], in: Siegfried Frech and Peter I. Trummer (eds.). *Neue Kriege. Akteure, Gewaltmärkte, Ökonomie [New wars. Actors, markets in violence, economy].* Schwalbach: Wochenschau, 33–52.

McQuade, Aidan (2007). Der Kampf für die weltweite Abschaffung der Sklaverei [The struggle to achieve the abolition of slavery worldwide], in: Jahrbuch Menschenrechte *[Yearbook of human rights] 2008*, ed. by Deutsches Institut für Menschenrechte. Frankfurt: Suhrkamp, 15–22.

Menashri, David (1991). The Jews of Iran: Between the Shah and Khomeini, in: Sander L. Gilman and Steven T. Katz (eds.). *Anti-Semitism in Times of Crisis.* New York/London: New York University Press, 353–71.

(2002). The Pahlavi Monarchy and the Islamic Revolution, in: Houman Sarshar (ed.). *Esther's Children. A Portrait of Iranian Jews.* Beverly Hills: The Center for Iranian Jewish Oral History, 379–402.

Merkel, Wolfgang (1999). *Systemtransformation. Eine Einführung in die Theorie und Empirie der Transformationsforschung [System transformation. An introduction to the theory and empirical practice of research on political transformation].* Opladen: Leske and Budrich.

Merritt, Davis 'Buzz' (1998). *Public Journalism and Public Life. Why Telling the News Is not Enough.* Mahwah/London: Lawrence Earlbaum.

Metzger, Albrecht (2000). *Der Himmel ist für Gott, der Staat für uns. Islamismus zwischen Gewalt und Demokratie [Heaven is for God, the state is for us. Islamism between violence and democracy].* Göttingen: Lamuv.

Meyer, Thomas (1977). *Bernsteins konstruktiver Sozialismus. Eduard Bernsteins Beitrag zur Theorie des Sozialismus [Bernstein's constructive socialism. Eduard Bernstein's contribution to the theory of socialism].* Berlin: Dietz.

Micksch, Jürgen (ed.) (2007). *Evangelisch aus fundamentalem Grund. Wie sich die EKD gegen den Islam profiliert [Protestant for fundamental reasons. How the Protestant church in Germany constructs its identity through contrasts with Islam].* Frankfurt: Lembeck.

Miller, David (ed.) (2004). *Tell me Lies. Propaganda and Media Distortion in the Attack on Iraq.* London/Sterling: Pluto.

Milton-Edwards, Beverley (2006). *Islam and Violence in the Modern Era.* Houndmills/New York: Palgrave Macmillan.

Mir-Hosseini, Ziba and Richard Tapper (2006). *Islam and Democracy in Iran. Eshkevari and the Quest for Reform.* London/New York: I.B. Tauris.

Moghadam Assaf (2006). The Roots of Suicide Terrorism. A Multi-Causal Approach, in: Ami Pedahzur (ed.). *Root Causes of Suicide Terrorism. The Globalization of Martyrdom.* London/New York: Routledge, 81–107.

Moore, Barrington (1966). *Social Origins of Dictatorship and Democracy: Lord and Peasant in the Making of the Modern World.* Boston: Beacon.

Mudhoon, Loay (2006). Muhammad Schahrur: Für ein zeitgenössisches Koran- und Islamverständnis [Muhammad Shahrur: towards a contemporary understanding of the Koran and Islam], in: Katajun Amirpur and Ludwig Amman (eds.). *Der Islam am Wendepunkt. Liberale und konservative Reformer einer Weltreligion [Islam at the crossroads. Liberal and conservative reformers of a world religion].* Freiburg et al.: Herder, 136–45.

Mueller, John E. (1973). *War, Presidents, and Public Opinion.* New York: Wiley.

Münkler, Herfried (2005a). *Imperien. Die Logik der Weltherrschaft vom Alten Rom bis zu den Vereinigten Staaten [Empires. The logic of global domination from ancient Rome to the United States].* Berlin: Rowohlt.

(2005b). Die neuen Kriege [The new wars], in: Siegfried Frech and Peter I. Trummer (eds.). *Neue Kriege. Akteure, Gewaltmärkte, Ökonomie [New wars. Actors, markets in violence, economy].* Schwalbach: Wochenschau, 13–32.

Nienhaus, Volker (2000). Islamic Economics: Dogma or Science?, in: Kai Hafez (ed.). *The Islamic World and the West. An Introduction to Political Cultures and International Relations.* Leiden et al.: Brill, 86–99.

Norris, Pippa and Ronald Inglehart (2004). *Sacred and Secular. Religion and Politics Worldwide.* Cambridge: Cambridge University Press.

Norton, Augsutus Richard (2005). Thwarted Politics: The Case of Egypt's Hizb Al-Wasat, in: Robert W. Hefner (ed.). *Remaking Muslim Politics. Pluralism. Contestation, Democratization.* Princeton/Oxford: Princeton University Press, 133–60.

Norton, Augustus Richard (2007). *Hezbollah. A Short History.* Princeton/Oxford: Princeton University Press.

O'Donnell, Guillermo and Philippe C. Schmitter (1986). *Transitions from Authoritarian Rule. Tentative Conclusions about Uncertain Democracies, with a Foreword by Abraham F. Lowenthal.* Baltimore/London: The Johns Hopkins University Press.

Parekh, Bhikhu (2002). *Rethinking Multiculturalism: Cultural Diversity and Political Theory* Cambridge: Harvard University Press.

Parel, Anthony J. and Ronald C. Keith (eds.) (2003). *Comparative Political Philosophy. Studies under the Upas Tree.* Lanham et al.: Lexington.

Paret, Rudi (2005). *Mohammed und der Koran [Muhammad and the Koran].* Stuttgart: Kohlhammer (orig. 1957).

Parsa, Misagh (1989). *Social Origins of the Iranian Revolution.* New Brunswick/London Rutgers University Press.

Pawelka, Peter (1985). *Herrschaft und Entwicklung im Nahen Osten: Ägypten [Power and development in the Middle East].* Heidelberg: C.F. Müller.

Pei, Minxin (2000). China's Evolution toward Soft Authoritarianism, in: Edward Friedman and Barrett L. McCormick (eds.). *What if China Doesn't Democratize? Implications for War and Peace*, Armonk/London: M.E. Sharpe, 74–97.

Pickel, Susanne and Gert Pickel (2006). *Politische Kultur- und Demokratiefor schung: Grundbegriffe, Theorien, Methoden. Eine Einführung [Political research on culture and democracy: basic concepts, theories, methods. An introduction]*. Wiesbaden: VS Verlag für Sozialwissenschaften.

Pilger, John (2002). *The New Rulers of the World*. London: Verso.

Pintak, Lawrence (2003). *Seeds of Hate. How America's Flawed Middle East Policy Ignited the Jihad*. London/Sterling: Pluto.

(2006). *Reflections in a Bloodshot Lens. America, Islam and the War of Ideas*. London/Sterling: Pluto.

Piper, Ernst (1979). *Savonarola: Umtriebe eines Politikers und Puritaners im Florenz der Medici [Savonarola: the activities of a politician and Puritan in Medici Florence]*. Berlin: Wagenbach.

Podhoretz, Norman (2007). *World War IV: The Long Struggle Against Islamofascism*. New York: Doubleday.

Porter, Andrew (2004). *Religion versus Empire? British Protestant Missionaries and Overseas Expansion 1700–1914*. Manchester: Manchester University Press.

Pridham, Geoffrey (2000). *The Dynamics of Democratization. A Comparative Approach*. London/New York: Continuum.

Prittwitz, Volker von (2007). *Vergleichende Politikanalyse [Comparative political analysis]*. Stuttgart: Lucius and Lucius (UTB).

Prunier, Gérard (2005). *Darfur: The Ambiguous Genocide*. London: Hurst.

Przeworski, Adam (1991). *Democracy and the Market. Political and Economic Reforms in Eastern Europe and Latin America*. Cambridge/New York: Cambridge University Press.

Rahman, Fazlur (1982). *Islam and Modernity. Transformation of an Intellectual Tradition*. Chicago/London: University of Chicago Press.

Ramadan, Tariq (2004). *Western Muslims and the Future of Islam*. Oxford: Oxford University Press.

(2006). *The Way (Al-Sharia) of Islam*, in: *Mehran Kamrava (ed.). The New Voices of Islam. Reforming Politics and Modernity. A Reader*. London/New York: I.B. Tauris, 65–97.

Rashwan, Diaa ((ed.) (2007). *The Spectrum of Islamist Movements*. Berlin: Hans Schiler.

Read, Craig (2006). Fascism and Paganism. *A Brief Comparison of Nazism. Communism and Islam, Xlibris (www.elibris.com)*.

Richards, Alan (1982). *Egypt's Agricultural Development, 1800–1980*. Boulder: Westview.

Richter, Helmut and Günter Trautmann (eds.) (1979). *Eurokommunismus – ein dritter Weg für Europa? [Eurocommunism – a third way for Europe?]*. Hamburg: Hoffmann and Campe.

Riehm, Juliane (2006). *Die öffentliche Debatte über Kriegsopfer im Irak 2003: Akteure. Strukturen, Themen [The public debate on war victims in the Iraq war of 2003*. Actors, structures, themes]. Master's thesis, University of Erfurt.

Riesenbrodt, Martin (1987). Protestantischer Fundamentalismus in den USA. Die religiöse Rechte im Zeitalter der elektronischen Medien *[Protestant fundamentalism in the USA. The religious right in the age of electronic media]*. Stuttgart: Evangelische Zentralstelle für Weltanschauungsfragen, Information no. 102, VIII.

Robinson, Glenn E. (2004). Hamas as Social Movement, in: Quintan Wiktorowicz (ed.). *Islamic Activism. A Social Movement Theory Approach*. Bloomington/Indianapolis: Indiana University Press, 112–39.

Roetz, Heiner (2006). China – eine andere Moderne? [China – another modernity?], in: Schwinn, Thomas (ed.). *Die Vielfalt und die Einheit der Moderne. Kultur- und strukturvergleichende Analysen [The diversity and unity of modernity. Comparative analyses of culture and structure]*. Wiesbaden: VS Verlag für Sozialwissenschaften, 131–49.

Rohde, Achim (2003). Von Kaisers Kleidern. Wechselfälle des Nationalismus im Irak [On the clothes of emperors. The vicissitudes of nationalism in Iraq], in: Kai Hafez and Birgit Schäbler (eds.). *Der Irak. Land zwischen Krieg und Frieden [Iraq. Between war and peace]*. Heidelberg: Palmyra, 172–86.

Rosen, Jay (1999). *What are journalists for?* New Haven/London: Yale University Press.

Rosenberg, Arthur (1983). *Entstehung und Geschichte der Weimarer Republik [The emergence and history of the Weimar Republic]*. Frankfurt: Europäische Verlagsanstalt.

Ross, Daniel (2004). *Violent Democracy*. Cambridge: Cambridge University Press.

Roy, Olivier (2006). Der islamische Weg nach Westen. Globalisierung, Entwurzelung und Radikalisierung *[The Islamic path to the West. Globalization, uprooting and radicalization]*, Munich: Pantheon (orig. 2002).

    (2007). *Le croissant et le chaos [The crescent and the chaos]*. Paris: Hachette.

Rufin, Jean-Christophe (1994). *Die Diktatur des Liberalismus [The dictatorship of liberalism]*, Reinbek: Rowohlt.

Rustow, Dankwart (1970). Transitions to Democracy: Towards a Dynamic Model, in: *Comparative Politics* 3, 337–63.

Said, Edward W. (1978). *Orientalism*. New York: Pantheon.

Salamé, Ghassan (ed.) (1994a). *Democracy without Democrats? The Renewal of Politics in the Muslim World*. London/New York: I.B. Tauris.

Salamé, Ghassan (1994b). Introduction: Where are the Democrats, in: Ghassan Salamé (ed.). *Democracy without Democrats? The Renewal of Politics in the Muslim World*. London/New York: I.B. Tauris, 1–20.

    (1998). Torn between the Atlantic and the Mediterranean: Europe and the Middle East in the post-Cold War Era, in: B.A. Roberson (ed.). *The Middle East and Europe. The Power Deficit*. New York: Routledge, 20–44.

Salter, Mark B. (2002). *Barbarians and Civilization in International Relations*. London/Sterling: Pluto.

Salvatore, Armando (1997). *Islam and the Political Discourse of Modernity*, Reading, UK: Ithaca.

Sardar, Ziauddin and Merryl Wyn Davies (2002). *Why do People Hate America?* London: Icon.

Saritoprak, Zeki (2005). An Islamic Approach to Peace and Nonviolence: A Turkish Experience, in: *The Muslim World* 7 (July). 413–27.

Satha-Anand, Chaiwat (1993). The Nonviolent Crescent: Eight Theses on Muslim Nonviolent Actions, in: Glenn Paige. Chaiwat Satha-Anand and Sarah Gilliatt (eds.). *Islam and Nonviolence,* Honolulu: University of Hawaii. Center for Global Nonviolence Plannung Project, 7–26.

Schäfer, Jan Michael (2008). Liberalisierung durch Fernsehen in Ägypten? Al-Jazeera und die Kifaya-Bewegung im Jahr 2005 *[Liberalization through television in Egypt? Al Jazeera and the Kifaya movement in 2005].* Master's thesis, University of Potsdam.

Schechter, Danny (2003). *Embedded: Weapons of Mass Deception. How the Media Failed to Cover the War on Iraq.* Amherst, MA: Prometheus.

Scheffler, Thomas (2000). West-Eastern Cultures of Fear: Violence and Terrorism in Islam, in: Kai Hafez (ed.). *The Islamic World and the West. An Introduction to Political Cultures and International Relations.* Leiden et al.: Brill, 70–85.

Scheuer, Jeffrey (1999). *The Sound Bite Society. How Television Helps the Right and Hurts the Left.* New York: Routledge.

Schmitt, Carl (2002). *Der Begriff des Politischen [The concept of the political].* Berlin: Duncker and Humblot (orig. 1932).

Schubert, Gunter, Rainer Tetzlaff and Werner Vennewald (eds.) (1994). Demokratisierung und politischer Wandel. Theorie und Anwendung des Konzepts der strategischen und konfliktfähigen Gruppen (SKOG) *[Democratization and political change. Theory and application of the concept of strategic and conflict capable groups (SCOG)],* Münster: LIT.

Schwedler, Jillian (2007). Democratization, Inclusion and the Moderation of Islamist Parties, in: *Dialogue* 1, 56–61.

Schwinn, Thomas (ed.) (2006). *Die Vielfalt und die Einheit der Moderne. Kultur- und strukturvergleichende Analysen [The diversity and unity of modernity. Comparative analyses of culture and structure].* Wiesbaden: VS Verlag für Sozialwissenschaften.

Scott, Peter Dale (2004). *Die Drogen, das Öl und der Krieg. Zur Tiefenpolitik der USA [Drugs, oil and war. On the deep policies of the USA].* Frankfurt: Zweitausendeins.

Segal, Ronald (2001). *Islam's Black Slaves. A History of Africa's other Black Diaspora.* London: Atlantic.

Shabestari, Mohammad M. (2003). *Islam und Demokratie [Islam and democracy],* ed. by Wolfgang Bergsdorf, Erfurt: University of Erfurt.

Sharabi, Hisham (1988). *Neopatriarchy. A Theory of Distorted Change in Arab Society.* New York/Oxford: Oxford University Press.

Sheehan, James J. (1978). *German Liberalism in the Nineteenth Century.* Chicago: Chicago University Press.

Shipler, David K. (1986). *Arab and Jew. Wounded Spirits in a Promised Land.* New York: Penguin.

Silvestri, Sara (2007). Europe and Political Islam: Encounters of the 20th and 21st Century, in: Tahir Abbas (ed.). *Islamic Political Radicalism: A European Comparative Perspective*, Edinburgh: Edinburgh University Press, 57–70.

Simons, Geoff (1994). *Iraq: From Sumer to Saddam*. London: Macmillan.

Singerman, Diane (1995). *Avenues of Participation. Family, Politics, and Networks in Urban Quarters of Cairo*. Princeton: Princeton University Press.

Sloterdijk, Peter (2006). *Zorn und Zeit. Ein politisch-psychologischer Versuch [Rage and Time. An essay in politics and psychology]*. Frankfurt: Suhrkamp.

Solingen, Etel (2003). Toward a Democratic Peace in the Middle East, in: Amin Saikal and Albrecht Schnabel (eds.). *Democratization in the Middle East: Experiences. truggles, Challenges*, Tokyo et al.: United Nations University Press, 42–62.

Sölkner, Andrea and Bärbel Heide Uhl (2007). *Freiwillige Rückkehrprogramme für gehandelte Menschen: Menschenrechtschutz versus Migrationsmanagement? [Programmes of voluntary return for former slaves: the protection of human rights versus migration management?]*, in: *Jahrbuch Menschenrechte [Yearbook of human rights]* 2008, ed. by Deutschen Institut für Menschenrechte. Frankfurt: Suhrkamp, 77–87.

Somjee, A.H. (2002). Non-Western Theories of Development: Critiques and Explorations, in: Howard J. Wiarda (ed.). *New Directions in Comparative Politics* (3rd edn.). Boulder: Westview, 119–40.

Soroush, Abdolkarim (2000). *Reason, Freedom, and Democracy in Islam. Essential Writings of Abolkarim Soroush*, ed. by Mahmoud Sadri and Ahmed Sadri. Oxford: Oxford University Press.

Speckmann, Thomas (2007). Die imperiale Verlockung. Rhetorik und Realität französischer Außenpolitik [The imperial temptation. The rhetoric and reality of French foreign policy], in: *Merkur* 11, 1014–25.

Springborg, Robert (1979). Patrimonialism and Policy Making in Egypt. Nasser and Sadat and the Tenure Policy for Reclaimed Lands, in: *Middle East Studies* 1, 49–69.

Stahr, Volker S. (1997). *Südostasien und der Islam. Kulturraum zwischen Kommerz und Koran [South East Asia and Islam. A cultural area between commerce and the Koran]*, Darmstadt: Wissenschaftliche Buchgesellschaft.

Steinbach, Udo (1979). *Das politische System in Iran unter dem Schah-Regime [The political system in Iran under the Shah]*, in: *Expertengespräch 'Gesamtanalyse der Ursachen und möglichen Perspektiven der Entwicklung in Iran' [Expert discussion: 'Overall analysis of the causes and prospects for development in Iran']*. Bonn 21–22 June 1979, ed. by the Friedrich Ebert Foundation. Bonn, typewritten manuscript without page numbers.

Steinweg, Reiner (ed.) (1989). *Militärregime und Entwicklungspolitik [Military regimes and development policies]*. Frankfurt: Suhrkamp.

Takeyh, Ray and Nikolas K. Gvosdev (2006). *The Receding Shadow of the Prophet. The Rise and Fall of Political Islam*. Westport/London: Praeger.

Taylor, Charles (1994). *Multiculturalism and the Politics of Recognition*. Princeton: Princeton University Press.

Tehranian, Majid (2003). Disenchanted Worlds: Secularization and Democratization in the Middle East, in: Amin Saikal and Albrecht Schnabel (eds.). *Democratization in the Middle East: Experiences. Struggles. Challenges*, Tokyo et al.: United Nations University Press, 79–102.

Tessler, Mark (2000). Democratic Concern and Islamic Resurgence: Converging Dimensions of the Arab World's Political Agenda, in: Howard Handelman and Mark Tessler (eds.). *Democracy and its Limits. Lessons from Asia, Latin America, and the Middle East.* Notre Dame: University of Notre Dame Press, 262–89.

(2002). Islam and Democracy in the Middle East. The Impact of Religious Orientations on Attitudes toward Democracy in four Arab Countries, in: *Comparative Politics* 2, 337–54.

(2003). The Influence of Islam on Attitudes toward Democracy in Morocco and Algeria, in: Amin Saikal and Albrecht Schnabel (eds.). *Democratization in the Middle East: Experiences, Struggles, Challenges*, Tokyo et al.: United Nations University Press, 103–23.

Tessler, Mark and Ebru Altinoglu (2004). Political Culture in Turkey: Connections among Attitudes toward Democracy, the Military and Islam, in: *Democratization* 1, 21–50.

Turner, Bryan S. (1978). *Marx and the End of Orientalism.* London/Boston: Allen and Unwin.

Thussu, Daya Kishan and Des Freedman (eds.) (2003). *War and the Media. Reporting Conflict 24/7.* London et al.: Sage.

Tibi, Bassam (1984). Orient und Okzident. Feindschaft oder intellektuelle Kommunikation? Anmerkungen zur Orientalismus-Debatte [Orient and occident: enmity or intellectual communication? Notes on the orientalism debate], in: *Neue Politische Literatur [New political literature]* 29, 267–86.

(1985). *Der Islam und das Problem der kulturellen Bewältigung des sozialen Wandels [Islam and the problem of the cultural assimilation of social change].* Frankfurt: Suhrkamp.

(1993). Der islamische Fundamentalismus zwischen 'halber Moderne' und politischem Aktivismus [Islamic fundamentalism between 'semi-modernity' and political activism], in: *Aus Politik und Zeitgeschichte [Politics and contemporary history]* B 33, 3–10.

Tumber, Howard and Jerry Palmer (2004). *Media at War. Iraq Crisis.* London et al.: Sage.

Understanding Islamism, International Crisis Group, Middle East/North Africa Report, no. 37, 2 March 2005, place of publication unknown.

von Prittwitz, Volker (2007). *Vergleichende Politikanalyse [Comparative political analysis].* Stuttgart: Lucius und Lucius.

Waterbury, John (1983). *The Egypt of Nasser and Sadat. The Political Economy of two Regimes.* Princeton: Princeton University Press.

(1994). Democracy without Democrats? The Potential for Political Liberalization in the Middle East, in: Ghassan Salamé (ed.). *Democracy without Democrats? The Renewal of Politics in the Muslim World.* London/ New York: I.B. Tauris, 23–47.

Weber, Max (2006). *Die protestantische Ethik und der Geist des Kapitalismus [The Protestant ethic and the spirit of capitalism]*, Erftstadt: Area (Orig. 1904–5).

Webster, Richard (1990). *A Brief History of Blasphemy. Liberalism, Censorship and the 'Satanic Verses'*. Southwold: Orwell.

Weinstein, Kenneth R. (2006). The Rise of Toleration in the West and its Implications for the War on Terror, in: Bradley C.S. Watson (ed.). *The West at War*. Lanham et al.: Lexington, 99–109.

Wickham, Carrie Rosefsky (2002). *Mobilizing Islam. Religion, Activism, and Political Change in Egypt*. New York: Columbia University Press.

Wiktorowicz, Quintan (2004a). Islamic Activism and Social Movement Theory, in: Quintan Wiktorowicz (ed.). *Islamic Activism. A Social Movement Theory Approach*. Bloomington/Indianapolis: Indiana University Press, 1–33.

Wiktorowicz, Quintan (ed.) (2004b). *Islamic Activism. A Social Movement Theory Approach*. Bloomington/Indianapolis: Indiana University Press.

Wittner, Lawrence S. (1984). *Rebels against War. The American Peace Movement, 1933–1983*. Philadelphia: Temple University Press.

Wolin, Sheldon S. (2008). *Democracy Incorporated. Managed Democracy and the Specter of Inverted Totalitarianism*. Princeton/Oxford: Princeton University Press.

Youngs, Richard (2004). European Democracy Promotion in the Middle East, in: Internationale Politik und Gesellschaft *[International politics and society]* 4, 111–22.

Zakaria, Fareed (2004). *The Future of Freedom. Illiberal Democracy at Home and Abroad*. New York/London: W.W. Norton and Co.

Zaki, Moheb (1995). *Civil Society and Democratization in Egypt, 1981–1994*. Cairo: Ibn Khaldoun Center for Development Studies and Konrad Adenauer Foundation.

Zapf, Wolfgang (2006). Modernisierungstheorie – und die nicht-westliche Welt [Modernization theory and the non-Western world], in: Schwinn, Thomas (ed.). *Die Vielfalt und die Einheit der Moderne. Kultur- und strukturvergleichende Analysen [The diversity and unity of modernity. Comparative analyses of culture and structure]*. Wiesbaden: VS Verlag für Sozialwissenschaften, 227–35.

Zelizer, Barbie and Stuart Allan (eds.) (2002). *Journalism after September 11*. London/New York: Routledge.

Zimmermann, Ekkart (2006). *System Transformation and Political Violence, Unveröffentlichter Vortrag gehalten anlässlich der 47th International Studies Association Convention [Unpublished lecture delivered at the 47th International Studies Association Convention]*. San Diego, 22–27 March 2006.

Ziring, Lawrence (2003). *Pakistan at the Crosscurrent of History*. Oxford: Oneworld.

Zunes, Stephen (1999). Unarmed Resistance in the Middle East and North Africa, in: Stephen Zunes, Lester R. Kurtz and Sarah Beth Asher (eds.). *Nonviolent Social Movements. A Geographical Perspective*. Malden/Oxford: Blackwell, 41–51.

Index